How to Make Johnny WANT to Obey

By Dr. Stephen E. Beltz

PRENTICE-HALL, INC.
ENGLEWOOD CLIFFS, N.J.

*This book is gratefully
dedicated to the memory of my father,
who did his best . . .*

Acknowledgments

The approach used in this volume represents an attempt to adopt the technology of Behavior Modification for use by parents and teachers as a general system of Behavior Management and Motivation. Because various aspects of the system upon which this book is based were drawn from the work of many other Behavior Modifiers, I would like to acknowledge here the men who have most significantly contributed to my own thinking and development as a Behavior Modifier. I owe Dr. Israel Goldiamond an eternal debt of gratitude for criticizing weaknesses in my language and thinking before he introduced me to the precision and systematic approach of operant work. I wish to thank Dr. Charles Ferster, not only for his brilliant contributions to my knowledge, but also for making me aware of the contributions of the clinical Behavior Modifier to the development of the total field. To Dr. Ogden Lindsley I owe a special, though bittersweet, appreciation for helping me crystalize the high goals to which I and other Behavior Modifiers have become committed.

To my clients and students who have so patiently borne with me in the long and difficult task of acquiring not only technical competence but compassion, and the understanding of the power and importance of human warmth and empathy in the development of effective management systems, I owe a special appreciation. Whatever clarity this book may have in its language and ideas is due entirely to the shaping processes I underwent in attempting to communicate with the many people I have had the privilege of knowing. There is nothing more humbling to a teacher than to find that his most complex ideas, with all their intricacies and subtleties, can be translated into clear English statements by a person without his advantages of higher education. In fact, careful examination of that most uncommon commodity called "common sense" has taught me that people have known the raw material of effective behavior management long before mankind invented "science" or psychology. There is no question in my mind that the "scientific knowledge" contained in this book is simply *refined* common sense with the superstitions, misunderstandings, and ignorances removed.

Many thanks and heartfelt appreciation must be extended to members of my staff and my colleagues, without whose help, suggestions, and patience this book would not have been written.

I wish to thank also the three women who "heard" the book first, as I dictated it—Mrs. Pat Castill, Mrs. Pat Megaegel, and Mrs. Anne Shaffer. Their enthusiasm and differential reactions helped to bring it even further along the road to clarity.

I wish to thank my wife, who has been my prime Behavior Manager, for her unusually great ability to see the first approximation of desirable behavior in me and to strengthen it with the most positive consequence of all—herself! And final acknowledgment must be paid to the five most important teachers I have had the privilege of knowing—my children: Lauri, Linda, Lisa, Leah, and David.

Philadelphia, Pennsylvania   S.E.B.

Preface

This is a book about how to motivate children. It doesn't attempt to tell you *what* to teach Johnny or what Johnny *should* do. It tells you *how* to get him to do what you, the parent, want him to do.

Its purpose is to offer a new way of getting Johnny to obey by helping him to *want* to obey. The method set forth here works by increasing his motivation. Most parents strive constantly for what they feel is a reasonable amount of obedience from their children. They try many ways to get it—asking, pleading, persuading, bribing, threatening, and punishing. Far too much of their time and effort is spent in methods that only occasionally work, and even then only with some children.

A few people are lucky; their children seem to obey almost without any effort. If you have such a child, you are probably doing the right things without even knowing it. This book will help you understand why you are already successful. If you are having trouble with Johnny, this book should show you how to improve your skill.

Children are treated as people in this approach, with all the rights, privileges, and obligations of people. Cooperative behavior is obtained in children in the same way as working adults are led to perform their work effectively. There is no resort to threats or punishment. This approach is based on the creative use of incentives to increase motivation. A good deal of time will be spent explaining the real and important differences between a system of bribery and a system of incentives.

I have organized the book to give you more than a cookbook of techniques. The techniques are there, of course, but so is the background, and the reasons behind each step. In Part One, "The Why of Behavior," I have tried to explain in depth what a family is and why it can experience difficulty with children.

In Part Two, "The What of Behavior," I have tried to provide a basic understanding of the principles of behavior. You may be tempted to skip this section in order to plunge into the actual methods and techniques, but I would suggest that you take the time to read the principles carefully. Any technique must be modified to fit your child. Without a knowledge of why the technique is designed as it is, you may be unable to adjust it for your own particular situation.

In Part Three, "The How To of Behavior," I have tried to give you a brief overview of the various ways in which behavior can be modified. However, the major emphasis is on the home contract system, since it has the greatest applicability in the management, motivation, and modification of children's behavior.

Lastly, in Part Four, "The Why Not of Behavior," I have included a short section on the role of children in our society and in your family. I have tried to clarify here the basic philosophy of the behavioral approach as I see it.

I have tried to anticipate as many as possible of the common situations and problems you may encounter in the use of my techniques; and I have given you what have proved to be practical solutions for many of the families who have successfully used this approach.

Contents

Part 1
THE
WHY of
BEHAVIOR

1

Times Have
Changed

Have you ever wished you could give your children away and not even have a family anymore? That's an honest "gut" feeling that most parents have at one time or another. Some parents have it all the time. My wife has it at least once a day. Usually it's when our five children are all screaming at once, our two-year-old has a kitten dangling from each hand (upside down, of course), our dog is busily trying to devour one of our daughter's little friends, and I've just arrived home for a hurry-up dinner before rushing back to the office.

At times like these you yearn for the good old days when children were seen and not heard, when a parent's word was law and Father demanded and got instant obedience. Children knew their place, did their chores diligently, and went smilingly off to sleep. That's the picture my mother described to me when I was growing up. I suspected, even then, that those days were gone forever because, like most of my friends, I was always in hot water, getting punished for one thing or another. Our parents seemed to be always screaming at us because we hadn't done something we were supposed to do, or had done something we weren't supposed to do, or because they thought we had done something we didn't do. As a matter of fact, we were never really sure which was which. To this day I still don't know if I'm supposed to hit back if attacked by someone my own size, bigger, or smaller. The rules seemed endless and unnecessarily restricting. Parents were the enemy and children banded together to ward off the enemy's encroachment on our secret world where truth, beauty, and joy reigned in the form of torn pants, secret hiding places, pockets full of junk, and "breaking the rules."

Now that I'm a parent myself and a consultant to many other parents, I realize how important rules can be and how necessary it is to bring some sort of order out of (or into) the chaos of those interacting energy systems commonly called children. A method of harnessing raw energy so that a home can attain some sort of harmonious existence has been the goal of parents since time immemorial. For centuries the method used remained fairly constant: "spare the rod and spoil the child." It worked. That is, it worked reasonably well. Remember Peck's Bad Boy? I was one, and I can personally attest to the existence of at least six others, who lived on my block (Wanamaker Street) while I was growing up more or less successfully. We must admit that even in the "good old days" parents had some trouble with the "spare the rod" system of child rearing.

How many people do you know who are able to raise their children today without major problems? I don't mean just the usual mischief and misbehavior that any red-blooded American Peck's Bad Boy gets into (we were the seven holy terrors of Wanamaker Street). I mean the kinds of alienation, rebellion, underachievement, and self-destruction so rampant today. How many parents feel confident their approach will work and produce not only well-mannered, well-behaved children but independent, self-governing, self-fulfilled adults? Isn't it time to draw upon the accumulated wisdom of mankind, the developments in modern science, and the new perspectives of a democratic society to develop a new approach to child-rearing?

The world has changed. No longer do parents have the total support of their neighbors, close family friends, and relatives, all with similar points of view, all working together to support a common set of ideals and goals for children. Today many different kinds of families live close together with opposing points of view. Children have access to television, radio, newspapers, and magazines in a way that their parents never did. It is possible for them to travel quickly and easily on both public and private transportation, extending their horizons even further.

Although poverty remains a problem in our society, it still can be said that we are an affluent society. People have more money to spend today than ever before in history; and children have more money to spend than ever before in history. It is no longer necessary for a family to do many daily chores. Dishwashers, vacuum cleaners, and freezers have changed the whole pattern of family living. So the children, who used to pitch in and help out, frequently earning money to help the family exist, plowing the fields, taking care of the store, or serving as at least part-time domestic help, are no longer an asset and frequently may be a liability in terms of the economics of a family. They used to be an essential part of a family's existence, necessary and respected for their contributions and occupied much of the time with helping the family survive.

Today, there is no longer a need for children to work around the house, around the farm, or around the store. Children have a good deal more free time and less is required of them than ever before. The combination of free time and the changing family patterns have provided the soil in which the new ideals of children's rights, their freedom to determine their own destiny, and their eventual emancipation at the age of twenty-one have flourished. But it has also led to the flowering of dissent and revolt in a way that has shocked parents all over the country. Parents have a notion of what a family should be, and they want to preserve that notion in traditional ways and traditional patterns. They are finding that their children no longer accept those values or the methods by which such values were once imposed.

While I was going to college I once told my father that I didn't need money to live. Being a very practical businessman, he was shocked and tried to persuade me otherwise. Since I wasn't willing to give up eating or going to the movies, I quickly found out he was right. But the young people today are less easy to convince. They are willing to eat brown rice and vegetables and find their recreation in playing frisbee, a very low-cost entertainment. The paradox of young people insisting on a return to a more simple style of life while at the same time being able to earn more money than ever before in history is perplexing to say the least. Maybe it explains a little of their confusion and that of their parents.

If you were to sit in my office day after day listening to the problems that arise in families, you would be amazed at how many different kinds of conflict and argument exist. Very often the conflicts revolve around the very nature of the family structure itself.

There was a time when we took for granted what structure a family was to have. For hundreds and hundreds of years, people lived in groups that existed over many generations with very, very little structural change. There was usually a head of the family, a patriarch or occasionally a matriarch. This was some older man or woman who was the last surviving member of his generation and who had accumulated a great deal of experience and wisdom. Their knowledge of the world, and of the family itself, was respected by all because of its relevance to the problems with which every family member had to cope. The various religions supported this veneration of elders and provided a cultural format to support this type of structure. The father was the king within his family, and kings were an accepted part of the way people lived. The mother was the queen. These two people had arbitrary rights granted by God and sustained by custom. Included in these rights was control of the decision-making process. All decisions of importance to the family and to each member of the family were referred to the patriarch or the matriarch.

Next under these rulers of the family was the council of elders. Occasionally, this element consisted of peers of the patriarch; more often, its members were of the next younger family generation—people who had not lived as long or had had as much experience, but were running a close second. This group of people usually constituted the sons and daughters of the patriarch together with their spouses. They were the brothers and sisters of the tight-knit family clan.

Their children, closely bound as first cousins, constituted a third generation within this extended family and were frequently mature enough to have children of their own as well as responsibilities within the community. The fourth and occasionally fifth generations were the children or young adults, who had little status or power within the family structure.

All decisions were referred upward and all edicts were handed downward. There was very little personal freedom and each edict was stated as a command. There were many variations of this particular structure and, in general, most of them also worked well.

This kind of structure preserved the family's wealth and gave the family group continuity over time. It gave the family's members close emotional support and a rich and varied emotional existence. People cared and would step in to help when trouble occurred to a member. In cities and towns the family usually stayed close together, living within a few blocks or miles of each other. On farms, houses were built side-by-side. Each child was responsible to all adults. First cousins who were older frequently had as much power over the child as did the immediate parent, grandparent, or patriarch. In a primarily rural society, where change came slowly, this system worked exceedingly well.

The method of discipline used was strong punishment made even more formidable by the constant attention of adults. Children were frequently too busy to get into mischief and many of our proverbs reflect this pattern. "Idle hands are the devil's workshop" is a good example of the overriding philosophy of the family. Keep the children busy. Children were often sent out to work (hired out) on a neighboring farm and, later, in the growing factory and business life of urban society.

But as times changed, and as people were transposed from rural to urban living, the extended family structure began to break down. For many families the move from Europe to America hastened this process, which was going on at its own pace anyway. New notions appeared; for example, at twenty-one a child was no longer to be held accountable to his parents. In the old extended family this would have been impossible. A child was accountable to his parents until the day his parents died. Frequently even senile patriarchs were afforded great respect and obedience, no matter how silly the commands they gave.

The patriarchal pattern still exists in many countries which are considered underdeveloped and more primitive in their techno-logical advances. It works best in a primitive society or in a rural culture. When it is transposed into an urban culture, we see the effects that we have seen in America. The extended family shrinks in size. Cousins move away, uncles and aunts are no longer next-door neighbors. As distance grows greater, so do differences in living conditions. It is more difficult to call a family together to decide a problem; besides, the separate parts of the family won't often share problems in common. People live longer, so that the second and third generations of a family begin to resent the older patriarch. The nature of the society around the family presents new problems so radical in concept that the old ways no longer work. The advice of the patriarch and the matriarch no longer seems as relevant as it once did, and the commands that they issue no longer have the authority they formerly had. The inherited wisdom and experience of a lifetime passed on from generation to generation, honed and refined, suddenly seems dull and unable to serve the family needs.

The final result has been the development of a nuclear family. A nuclear family is simply the parents and children as a single unit, separate and detached from the extended family, maintaining their contact with the larger group only at births, weddings, funerals, and other special occasions. The young mother and father have no one to whom they can turn for guidance or support except their own peer group, the young friends who got married at the same time and who have as little experience as they do. They resent the advice offered by their parents because they quickly find that much of it seems biased, inadequate, irrelevant, or apparently designed to ensnare them again in the dependency of their childhood. Whereas at one time dependency was a way-of-life, accepted and acceptable, it is no longer considered desirable. We have changed our societal goals and values, and we now require that a child of twenty-one become a patriarch or matriarch in his or her own right, without the years of training and experience and seasoning that were required for the role in past days. Today's young couple is almost forced to refuse advice because, by definition in our culture, anyone who takes direction is dependent and childlike. The adult gives direction. This profound change in the structure of our society in general and within the family in particular has produced an increasing rate of alienation between parent and child, of conflict and struggle over simple matters of obedience that never were a problem in the past.

I remember once at a workshop talking with a woman principal from New Delhi, India. The question arose as to how Indians disciplined their children. And her reply was "we don't." The startled group turned to her and asked for further information. One lady in total shock said, "Don't you punish your children?" and she said, "What for?" Another member of the group cried out, "When they misbehave, of course." And her reply was, again in a quiet voice, "They don't misbehave." By this time, the entire group was disconcerted and showing a great deal of disbelief, amounting almost to annoyance at this woman's very matter-of-fact tone. When pressed to explain further, she finally did, in the following way: "Our family lives together in one large complex," she explained in answer to our questions. "The older members are always in charge. In any given room, at any given time, the oldest member of the family present is in charge. No one disobeys. There is no model for children for disobedience. The minute a child starts to disobey, some adult is always present to take him by the hand and lead him to obedience. Without a model of disobedience, with prompt and rapid attention by an adult, there is no need for punishment. The children simply do not disobey." And then with a chuckle, she added, "Of course, that was before the British came. Now we are becoming modern and families are starting to have difficulty."

Her point was very well taken. There was no model for disobedience. Adults were always present and children were not allowed to disobey. There was no need for discipline or punishment in the usual sense that we understand by these terms in our society. There is a memory of this kind of system in all of us. We have the mistaken belief that children are supposed to obey, almost as if by nature. We believe that we really don't have to do very much to get obedience except to be parents. We become shocked and angry at our children when we find that they are not obeying us. We have no one to turn to for meaningful advice.

Many families turn to the books and magazine articles written by psychologists and child experts during the 1930s and 1940s. The prevalent notion at the time was that it was dangerous to traumatize a child, to hurt him in some way by restricting him. The theory was that if he preferred to do something he should be permitted to do it; otherwise he would grow up having many kinds of problems, complexes, and neuroses that would make his life miserable. Parents were admonished not to inhibit a child. This procedure worked no better than did the one before it, which extolled the virtues of extremely violent and harsh discipline through punishment. The net result of the newer theory (poorly interpreted, of course) was a generation of confused and bratty children with tormented and tired parents who spent most of their time sitting on their rage and anger so that they wouldn't "traumatize" their child.

As America grew and more and more of the responsibility that once belonged to the parent and the family group was delegated to schools, community centers, boy scout troops, churches, and the gang, the problem grew worse. The only solution that seemed to make any sense to parents was to turn their child over to some professional who magically would change him into a traditionally obedient child. Even as the young parents were protesting the interference of their parents, they continued to interfere with their children. There was no clear definition of family boundaries and family freedoms for each generation. To this day the confusion persists. This is the background behind the problem of how to make Johnny want to obey.

Almost all the families that have come to me over the years, no matter what the presenting problem, have been concerned with children's obedience. "If only my child would obey, everything could be solved." Then all problems could be solved through the coaching and guidance and advice of the parent. If the child would obey the teacher, everything would be all right; if the child would obey the policeman, the scout leader, the minister, the neighbor, the librarian; if the child would only obey.

A mother once told me that she wanted her five-month-old child to obey her by keeping his hands out of his mouth when he ate. She proudly told me that she had succeeded by slapping his hand every time he put it in his mouth. Her inexperience and the inappropriateness of her method are obvious.

On the other hand, I have had parents tell me that they wanted their child to refrain from sniffing glue and destroying his brain cells. Not all parents want the worst for their children, not all parents are selfish in requiring that a child obey them for their own personal gratification. Of course, all parents do this at some time, but most of the parents that I have known over the years have been concerned with getting their children to obey reasonable rules, to learn behaviors that were in the child's best interest, as well as the parents. In general, they demanded the obedience not for their own selfish ends, but for the child's growth and maturity. I have had no hesitation in working with these parents to help the children learn to obey.

I have always cautioned each family, however, that they should work just as hard to teach the child constructive disobedience, for this skill is also necessary. A child must learn to obey and must learn to refuse to obey, wisely. There are times in every person's life when obedience would be detrimental and destructive, when the simple act of obedience could cause great harm to himself and to others. No mother wants her children to obey a stranger who entices them into a car with candy, no mother wants her children to obey the gang leader who suggests breaking into a store, no parents want their child to obey an adult who offers allegiance to a creed or an ideology that the parent abhors and finds repugnant. What most parents really want are children who obey when it is reasonable to do so and who defer to the parent's judgment in areas where their own competence is poorly developed. Most parents today would allow their children, as they become competent, to disagree and disobey in ways that the parents can accept and respect.

All parents, of course, are human beings; they have their biases and prejudices and blind spots. At times there will be clashes between parent and child, no matter how effective is the relationship and the methods by which the family resolves differences. Most parents want their children to continue the nuclear family pattern, to stand on their own feet when they become adults, to make their own decisions and live their own lives.

That's enough history. Many families are in trouble today; the conflicts and unhappiness are going on right now. If your family is in trouble, you want to know why and what to do about it. But before we can get to the "what to do about it" we need to go deeper into the current causes of the "why." The next chapter will explore some important problems of families in trouble to see if we can search out the essential causes.

2 ❦
Formulas
for Successful

Families

Have you ever tried to figure out why one family seems to get along so well and another seems in constant turmoil? Have you ever wondered about your own family? I would be very surprised if you haven't often tried to find the essential formula for a successful family.

Just a few moments ago, I spoke on the telephone to a father who blurted out in anger, "I'm going to really belt that kid. My father did it to me and I'm a better person for it. That's what that kid really needs." This father really believes that direct and violent punishment is the essential factor in successful child-rearing.

Other parents will argue just as strongly that the essential reasons for success lie in such things as parental consistency, or loving discipline, or specific and concrete rules, or flexibility, or a variety of other formulas. My own mother is convinced that plenty of rest, lots of good food, plenty of chores, and clean bowels produce good children. For her generation sleeping, eating, working, and defecating were the essential components of mental health, just as respecting your parents was the cardinal rule of childhood. A child who respected parents could be forgiven most other things—even keeping disreputable hours, being lazy or irregular.

Let's examine some of the usual explanations of successful child-rearing suggested by many parents and see if we can discover what the really essential rule for child-rearing turns out to be.

WHO'S THE BOSS? ～

I can remember one family—I'll call them the Browns—who came to see me. It was an emergency call; they asked me to meet them at my office late at night. When I arrived, I found the mother hysterical, the father sobbing, the two children sullen, angry, and withdrawn. As we entered my office, I heard the father mumbling to himself over and over again, "There's gotta be a better way, there's gotta be a better way."

The Browns were in conflict over who was to be in charge of the family. This family had been father-dominated. Over the years, the father had assumed the role of patriarch and had insisted that each of his two children become the kind of person he decided he

11

wanted them to be. He would broach no interference from his wife who, however, continuously persisted in trying to soften his demands and protect the children by serving as a buffer in all the family arguments and disputes. To her surprise, the children did not line themselves up with her and support her; they did not even appear grateful for her defense of them. While she defended them from the father, she herself attempted to dominate them and determine what they should be. The real conflict then was simply in which kind of mold the child was to be set, her softened requirements or the father's harsher demands. There was never any question that the parents would decide the future lives of their children. The conflict between mother and father, as to who would dominate the family, confused the children and they became angry and very uncertain as to what they were supposed to do. As they got older and entered their teens, they tried to reject the whole idea of their parents' determining their lives for them, but they did not win. Their father was strong and aggressive and sometimes violent. He would fly into rages and then into tears, dominating the family by the very violence of his emotions. The children were fighting a losing battle.

All of us know of families, though, where the father is in charge and where there is no open conflict. Yet the parent-dominated system does not always work there either. The children may be failing in school or even getting into serious trouble in the community. Obviously parent-dominance, whether successful or not, is not the complete answer.

If we were to go to the other extreme and look at a child-dominated family, we would find similar kinds of problems. For example, I know of a family which had only one child, a young girl, who completely dominated the family. She decided whether her parents were permitted to go out or not by simply throwing tantrums, whining, complaining of feeling ill, or employing a variety of stratagems which completely frustrated the parents from any social life. Their every waking moment was dominated by acceding to the child's wishes in order to avoid her tantrums or the withdrawal of her love that the child held like clubs over their heads. In addition to these devastating effects on the parents, this child-dominated home almost destroyed the child. Her emotional reactions had gotten out of control and she had few effective social skills. She was certainly not capable of deciding for herself what were the most effective style of life, patterns of behavior, or personal characteristics she should acquire. She was too young to have the necessary experience and judgment. The parents, however, who lived in such terror of this child, gave in continuously, passing on to the child (without even realizing it) the decision-making process of the family. They could not move because the child preferred the current neighborhood. The child did not like the kind of car they wanted, so they bought the kind of car the child wanted. The child did not like certain friends, so the parents stopped seeing them. This is, of course, an extreme case of a child-dominated home, but it is by no means unique.

We have all seen families, of course, in which the children are given great weight and respect in helping to make the family's decisions without the situation becoming pathological as in the case I have just described. And yet, here too the child who is given a great deal of freedom in choosing clothes, friends, activities, and goals often turns out badly. The parent who tries to determine which extreme is best, a parent- or a child-dominated family, is frequently frustrated. When observing a liberal family with children who are given freedom and use it badly, he becomes perplexed as to whether he or the child should decide how things are to be. Neither way seems to work more than the other. Thus we can conclude that this whole area of "who's the boss" does not contribute a great deal of clarity to an understanding of what makes families happy and successful and how to make Johnny *want* to obey.

HOW ABOUT PUNISHMENT? ⌒

Frequently people will point to the issue of punishment versus no punishment as being the essential criterion for determining what makes a successful family or an unsuccessful family. They point out that the use of weak punishment rather than strong punishment is the chief cause of what's wrong with families today. Invariably, they will point to the old days when strong punishment was meted out to any child who disobeyed and children lived in fear of this punishment. They claim that this was the reason the children obeyed well.

I'm reminded of one family in particular who came to me because of a learning problem in one of their children. They claimed they had no problems whatsoever in the management of their family and in their relationships with each other. I was appalled, however, to find out that their method of discipline had literally stripped all the children in the family (there were four) from any of the privileges of childhood whatsoever. Any infraction of the many rules that characterized this family was met with strong punishment which bordered almost on cruelty. The parents believed that punishment was religiously sanctioned and was necessary for their children's character development. Any child who stepped out of line was either physically punished with a strap, frequently leaving welts, or deprived for long periods of any of the pleasures of childhood. This family would have fit very well in earlier times in which pleasure was considered sinful and the ability to withstand pain and torment were considered noble and religiously sanctifying. The children were fighting back in the only way they knew how—by failing.

Frequently, children will choose this route as a method of creating upset, turmoil, frustration, and anger for their parents. They cannot stand up to the discipline and punishment directly, because to do so would lead to guilt and even more severe punishment; but they can stand up to it indirectly. I found one child in this family withdrawing increasingly into a shell. It was easy to see that at some point he would give up the game of trying to live up to the rules and avoid the punishment; instead he would simply withdraw totally from society and the world itself. Another child was becoming a failure, choosing the route of infuriating everyone around him by his incompetence and inability. This was the one the parents had brought to me, but each of the children was fighting back in his own way. The apparent illusion of a sound family was quickly dispelled upon closer examination. The parents consistently denied that anything was wrong, for to admit this would have brought the whole house of cards down around their ears. It took a very long process of gently leading them to an awareness of the problem before they could tolerate simply knowing that their family was in trouble.

If problems tend to remain hidden in families practicing strong punishment, they are often obvious in families where weak punishment is the rule. The children ignore the threat of weak punishment and proceed to go their merry ways, frequently to the detriment of themselves and the family. The fear of traumatizing children, mentioned earlier, plays a large part in some parents' reasons for the avoidance of punishment as a method of control. The strong punishment experienced in their own childhoods probably has led many parents to avoid perpetuating the punishment system and they have gone to the other extreme to avoid it. Their punishments are futile and often laughable. The children quickly learn that the parents can be easily controlled by making them feel guilty.

I met one little girl who was an expert at this. Every time one of her parents scolded her, touched her, or deprived her in any way, she would begin the most pitiful weeping you could imagine. It would bring tears to the eyes of an unwitting observer. Her parents were terrified of setting any limits, imposing any conditions, or providing any punishment for her behavior. She was the most unlikeable monster I have ever met. A great deal of patience and understanding on the part of several therapists was required to turn off the tears and teach her more effective ways of dealing with people than by manipulating their feelings of guilt.

All of us can think of various families which have been equally unsuccessful with strong or with weak punishment. This issue of punishment versus no punishment does not seem to be the essential element in explaining successful and unsuccessful families either.

HOW MANY RULES? ∽

The problems of family structure that we are considering can be helpful in our understanding of Johnny's disobedience. But so far the most important one eludes us. One of the most frequently chosen explanations of family success has to do with the number of sets of rules or the number of specific rules the children have to obey within the family. Many people believe that if each situation is not carefully specified in advance with a set of carefully laid out "do's and don't's," a child will somehow run wild and fail to develop an effective character. Sometimes the rules are imposed after the fact, so that a child only discovers them as he progresses through the situation and errs.

Often there are several sets of rules in a family: one set of rules which the father must obey, specifying his rights and privileges; one set of rules for the mother, specifying her rights and privileges; a set of rules for the male children as to what they may and may not do; and a final set of rules for the female children. Arranged in a hierarchy from father to girl-child, each of these sets is more restrictive than the one ahead of it. Fathers in many cultures are given greater freedoms and privileges than any other member of the family.

A woman came to me and complained of difficulties with one of her children. Upon questioning her, I found an extremely unusual family situation. Her husband would drink excessively, frequently abusing her and the children physically; on many occasions during the course of a week he would bring strange women home and frequently have intercourse with them in his bedroom without even bothering to close the door. When I asked about the effect of this behavior on the children in the family, she was amazed that I would even bring up such a question; in her opinion she had a very good husband—why was I even questioning his behavior? I discovered that his set of rules permitted him all of these behaviors as long as he brought his paycheck home every Friday night, which he did! He was a good financial support for the family, and no other conditions were set on his behavior patterns. This case may seem extreme in our culture, but in many cultures it is quite permissible for the male to live in any way he deems proper; his set of rules is very nonrestrictive.

It is, of course, essential that there be rules for families to live by. In more modern homes, the rule structures are usually differentiated between those for adult and for children—two-rule home in other words. The rights and privileges of the adult are seldom granted to the children. As long as they are designated children, they must live by the children's set of rules, no matter how competent they are, no matter how prepared they are to assume adult responsibility and privileges.

In my opinion, the most desirable structure would be that of a one-rule home—where both parents and children are required to live by the same, single set of rules, and where competency is the determining factor. If an individual is competent within a particular area, he will assume the obligations and the privileges pertaining to that area. Thus, in my own home, a child is as privileged as I am to request that I leave his or her room; and each child is free also to offer criticism to any adult present. All members of the family are obligated to report on their comings-and-goings to every member of the family as a matter of sheer consideration and courtesy, as well as of necessity. In many homes, of course, particularly in homes with two sets of rules, children are required to report on where they are going, but parents are not so obligated.

I have pointed out earlier that the existence of too few specific rules within the sets of rules in a family can be very detrimental, and a husband who is not required to observe the simple decencies that our culture requires, even if he has a special *set* of rules, frequently causes great difficulty within the life of the family, often showing itself in the problems that develop in the children.

But what of the family that has too many specific rules, too many requirements? One family I knew many years ago was almost incapacitated by the number of rules that had to be obeyed before each day was successfully finished. There was a right way to talk to each other, for instance, and any deviation from this led to great turmoil; as a result everyone was constantly apprehensive and fearful about the correct form of speech, the content of speech, and any other aspect of communication that might exist among the members of a family. Notes had to be left in just the right way and at just the right time. The prescribed behavior patterns continued even into other social settings that the family might visit. Even while at play the children were constantly being evaluated as good or bad, right or wrong, by an elaborate set of rules. Yet the parents complained of the fearfulness and the anxieties of the children; they could not understand why their children were lacking confidence and were not assertive enough in life. It appeared so obvious that under such a system no individual could ever relax because there was always the nagging question: "Am I doing right or wrong?"

In cultures where such patterns are prevalent—the cultures of the Far East, for example, particularly those of Japan and other countries which have a high degree of ritual—all members of the culture maintain the same ritualistic pattern; the many rules are explicit and models of correct behavior are constantly being displayed. It is very easy, then, for children to acquire skill, very early in life, in maintaining the necessary behaviors to conform to a complex pattern of rules. But in our society, where there are such varying degrees of rule structure and so many varying kinds of rule systems, it is almost impossible for children to accommodate themselves to a very complex set of requirements. The solution for this American family with its excessive number of rules was to simplify, simplify.

It would seem then that the number of rules is still not the determining factor of a successful family structure and the development of effective behavior patterns within children. While knowing about the rules system a family uses contributes some understanding of family conflict, rules themselves still do not appear to be the most essential area for explaining successful child-rearing.

WHO OR WHAT IS IMPORTANT? ☽

A frequent cause of family conflict is the relative importance assigned by different members of the family to various people or objects. Children want to be considered more precious to their parents than the furniture they break or the toys they abuse. The feeling of playing "second fiddle" to an object leads many a child to wreak vengeance on the parent in the form of tantrums or sullenness, resentment or resistance.

It is a useful rule of thumb that if people are more important than objects, the family is probably doing a pretty good job of raising children. If objects are more important and children are required to defer constantly in their play or in their general living habits to the care and maintenance of living rooms and toys, then serious difficulty *may* exist within the family.

Families which place greatest weight on the children often appear to be doing a more effective job in raising children. Some parents may even allow their children to destroy family objects and their own possessions, or allow their children to lose or abuse their own and other people's possessions without serious repercussions. In my own home, we try to teach respect for people and for possessions, unlike one family I knew who almost made a crusade out of possessing little and showing indifference to what they did possess. They prided themselves on tattered clothing, sprung chairs, and dust on the floor. They claimed to be free of excessive concern for material things. Their constant emphasis was on the emotional relationship among the members of the family and on "doing their own thing." However, their children had been brought to me because of involvement with drugs and some serious sexual misbehavior on the part of the older children. I am not implying that the lack of concern for objects produced the problem; I am saying merely that this family was in conflict and that their elimination of the importance of objects did not save them from problems. Thus the issue of concern or lack of concern for objects proved to be irrelevant with respect to understanding why these children had failed to develop more mature self-control that would have prevented society from jumping on them for misbehaviors.

There is no magic panacea in making objects less important than people, since we find that this area, also, is not essential in understanding successful family living and child-rearing. At both xtremes we can find examples of families who are making it and families who are not.

For centuries people were required to value objects, to maintain them, and to hand them down from generation to generation.

Children were carefully taught that objects were irreplaceable and must be cared for. In some cultures more primitive than ours it was easier to replace people than their possessions. This is no longer true in our culture and no longer a critical problem. And yet there are still people who behave toward their children as though it were easier to replace them than the objects which the children have broken.

DIVIDED WE FALL ❦

Most sociologists and students of families point to the problem of parental disagreement as being one of the most essential factors in understanding why children develop conflicts and fail to achieve mature behavior patterns. They point out, rightfully, that quarreling parents, who cannot agree on a single set of standards for their children, frequently produce children who are themselves confused and in serious difficulty. The principle that the ideal goal of parents is always to agree in front of the children and disagree when the children are not present is seldom realized by most families, although some come awfully close to that pattern. In some rare cases you can find almost total agreement between both parents as to what is desirable and proper behavior for their children to learn.

In cases where there is not such agreement between the parents and among the family members, children frequently use the disagreement as a means toward an end. They manipulate the parents into a conflict situation and then temporarily favor the parent who agrees with them. This pattern can become so serious that the constant irritation leads to a break-up of the family, with either the children leaving, the parents separating, or a combination of the two. Because this is a dramatic kind of confrontation and a dramatic kind of solution, it has given rise to the popular myth that parental disagreement, of necessity, must cause damage and that parental agreement, of necessity, must prevent problems in children.

Where there is no true parental agreement, efforts to maintain appearances for the sake of the children usually fail badly. Children become aware of the subtle disagreements as surely as if the parents were shouting across the table. Although Mommy seems to agree with Daddy and goes along with his decisions, she subtly erodes them by failing in little ways to implement the decisions, by looking differently when Daddy is laying down the law than when he is not. And although his father will back up his wife frequently in points where his opinion is in conflict with hers, the children are quick to grasp his disapproval and dislike of his wife's style and manner in maintaining order and discipline. They quickly become aware of the fact that he will soften upon appeal and that he will stand as their defender at a later time.

But again, I can think of families in which there has been open strong parental disagreement with respect to the proper and desirable ends for children in which no damage was done to the children. In these families the children recognized the differences and the family accepted the differences. Compromises were reached or children learned easily how to use alternate patterns in the presence of one or the other parent.

We can also think of families in the slums, the typical stereotype of the bad home in our culture, in which the father was abusive and an alcoholic who held values for his children that either were too low or were asocial in some way; and in which a strong and determined mother was able to influence the child to throw off his past and become an outstanding member of his community.

Many families in which both parents agreed and tried to work in perfect harmony to develop the required learning of skills and behavior for their children have ended in my office complaining that while they agreed, the children disagreed and the children were winning.

There are many conflicts which children should not win for their own best interests. Frequently parents are right in what they require of the child. Parental agreement, by itself, produces no miracles. Without other essential factors present, parental agreement cannot, in itself, determine effective family living and effective child-rearing.

THAT'S THE RULE ∽

Another frequent concern alluded to as a basic cause of child-rearing problems is the question of consistency. Parents are admonished always to be consistent when rules are laid down and when punishments are set. The inconsistent parent who vacillates from day-to-day, depending on his or her mood or the expediencies of the moment, is pointed out as the producer of disturbed children or of children with patterns of behavior unacceptable to themselves or to the society in which they live. Consistency is always held to be the most desirable possible characteristic.

While it is certainly true that consistency is a desirable characteristic of any management system and that inconsistency can generate anxiety and uncertainty on the part of unskilled and untrained children who require structure, routine, and continuity in their lives in order to be comfortable, it is, however, not true that consistency, by and of itself, can produce any magic results in child-rearing.

Consistency is simply a component of a larger approach. Too many parents believe that being consistently wrong is better than being inconsistently right. They have refused to change their style or manner, their ideas, or their expectations of children even when these appear almost absurd. The mother who wants her fat little daughter to be a great ballerina and consistently pushes her toward accomplishment in a field in which she has no natural talent may be consistent in her expectations and in her method of trying to obtain it. She may end up with a little girl like the one who sat in my office, tearful and hysterical (after she had run away from her parents), asking if she could live in my office because at least here she could be herself.

I am not condoning inconsistency. Children become tense and develop many emotional difficulties in a home where they never know what to expect, in which a certain behavior will be permitted, condoned, or praised sometimes and at other times punished suddenly and arbitrarily because the parents that day became upset at something else.

Too many children have sat in my office complaining about the inflexibility of their parents when it would have been more humane and meaningful as a human experience for the children if the parents had broken their patterns and permitted an exception, perhaps as a special treat or as a special example of their care and concern. Rules are made to be broken sometimes. It is the over-all pattern that is important. Total consistency in my opinion would be as bad as total inconsistency. But again, the point must be made that this area of family conflict is not the one which can determine effective child management.

IT'S ALWAYS BEEN THIS WAY ∽

Let's look at the problem of tradition. There are families who live by the tradition of centuries and generations and families who adapt to fit the changing times. There are fathers who wear a striped school tie and hair cut short in order to maintain conformity with the past and with their peers, and there are fathers who appear in the fashion of today, with long hair or bell-bottoms, and whose styles of family life change from year to year. Which father can guarantee that his children will not have problems of disobedience or social development?

Some people cite the idea of maintaining a rigid pattern within the family rather than adapting or changing or modifying with the times as a condition for success in child-rearing. It is most certainly a frequent area of conflict within families I have known. The unbending father who gives his child until Friday to cut his hair with no recourse to rational decision, with no possibility of modification, and with no way out for the child, frequently provokes open hostility as the child gets older, until there is eventually a final rupture in the family structure. It is easy to see such families and decide that rigidity, the inability to change, to acquire new ideas, to modify the requirements according to the times is a prime cause of family tragedy, and that rigid conformity to traditional ways is to be avoided at all costs.

Flexibility is given high status in our culture and is frequently described as desirable and necessary for an effective family. While I'm certainly in favor of flexibility, I do not find that by itself it will make Johnny want to obey. Flexibility is a difficult skill to learn, requiring an individual with a firm grasp of principles and general broad outlines of living, a philosophy of life that allows for change, and a set of ideals and values which in and of themselves are receptive to change. It requires an individual with many skills for handling anxiety because when patterns are broken, the resulting ambiguity and uncertainty will produce anxiety until new ones are formed. This, perhaps, explains why so many families would rather be "dead than red" or "right than happy."

OF COURSE I LOVE YOU! ⌒

Very often the cold, aloof family is pointed to as a type particularly likely to experience ineffective child-rearing. We are told that a great deal of expressed love and emotionality is a necessity in the rearing of children, and that either the absence of strong positive feelings or the presence of large amounts of feelings of anger and fear are corrosive and destructive in the development of children.

Children must have love, ever-constant, ever-flowing, for the successful growth and development of mature behavior patterns. Many fathers have sat in my office, listened to their children talk, and then blurted out in amazement, "Of course, I love you." They can't seem to understand that their children do not interpret their behavior as loving. Their nagging, their scolding, their criticism, their ignoring of the child for months and years in order to earn sufficient income for their family, their tiredness and irritability because of their attempts to manage the economics of their family, their harsh and severe discipline and punishment and the frequent application of spankings are all signs of love to the father, but not to the child.

The father, who knows that all he does is being done for the children, cannot understand why they do not appreciate it and reciprocate with a great deal of love and affection. The mother, who is constantly pushing the child to develop talents and skills that elevate her status in the eyes of her friends, cannot understand why the child does not appreciate this as a sign of love.

Watching from the outside, it is easy to understand the disparity between angry discipline and loving affection. Parents are afraid to spoil their children, are embarrassed at their positive feelings, and believe that an occasional reassurance such as "Of course, I love you!" is sufficient to establish close family ties and bonds of love and affection.

In some cases this pattern is culturally determined, depending on where the parents have come from and their own upbringing, what ethnic group they belong to, and in which section of the country they live. Many groups carry on the tradition of aloofness and restrained feelings, believing that love and laughter and joy are somehow not as acceptable to God as hard work and seriousness and purpose. But more often, withholding affection and minimizing physical touching and displays of concern result from personal problems of the parents. Parents who are constantly frustrated in the raising of their children end up angry, and many a child has sat in my office complaining that "all my father and mother ever do is scold me, yell at me, or reject me."

Although the need for love looks essential in the development of children, it is becoming clearer and clearer as we learn more and more about families that the phrase "love is not enough" is all too true. Many a family has sat in my office able to express love and affection toward each other, genuinely liking each other, sitting close and tight on the chairs of the office so that they are almost in constant physical touch. But they are nevertheless unhappy and concerned about serious deficits in the children's repertoire of behaviors, and in some cases even concerned with seriously damaging kinds of behavior the children have developed. How does this happen? Why can't a loving family automatically do all the right things to help their children avoid the pitfalls and gain the rewards of our society?

This was the question asked of me by one family that came to me with the problem of a child whose previous goals and values, involvement with the family, and effective social patterns were all gradually deteriorating. They were a close-knit family in which many kinds of activities were done within the family almost as a matter of course; they traveled together, they played sports together, they expressed their feelings toward each other freely and openly in a European manner. The boys—there were two sons—were not ashamed to kiss their father, nor he them. They could be frequently found arm-in-arm walking down streets on their way to some activity, laughing and joking together. From all outside appearances, this was a strong healthy family unit. There was no doubt about the strength of their feelings or the fact that they were primarily positive.

What was not apparent, however, were the expectations of the parents for the success of the children. One child made it. He had the natural ability and talents that made it possible for him to achieve at a very high rate. The other child did not. They were constantly tolerating his failures, accepting them graciously, and reassuring him. But the constant failure led him to seek other sources of success and approval which led to his eventual downfall and almost to self-destruction. He turned to people who had low standards or expectations, with whom he could feel successful (since success was such an important part of his family's structure). At home it was not enough to play a sport; it had to be played well. It was not enough to join in the conversation; one had to dominate it or at least hold up one's end. Passivity was frowned upon, failure was somehow wrong, and while the family expressed strong positive feelings which it genuinely felt, the toleration expressed toward the younger son led to bitterness and resentment that on the surface would have appeared entirely irrational.

On the other hand, I know of a family in which the negative feelings were so strong and so frequently expressed by the parents as outbursts of anger and irrational rage amounting almost to temper tantrums that the children simply had adapted to the situation. For them it became a part of the background noise, although in fact it functioned at a level that would have been deafening to most of us. I could hardly believe this family when I first met them, and yet after long years of association I was forced to admit that it is possible to live in the midst of what to my ears sounds like a jetport yet to their way of life is just casual, everyday interaction. There was love and good management present, of course, and this made it possible for such a family to give constant evidence of strong angry feelings, irrational rages, or tantrums, without destroying either the children or the tight family bonds that existed.

The presence of intense love or anger do not, in themselves, supply an answer as to why some children develop well and others develop badly. Why do some parents find the job of child-rearing exciting, pleasurable, and a constant source of gratification while others find it a chore so difficult they cannot wait to put down the reins of family management? How does this difference come about? What causes it?

WHAT'S THE WORLD COMING TO? ᘛ

Many people point to the old life style of the extended family with respectful children who were seen and not heard as a potential solution to all of the problems that plague modern society. The modern design for families, in all of its different variations, is seen as the cause for the breakdown in parental authority and discipline and the development of increasingly large amounts of maladaptive behavior in many children. Many people say it's all because we've changed our values and our family patterns. And yet this issue, too, like all the others we've considered so far, does not answer the basic question of why kids go wrong. There are too many examples of families with traditional design patterns, even including the extended family, who have failed. Some traditional families are successful; others are not. Modern families are making it; modern families are failing. Whether we give children equal status and rights within the family, or subject them to second-class citizen status does not seem to be the answer. Both extremes seem to work and both extremes, too often, fail. No simple answer that we have considered so far appears to be the real solution. It takes a knowledge of how people learn and what really constitutes the essential ingredients of a management system to provide the answer we have been looking for.

THE MIDDLE WAY ᘛ

By now it should be apparent that the extremes of family behavior can frequently cause more harm than good. But what of a compromise solution, what of the middle way? What would families be like which were neither parent-dominated nor child-dominated, but something in between; in which neither strong punishment nor weak punishment was the major characteristic;

where the structure was neither too simple nor too complex; in which people had greater worth than objects; in which parents neither agreed all of the time nor disagreed consistently; in which consistency was tempered and total inconsistency was avoided; in which either constant positive feelings or excessive negative feelings gave way to a more balanced emotional pattern; in which modern design was tempered with traditional values? Would this ideal family arrangement automatically produce effective families in which the parents found child-rearing easy and effortless, in which problems, pitfalls, and tragedy were all avoided? Let's examine such a family and see whether it would still have problems, whether even the moderated combination of all of these criteria proves to be the essential ingredient which explains why some families make it and some families don't.

Our hypothetical family would have a set of parents who were sure of themselves, assertive without being aggressive, proud of their accomplishments, humble in the face of their inadequacies, with many interests and long-range goals, compatible with each other and with their family. Their children, on the other hand, would be seen as members of a family group rather than as possessions, and would be entitled to respect, freedom, and privileges in the same measure as their parents. Their counsel would be sought and respected in family decisions. They, in turn, would feel in a similar fashion toward their parents. The punishments utilized by this mythical family would be in keeping with the crime, neither too harsh nor too weak, and would occur reasonably quickly and consistently. All the members of the family would live by a set of rules that made sense, were not burdensome, and yet served to spell out the requirements of daily living, both within the family and in dealings with the outside world. Care would be given to the objects and possessions of the family and the children would be required to exhibit not only neatness but also carefulness in the handling and use of the family's possessions. Excessive polishing and primping would be avoided, and yet the entire impression would be one of harmony and order.

While the parents occasionally would disagree in front of the children and the children would be aware of certain major differences between the parents, a system would be established whereby one or the other's preference would dominate a given situation, so that the over-all effect would be of a single set of expectations with variations and alternatives possible under different conditions, depending on which parent was in control at the moment or in which situation the child found himself. The patterns would be established with reasonable consistency, so that the children would know that what held true today would, for the most part, hold true tomorrow. Any inconsistencies arising out of the natural frailty of people or because of a changing situation would be acceptable and understandable. The family would be growing and changing in its requirements and expectations as society shifted and changed. Tradition for its own sake would be rejected, but tradition would be utilized for its richness, the help it provides in establishing a way of life, and its ties with the past. The family, therefore, would change, not wildly or impulsively, but reasonably and with thought.

Real feelings would be expressed, but the general tendency would be to express positive feelings since these in fact would reflect the predominant attitude of each family member. People would like each other and express that liking. They would feel and express strong love and empathy, but no one would avoid expressing anger, irritation, or fear when he felt them. The resulting mixture would provide a sense of reality, rather than a sense of saccharine sweetness or harsh dissidence. Finally, in this mythical family the traditional patterns of the extended family would have been modified to those of the nuclear family, the modern design. But it would have had added to it a circle of friends which satisfies the needs traditionally met by the presence of uncles and aunts and cousins. It would have a pattern of ritualistic observances that holds the family together, in some measure approximating the pattern of the old extended family, so that, to all intents and purposes, the family would be a combination of the strictly isolated nuclear family and the old complex extended natural family.

Is it possible for such a family as I have described to have problems, and if so, why? The answer to the first part of this question must be a resounding "of course, it can have problems." Nowhere in this description is there a guarantee that the children will develop all the necessary skills and attitudes for effective family or societal living. Within the outline I have described there are still strong possibilities for the development of unadaptive behaviors or serious maladaptive behaviors, and even for the disintegration of the family structure itself. The glaring deficit in this hypothetical ideal family pattern is the absence of any mechanism for controlling how new behaviors are to be taught,

how old patterns are to be managed, and how to make Johnny
want to obey.

Certainly the hypothetical family described is appealing and
seems to offer a desirable design for living. But it is doomed to
failure unless one additional factor is included and carefully
worked out. This important and basic factor I call *contract
management.* It can be defined simply by the question, "What
happens when Johnny obeys and what happens when he disobeys?" What happens when he is correct and what happens when
he is incorrect? What happens when he is exhibiting appropriate
behavior by whatever standards the family has set, and what
happens when he is exhibiting inappropriate behavior? The single
most important question that can be asked of any family structure
is *what happens when?* Contained within this question is the
whole contract management system and the whole modern
approach to child-rearing that this book is about. If the family
does not understand that each child must be handled differently
and that the question "what happens when?" must be answered
differently for each child and adjusted to fit each child, there will
be difficulties. Our hypothetical family makes no provision for
altering its system to fit each child, and thus the element of
effective contract management is absent.

I hope that all of the issues of family style that have been
discussed in this chapter become an important part of your
thinking and are taken into account in reevaluating your family
design. Each family must decide for itself what kind of family it
wants to be, what its characteristics will be. We can no longer rely
on doing things the way they used to be. We can no longer rely on
having things handed down to us. We must take on the responsibility of redesigning our own behavior repertoires both as
emancipated people in a free society and as members of a family
unit in a society which permits families great latitude in designing
themselves.

I began this chapter with the question of what leads to the
development of a successful family with obedient children. I am
ending it with the question of how one is to achieve that
obedience. I have indicated that it is based upon a concept of
contract management yet to be fully explained. But before
explaining it in greater detail, I think it is necessary to examine the
prevalent management system of our society—the system of
punishment to achieve discipline. This will be the subject of
Chapter 3.

3 🦋

Spare the

Rod

A very common problem that besets the question of discipline in our society is the conflict between the desire for respect and the desire to be loved. Some parents are content to have their children fear and obey them, defining respect in those terms. Others, finding that such a system frequently leads to a loss of love for the parents, insist that their children love them and worry less about "respect" than about the ever-constant problem of losing the love of their children. The two extremes seem irreconcilable.

In more traditional families with old-fashioned value systems and points of view, children are seen as possessions under the ownership of parents, who require of the child the kind of unquestioning obedience and loyalty that one would expect of an indentured servant. The child has to obey because "it's the right thing to do," because tradition and religious conviction demand it. It is quite convenient for the parent to resolve all difficulties by playing the absolute monarch. The effect of this system may be to create the illusion of a tightly-knit family with strong emotional bonds, but very often the bonds are based on fear, guilt, or shame, rather than on the more positive basis of love and affection.

I have seen families where the children are in such awe of the parents that they are afraid to voice any disagreement, objection, or criticism. They allow the parents not only to guide and coach them, but to determine every step they take in life. Very often these children are lauded as perfect models of what children ought to be. It is not hard, however, to discover the underlying strains and stresses in such a situation. The children feel deep resentment at being forced into this particular kind of relationship. The parents constantly bemoan the fact that their children avoid them, show little love or affection, and in fact simply tolerate them.

Let us examine the word "respect" and see what it means. Respect is really an awareness of the worth of another person's position, ideas, feelings, and actions. It does not necessarily imply agreement, but rather the ascribing of *worth* to the other person. Out of that sense of worth comes a willingness to compromise, to obey under certain conditions, and to disobey when appropriate. In our culture we have distorted the concept of respect by using it to justify a demand for obedience.

In contrast to the parents who demand obedience as a sign of respect, we have the parents who concentrate on getting their children to love them. Picture such a family in action. The mother hovers around the child, constantly asking, "Are you happy, are you satisfied, do you love Mommy?" The child quickly understands that an easy way to control Mommy is to threaten her with the loss of love. "I will love you if you give me a lollipop," the child frequently says. "You don't love me because you won't let me stay out late," the young boy often says accusingly to his parents. The parents constantly attempt to satisfy the whims and desires of the child in order to maintain his love. I have seen the end result of such a system in my office when the child, who has never known any limits or boundaries and has finally been caught in an act of wanton destruction or theft, turns to his parents and says, "You never gave me anything, you never loved me at all." The parents, bewildered, often say, "We gave him everything. Of course we loved him."

A deeper examination of this kind of situation reveals that the parents did give everything—except discipline, the most important gift of all. The parents were attempting to live up to an unrealistic standard that says a parent should be giving all the time in order to receive love. In this kind of family, in which the constant emphasis is on the parents' being appreciated, being loved, and being liked, the parents actually may be helping to destroy the child by constantly giving in to the child and never setting any boundaries or limits.

A love relationship is a give-and-take relationship which must be maintained by appropriate behavior. The parents who give material things for the purpose of receiving love are not really giving love. They are attempting to reassure themselves of their own effectiveness and worth as parents. In many cases, they may be attempting to hold back their own aggressions, very often the excessively loving mother feels that she might lash out if she did not keep herself in check by constant giving. The frenzy of giving in order to receive love is a result of the mother's search for reassurance that she is really a good person, after all.

Either extreme fails to promote effective discipline. The child who is forced to "respect" (which may really mean fear and obey) begins to resent, hate, and, in many cases, rebel. The punishment grows harsher, the pleas of the parents for respect grow more strident, until there is a constant flow of accusations back and forth. On the other hand, the parent who attempts to resolve the problem of "respect" by not requiring any at all soon finds a monster on his hands—the kind of a monster who has love and respect neither for himself nor for anyone else. Some parents vacillate back and forth between the two extremes, alternately demanding love or demanding obedience, and the child grows bewildered in the process.

The effective parent understands that feelings are one level of a relationship, obedience is another, and respect still a third. This type of parent distinguishes between obedience and discipline in terms of the methods to be used and the goals to be set. Respect is the basis of the entire process, for each individual's primary worth is recognized as having value. Thus the child feels a sense of his worth even when his parents disagree with his opinion. Under these conditions parents may disagree in front of the children without creating havoc. Disagreement, in and of itself, is not a lack of respect. The individual who maintains that respect implies total obedience or total agreement is constantly in turmoil. For he must go to great lengths to rationalize his arguments in order to avoid any disagreement or criticism. In the process he frequently causes more harm than good.

The end result of a system of discipline based on punishment and demands for "respect" is to produce the three witches of fear, guilt, and shame as the presiding spirits of the household. Fear may be expressed as anxiety, tension, or as "being nervous." If the control system is based on punishment for a simple failure to reach the standard, guilt or fear is felt. The failure is experienced as sinful and as meriting punishment. If the control system is based on rejection or ridicule, shame is felt. When shame is felt, it leads to attempts at concealment and withdrawal from others. Shame is most often described as embarrassment.

For too long, society has used the subtle manipulation of fear, guilt, and shame to control human beings. The admonition is "behave or else," where "or else" means punishment, rejection, being ostracized, or being ridiculed in public. Thus people have been forced into a pattern of conformity that is so subtle that they are hardly aware of it. Physical means of control are generally not necessary because fear, guilt, and shame act powerfully to enforce the required behavior. Only when people violate the requirements, in spite of these sanctions are stronger measures needed. We do not bring out the police, the national guard, or the army until the system of fear, guilt, and shame has broken down as a method of control. When that happens, we are forced to bring in physical means of control.

Most parents begin early in life to train their children to these three methods so that the children will not find themselves in a position of experiencing overt punishment. Parents want their children to be fearful of the teacher, to feel guilt for misbehavior, and to be ashamed of doing anything wrong. "If these three systems operate," parents reason, "my children will be safe. They will be protected from transgression and the more violent forms of punishment will be spared them." When you say to your children, "You ought to be ashamed of that. What would the neighbors say? What would people think?" you are using shame as a principle of control. As a result the child does not really learn that the behavior you are criticizing is wrong in itself. He learns only that he should be ashamed of letting people know about it; the only sin is being caught at what you're doing. In the end he will not behave better, but he will grow more secretive.

At other times you believe that the act itself is wrong and therefore you want the child to feel guilt. How many times have you looked at your child and said, "Don't you feel bad about this? Don't you know you've committed some kind of sin?" Have you ever tried to teach your child to feel bad inside and tried to intensify those feelings of fear or guilt by painting pictures of future punishment in Hell or when Daddy comes home? Have you ever used the term "You're a *bad* boy" with your child? When you hang that label on a child, you are making a moral judgment and you are trying to intensify the feeling of guilt. Without realizing it, you are helping to build the foundation for many kinds of problems later in life.

The child who feels fear, guilt, or shame will always be trying to avoid things rather than striving for things. He will be doing good in order to avoid punishment, the sense of guilt, or the sense of shame—not because he necessarily enjoys doing good or believes in doing good.

The fearful person finds it difficult to add new behavior to his repertoire, to change, to grow, to explore new ways of being. People controlled by this pattern very often find themselves shy, unsure of themselves, or even avoiding enjoyable situations. How many parents realize that in the very process of attempting to teach their children to deal with life, they are crippling them by their method of discipline or by the use of a concept of respect defined as obedience? We do not like it when other people try to manipulate us by using fear, guilt, and shame. We resent the threat of armed aggression. We resent the threat of rejection. We strongly dislike individuals who attempt to make us feel guilty and we bitterly oppose those who tend to shame us. Yet we use these very weapons as the three major tools in attempting to control our children.

By the time we must spank a child or send him to his room, we have lost control. Spanking or the use of deprivation are attempts to reinstate that control by making the child fearful of us or by making the child avoid our ridicule, our accusations, or our punishment. Our belief is that, somehow, as a result of punishment, the child will be better disciplined and better prepared to meet life and that our task as parents will be easier. Is it any wonder that our children avoid us and build their own worlds and prefer to be with their peers rather than with their parents? Is it any wonder that our words of praise have little meaning? Children see us very often as vengeful and judgmental. They accuse us of a lack of understanding. They see us as the policemen of their lives, rather than as friends, counselors, and loving parents. We rationalize the technique by believing that "some day they will understand and will love us." Too often, that never happens.

Many people believe, however, that we are forced to use punishment, despite all of the negative side effects, because there is no other way. I once was asked to examine a father who wanted to prevent his child from urinating in the diaper at the age of two weeks and scraped her bottom raw with a steel brush. He was insisting on discipline and on the child's living up to standards he had set. The tragedy in this case, of course, was that his expectations were bizarre and his lack of knowledge of a child's abilities extraordinary. Yet he is not unusual. There are on record numerous cases of child abuse in which the parents inflicted severe, harsh, and unusual punishment that appalls us when discovered. Somehow we feel these people are monsters; we could never do anything like that. Yet the researchers who have looked into this problem tell us over and over again that these parents are not monsters. They are not insane. They are simply very immature people with a background and a history in their own childhood of severe discipline and physical abuse. They are convinced that their rights as parents to punish their children are unbounded. Frequently the severe and cruel punishments occur as outgrowths of rage and frustration because the parents unwittingly are asking impossible behavior of their children.

But even where they are asking for reasonable behavior, they make no provisions for mistakes or errors or the just plain incompetence of growing children. Of course, our society grants parents the privilege of punishment and admonishes them to discipline their children and to maintain control over them. Supposedly in this way parents can encourage good character and rapid learning.

The notion of punishment is an ancient one in man's history. It parallels an equally ancient notion that punishment is not necessary. In the Old Testament there are at least two distinct points of view about the method of discipline. In one case, God is seen as a loving parent who either gives or withholds his love, depending on the behavior of his children. In another part of the Old Testament, we discover that God is vengeful and punishing to the point of taking the first-born children of the Egyptians as a punishment for the refusal of Pharoah to let the Jewish people go. As far as we can determine, these two attitudes about the nature of control go back into prehistory and can be found in the written records of all people.

Punishment, however, has always been the dominant method of control, perhaps because it is so seductive in its ease and simplicity—after all, it usually does achieve a temporary halting of undesirable behavior; perhaps because it also relieves the anger and frustration of the person doing the punishing. If we are honest with ourselves, we must admit that it feels good to let go, scream, yell, strike, or deprive. It feels good to work off our feelings. If it can be further justified as necessary and effective in producing desirable results, so much the better.

What of the other method? What of the differential giving of love? Perhaps this has not appealed as much to people because of the mistaken understanding of the nature of discipline. Discipline has so frequently been equated with punishment that the two seem almost synonomous. And yet discipline is not punishment. The dictionary defines discipline as "instruction or training, to instruct or to educate, to inform the mind of, to prepare by instruction, to train." Only one minor definition can be found equating it with punishment. Why, then, do we insist upon equating necessary discipline with punishment? Perhaps again because punishment is so attractive. It legitimizes our tendency toward aggression as a solution for our own frustration and as a way of reducing our own anger. Instinctively realizing this, children sometimes beg a parent to punish them, to reduce the parent's frightening anger. Perhaps we equate punishment with discipline because the utilization of other methods requires more knowledge than primitive man and even many modern parents have.

Discipline is, of course, necessary. There can be no question that children need structure, boundaries, and limits, and need them enforced. They cannot be allowed to flounder, to try out certain behaviors which can end only in tragedy for themselves and for others. They must be guided and led. No one can deny this fact. The arguable points have to do with how long, in how many areas, and by what method discipline is to be achieved and guidance and education are to be implemented.

According to scientists, punishment is a complex process involving two main parts. The first is the absence of any reward, positive feeling, or positive consequence. One cannot be loving and punishing at the same time. One cannot simultaneously give love and inflict some kind of undesirable outcome. Let us call this absence of positives a *time out*. It is a time out from any possibility of positive consequences. But during the time out period something else happens—something other than the mere cessation of positives, usually something painful and highly undesirable to the person who is being punished. The ingenuity of mankind in coming up with the undesirable is legion. In ancient times the undesirable outcome could entail amputation of a hand or the more permanent "time out" of amputating a head. It could involve the deprivation of liberty by locking someone up for a period of time or the taking of a possession as a penalty or fine. It could be the subjection of an individual to rejection over which he had no control. Some societies refined this to a fine art, ostracizing the child or removing him from the circle of family and friends and keeping him in isolation, far from the source of any love or affection or attention.

All of us have experienced punishment. It is difficult to avoid, and its characteristics occur naturally. If we place our hand on a hot stove, we experience natural punishment, involving the temporary absence (time out) of good feeling in our hand and the simultaneous infliction of pain, which is quite aversive.

Most people are unaware of the dual nature of punishment. Scientists have attempted to isolate these dual characteristics in order to study which of the two is the more important—the absence of a positive pleasure or the infliction of pain (or severe deprivation). They have studied it in carefully controlled, unemotional ways, attempting neither to defend the punishment nor to condemn it, but simply to understand the process. Animal experiments were conducted and repeated over and over again in an effort to determine the true nature of punishment. For example, in a study of the effects of punishment on a pigeon, the pigeon was required to peck on a disc only when a light was green. If it did so, it received corn as a consequence of its pecking. If, on the other hand, the pigeon pecked when the light was red, it received a severe electric shock. Needless to say, the pigeon was quickly discouraged from pecking when the light was red. It acquired, quite rapidly, the ability to differentiate between the green and the red light and soon made no errors in pecking upon the correct signal.

The rapid learning which results from the quick discouragement of inappropriate behavior has frequently been used as a justification for punishment. Certainly we can say that our pigeon has learned rapidly and that punishment appeared to be justified. But the analysis of punishment shows that there are two parts. During the incorrect behavior of pecking when the light was red, no corn was given as a consequence. There was a *time out* from receiving a positive reward. In addition, a punishing, painful outcome occurred. The pigeon received an electric shock. But was the shock necessary? Would the time out alone have been effective in teaching the pigeon his lesson? If the emphasis had been put on the granting or the withholding of corn, would the behavior also have been learned?

When an experiment was conducted to answer this question, it was found that the giving or withholding of corn also produced learning in the pigeon, but not as rapidly. Had the experiment stopped at this point, punishment would have been justified once more as a rapid method of teaching or discipline. But the astute experimenter recognized that one additional component was missing in his study. There had been, in fact, no readily identifiable time out period, no differentiation sufficient to really separate out the two components of punishment, the absence of a positive reward *and* the presence of a painful outcome. He repeated the experiment but this time, instead of simply giving or withholding the corn, he added a distinctive time out period. He did this by turning off the lights and equipment for a very brief time interval sufficient to indicate that a time out was occuring. The effect was astounding. Almost the same rate of learning was achieved as when the electric shock was used. The pigeon quickly learned the appropriate behavior to be used under each condition. There are many other such experiments to show that while punishment increases the rate of learning, so does the granting of a time out. The introduction of the pain is unnecessary since pain actually functions in the experiment as a time out.

The implications of these experiments for child-rearing are enormous. First of all, as we have seen, learning can be achieved without the introduction of time out by simply giving or withholding a reward. Such learning is slower, but just as sure and, as we shall see presently, infinitely more effective in the long run than learning produced by the use of punishment. Where a stronger negative consequence is required, half of the component of punishment can be used, which is simply a brief and dramatic time out interval during which no positive reward can be earned no matter what the individual does.

At this point, I hope it is clear that the nature of punishment is dual and that the first part of it, the temporary absence of the right to earn a positive reward, is much more effective, or at least as effective, as the combination of the two. The infliction of pain or deprivation is truly unnecessary from a scientific point of view. What is more, if we examine some of the other effects of the use of punishment we shall see that it is further to be avoided because of undesirable side effects. Remember that punishment contains elements of aggression, pain, or deprivation. What effect does this have upon human beings or upon any living thing? Scientists have shown us that punishment produces an emotional reaction in the living creature upon which the punishment is being inflicted, be it animal or child. This emotional state frequently is one of anger or fear, usually anger. Very few people respond positively to the infliction of pain or deprivation upon themselves.

I can remember my father taking me down to the cellar, stripping off his strap, and uttering those immortal parental words, "This is going to hurt me more than you." How did he know? I knew that the darn thing stung. Half the time I wasn't even sure why I was getting hit, but there was one thing I knew for sure; I was angry and I hated him for doing it to me.

The effect, then, of punishing any person is to create anger and to increase the likelihood that the anger will be expressed either as overt aggression or as passive aggression. Once a child is punished in the way we are describing, once the effort is made to discourage behavior by the infliction of pain or deprivation, we have created the beginnings of another problem and we then must find some way of removing the anger before it shows itself in agression in the child or other undesirable side effects. For example, my favorite way of getting even as a child was to come late to everything. I always had an excuse, but dragging my heels was a wonderful way to get even. As I got older, I found other, more subtle ways to get rid of my anger at parental punishment. One way was to withhold information, to become hostile and short-tempered, to drive my teachers to distraction.

Punishment is usually the result of the child's undesirable behavior. Clearly, however, because inflicting punishment relieves tensions and frustrations many people will find excuses to inflict punishment. Rules frequently will be arbitrary and changing. The effect of such arbitrary punishment is to produce a continuous state of anxiety in the child which, together with the anger resulting even from deserved punishment, leaves the child in a condition that certainly does not contribute to his physical or emotional well-being.

Even where the punishment is part of a structured, consistent, and rational system of management, the child still must constantly evaluate everything he does in anticipation of pain or deprivation. He cannot assume a relaxed attitude about life, but must always be alert to avoid the infliction of pain or deprivation.

Punishment also produces another set of problems stemming from the fact that human beings are quite capable of adapting to any level of punishment and accepting it as palatable. Therefore, to be effective, punishment must be so undesirable that the individual will avoid it and its effects and will actively suppress certain behavior. If the child adapts to the punishment level and begins to ignore a mere scolding or the threat of a scolding, the parent is forced to increase the loudness of the scolding, to add physical stress with a slap or the tap of a hairbrush. Escalation becomes a way of life. And since, as scientists tell us, no punishment can eliminate the tendency toward undesirable behavior, but at best can merely suppress it, the likelihood of its reoccurrence still exists. What is more, new kinds of misbehavior, failures, or errors will occur in the normal process of living.

As the child adapts to each level of punishment, the parent is forced into more and more extreme forms of punishment. The parent with the two-week-old baby, mentioned at the beginning of this chapter, rapidly went to an extreme form of punishment. Most parents must be driven there by sheer frustration because of their failure to produce obedience. It may take years for the escalation process to reach its ultimate peak when the parent has exhausted his bag of tricks and deprived the child as severely as he could justify doing. He has hit as hard and as often as he could, and has screamed for the last time. The day of reckoning almost always comes when the child looks the parent straight in the eye and dares him to go further, saying, in effect, "Your current level of punishment no longer bothers me."

Thus for a control system such as punishment to work, it must be backed up with the threat of total annihilation. In the Army, the sergeant is prepared to shoot you; in prison the death penalty stands at the end of the line of escalated punishment. Of course, few parents are prepared to go that far. They are willing to punish so long as they can justify it and are willing to get more severe so long as the child's behavior seems to warrant it. But they are totally helpless when the behavior of the child is not so far out of line as to justify a new level of punishment while the available punishments in their repertoire are regarded by the child without fear. At this point control is lost. It can happen at the age of seven or the age of seventeen. It depends on the child, the number of trials, the number of times that the parent has had to punish, and many other complex factors. But one thing is certain: escalation *will* occur. Few children continue to be afraid, as they get older, of mild disapproval or a harsh kind of threat. They require demonstration.

Some of the children who do adapt are the ones to be pitied more than any others. The escalation takes place inside. In many ways the slow withering of the spirit and the destruction of confidence are worse than the overt conflict I have been describing. The child is so terrified early in life by the fear of total rejection and ultimate death that he is afraid to challenge the parent and experience the punishment. He never has the chance to adapt slowly. Like the person who has uncontrollable fears of height or crowds, he will not even face a threatening situation. He constantly strives to avoid any punishment. His life is a continuously terror-filled day-by-day existence in which he has been successful only if he has not been scolded or rejected. Such a pattern almost always develops when the parent uses ostracizing the child as a method of rejection, withdrawing from him in such a way that he feels terrified, totally inadequate, and incompetent to bring the parent back. The child may accept the loss of the parent and withdraw completely from the struggle. There are many cases of severe disturbance in children who no longer seek support or acceptance from adults, totally convinced that they are unable to get it or so fearful of its loss that they would rather not risk exposing themselves to this situation. There are far too many cases of children who constantly live with the fear of rejection by everyone because an early traumatic experience of rejection, long forgotten, has convinced them that if they are not loved and approved they will die—because of the absence of the parent without whom every child knows he will die. In cases like these, escalation took place inside the child rather than outside in open conflict with parent or teachers.

Frequently, neither the parent nor the child is aware of that early confrontation, although they live under its shadow for the rest of their lives. Parents often are confused and amazed at the problems that have arisen as the side effects of a massive use of this kind of punishment early in life, for their children seem to be obedient children who never need punishment. In fact, it may seem that they never have been punished, and even the children will deny that they have ever been punished. They are confused as to why they live in a continuous state of anxiety and fear and why their lives somehow seem blighted and shadowed. It is almost better that the escalation takes place more slowly and more overtly, so that a child has a chance to develop behaviors and defenses to deal with the situation.

But let us return now for a moment to the use of time out mentioned earlier. Can escalation occur here? What is the difference? By its very nature, a time out must be coupled with positive consequences for it to be effective. Later, we shall see how important it is for the parent to help the child *earn* something he or she wants (positive consequence) after the time out is over. By its very nature, the use of a time out must involve recognition of the fact that the parent can only teach and can never eliminate behavior. Thus the purpose of the use of the time out is only to occasionally suppress the undesirable behavior. At the very worst the time out is temporary, for generally the child ends it, not the parent. Occasionally during a disciplining conflict the parent may have to designate a brief time out similar to the use of the penalty box in hockey games. I often have to send one of my young children away from the table for misbehaving. They may return when *they* feel they can control themselves and behave appropriately. If, after several trials, I find they are not staying away long enough to calm themselves down I may then impose a brief (several minutes) time out which *I* control. An important point is who decides when time out is over, my child or me, and most often it is the child. When I was a child I missed many a complete meal, radio privileges for a week, or the use of the car for a month. My father always controlled time out, it always lasted for a long time, and no matter how good I became I still had to suffer the punishment through till the end. Whenever time out lasts more than a few minutes, it becomes a punishment.

In the Gilbert and Sullivan opera, people were admonished to make the punishment fit the crime. This is a very difficult thing to do. Our legal system has wrestled with the problem for centuries. Depending on the mood of the parents, the punishment may be too harsh, too easy, or even not inflicted at all. But in any case, the effect of the parent's controlling the punishment is to create feelings of helplessness in the child. There is no way to stop it once it is happening. The inevitability of the doom is felt almost as a nightmare. Once you are caught, the process begins; no matter how much you repent or change your ways, you must suffer through the pain and the deprivation.

We forget how it must feel to be a child under such a system. Our memories become blurred with time and we accept the morality of such a system. We justify it as effective and put up with the cruelty because of our rationalizations. But if we remember what it felt like to be a child facing punishment without much experience, without a general sense of accomplishment, without a certainty of the punishment's ending, and without the time perspective of the adult, we will recognize what a terrible feeling it is to be helpless, awaiting punishment, and then experiencing that punishment.

Time out, on the other hand, as it will be used in this book, is so temporary and so intimately related to the behavior in question that the child can accept it as a necessity. No aggressive feelings are created and there is little fear because the child knows that as soon as his behavior shifts he can return to receiving positive consequences (just as the pigeon knows he will receive his food if he makes the correct response after the time out is over). The incentive to do so is very strong, inasmuch as no resentment or rebelliousness has been generated in the child since no aggression was used on him.

Most parents use punishment only because their goal is elimination of undesirable behavior. We don't want the child to steal, to fight with his sister, or to talk back to us. We want the child to avoid behavior that will endanger him, such as running into the street, playing with pills in the medicine cabinet, or picking up a knife from the table. We find ourselves constantly horrified at behaviors that children seem to gravitate to easily and naturally. Many new parents are certain that if their supervision and surveillance let up for a moment the child will destroy himself. Their life is a constant round of do's and don't's in which it seems the don't's far outweigh the do's. So much is this so that parents themselves begin to wonder why they even thought being a parent would be fun. The emphasis on elimination and suppression of behavior in some families becomes almost a mania, a constant round of criticising the child, saying "no, no," and trying to find stronger means of eliminating his undesirable behavior.

Family life thus becomes a constant struggle and battle as to who will win, whether the behavior will be suppressed, and whether the child will ever again resort to that approach. The answer usually is that punishment only works for a little while. The myth of the success of punishment persists because some "model" children get the message early in life. We saw why this is so and the problems that it creates. Efforts to use punishment as a means of control end in a situation in which you're damned if you do and damned if you don't. If you succeed, you've created a problem and if you fail, you have a continuous problem. Every behavior we've ever learned is still in our repertoire and capable of returning under the right conditions. Suppression is not an effective method.

Let's examine one very prevalent case, the child who steals. Initially, he is simply taking what he wants because it's there. The concept of the ownership of private property and its rights is very difficult for most adults to understand and almost impossible for children. So the young child reaches out and takes. As parents we immediately see it as the opening point of the wedge. If we allow it to continue, he will become a thief and a bum and a crook. Parents look upon the first stealing excursions of childhood with horror. The parents' response, of course, is to punish. The younger the child, the milder the punishment; the newer the problem, the milder is the punishment. But escalation has to take place. The mild punishment will suppress the behavior temporarily, it is true, since it is part of the family of negative consequences which do suppress behavior. But since there is no alternate behavior of which the child is capable, it will return. He has no other way of getting what he wants other than by taking it. He is very limited in skills and in his ability to delay gratification or to find alternate sources of gratification. He wants it now and he wants it strongly and you are blocking him. He will fight you at first; he will persist in trying to get around the obstacle. If he finally discovers that when you're present it isn't possible for him to get what he wants, he simply will wait until you leave. The suppressive effect occurs only while you are present. Very soon the child begins to gravitate toward other means of getting that gratification. He may lie or steal more efficiently or find someone else to do the stealing for him so that he can remain innocent of the actual happening. The ingenuity of children is amazing in solving the problem of getting what they want and avoiding the punishment. They discover very quickly that the real crime is in being caught and that the punishment really comes not so much from stealing as from being caught.

The terrors of Wanamaker Street once discovered the rich mother lode of candy at the corner store. We found that our limited resources of money did not meet the gnawing hunger of our bellies. We organized a shoplifting expedition that was simplicity in motion. We grabbed the stuff and ran. The druggist knew us and our parents and immediately picked up the telephone and made seven urgent phone calls. That night we slept standing up. Our solution was simple: steal from strange stores only, distract the shopkeeper, and always pay for something, even if only a penny piece of gum. We never got caught again and eventually dropped the stealing in favor of touch football.

Very little of what is desirable can be taught to the child simply by punishing for the act of stealing. What is more, punishment has its side effects which often result in the child's learning a great deal that is undesirable. The goal of permanent suppression simply is not scientifically valid. The only method known to science to eliminate a behavior permanently is to replace it with another behavior which is incompatible with the undesirable one and which remains at a very high strength throughout the lifetime of the child. That is, if we teach a child to be honest 100 percent of the time and if we carefully define honesty for him by teaching him various skills and maintaining honest behavior at a very high level, it will take care of the stealing.

When replacing rather than suppressing an undesirable behavior the emphasis, of course, is on the positive. The problem truly is never the undesirable behavior, but the absence of a desirable behavior. It is not the fighting between children that should concern us, but the lack of cooperation. If children are being cooperative 100 percent of the time, fighting cannot occur.

It is amazing how often this simple fact of human nature is overlooked, both at the level of the family and at the level of nations. The notion of using deterrents to eliminate behavior is an appealing one, because it makes us feel strong and powerful and it seems to work at first. If we just threaten the other person with a bigger stick long enough, we will be safe. Unfortunately, it has never worked. In mankind's recorded history, there are less than three hundred years when no war has occurred. In the lifetime of the average family, there are less than three hundred days in which a conflict of some sort does not occur at least subtly. It is time that we reexamine the goal of permanent suppression by the method of punishment.

Furthermore, for punishment to work, certain conditions are needed. For punishment to be even partially effective as a management system, the neighborhood and the extended family must support it. Remember the druggist who knew us and our parents? He knew just whom to call. Does the manager of your cut-rate drugstore in a far-off shopping center know your children and you? Where there are conflicting family systems in operation around the child, as there are in any neighborhood, and where he can contrast methods of control, the justifications and rationalizations used to support a punishment system no longer have the same effect. As long as the child can be told that God wills it so by his minister and as long as he sees that punishment is used all around him and has no other system to compare it with, it will work at least partially and for a time. It may even work reasonably well for most children most of the time, if there is the back-up of the local shopkeeper, the next-door neighbor and the cousins and the uncles and the aunts. But where a nuclear family exists in a neighborhood with many different kinds of systems, where there is no longer a tightly knit community, where the extended family has broken down, and where children are free to compare, they very quickly see the fallacies of punishing.

The tragedy is that when they become parents they in turn may use punishment on their children since they have never learned any other kind of management systems. They may find themselves slipping into the same rationalizations, so that the process will repeat itself.

Are there any occasions on which punishment makes sense? Are there any kinds of families that should consider the use of punishment as a method of suppressing behavior? The answer to the queston is "yes." I can think of occasions on which punishment makes real sense. For example, a study was done in California with autistic children. Autistic children present a rare kind of problem in that they never develop normal human social behaviors. They remain at the animal level and may even reject any contact with human beings. Frequently, they engage in self-destructive behaviors to the point where they will bite off their own fingers, gnaw their shoulders to the bone, detach a retina by constantly hitting the head with a hand or against a wall, and other similarly horrible behavior patterns. The autistic child fails to learn speech. Even the simplest kinds of activity, such as play, do not seem to appear. He will frequently rock for hours, making animal-like noises and his attention span seems to be a few seconds, at the most, for any constructive activity.

These are tragic cases and represent the most extreme kind of maladaptive development that we know. Almost all methods of treatment have failed to improve these children's behavior. On rare occasions, child therapists have been able to bring about reasonable changes in humanizing these children. The causes of autism remain obscure and perplexing, but one thing is certain—autistic children have failed to develop normal human behavior.

In the California experiment, an attempt was made to stop the children from biting off their fingers or engaging in other self-destructive acts. Many of these children had been in restraints for years as the only known method of preventing such behavior. When the psychologist conducting the experiment analyzed the problem, he came to the conclusion that one of the main factors in perpetuating this behavior was the tender loving care being given the children by sympathetic nurses, doctors, and parents when they engaged in various acts of self-destruction. He decided, therefore, to require of the nurses in attendance that they only give tender loving care (sympathy, warmth, and empathy) when the children were *not* engaged in self-destructive behavior patterns.

There was only one problem with this new program. This behavior had developed into such an intense habit, its practice was so rapid and constant with these children that at no time when they were out of the restraints did the behavior cease even for a moment. The man doing the experiment chose to shock the children with a cattle prod. Unquestionably, the electric shock served as a punishment. He used it to suppress the self-destructive behavior, but only long enough to give a great deal of tender loving care when the children were not engaged in the self-destructive acts. Within twenty-four hours the experimenters had successfully eliminated the self-destructive behavior in all of the children with whom the experiment was done and it has not returned since.

It seems to me that the use of punishment in this situation can be adjudged moral and effective. It can be seen as moral because it returned these children to the real world. They could now be free of restraints. And it was effective because it coupled punishment with good positive control, effective teaching, and a great deal of understanding and love on the part of the experimenter.

In a related experiment a child with similar kinds of problems was let into a room in which electric wires had been placed on the floor. The child was barefoot and allowed to run about freely in the room. The experimenter then turned on the rather unpleasant current. The child frantically dashed around the room and finally ran toward the experimenter. As she approached him, he turned off the current, ending the shock. She clutched at him and remained close. A little while later, she wandered off again and again he turned the current on. This time she immediately rushed back to him, hugging him and clinging closely. She had learned in a process of approximately sixty seconds what used to take a year for such children to learn—that adults could protect and safeguard the child against the unpleasantness of life. Adults rapidly developed value for the child.

Beginning on this base, the experimenter was able to help the child discover reality and begin to notice and take advantage of her environment. In relatively short order, using this technique as the opening wedge, he was able to help the child develop more nearly normal human behavior. This case also seems to me to be a justifiable use of punishment because the punishment served as only a very small component of a larger system and saved as much as six months of this child's life. The experimenter could have achieved the same results with six months of patient effort by gradually feeding her and acquiring in her mind value and worth. But he accomplished this in sixty seconds, using this punishment technique. The saving of six months in the short life of a child made it a moral act, and the fact that the punishment was a part of a well understood and carefully worked out positive-negative system made it effective.

Of course, the average person is not faced with problems as serious and severe as these. The average parent easily should be able to bring about effective control of his or her children without ever having to resort to the infliction of pain or arbitrary deprivation. The strongest technique needed by the parents of children who do not have serious problems is the use of the parentally controlled time out. In my opinion, the introduction of pain as a suppressant is justifiable only when no other technique will work or when the saving in time is so profound as to make it a reasonable choice.

Two other examples can illustrate situations in which punishment may be seen as necessary, moral, and effective. A boy was brought to me who had been hiccupping steadily, consistently, and quite loudly for over a month. This condition had caused his absence from school and finally necessitated hospitalization. When I first heard of the case over the telephone, it seemed inconceivable to me that a pupil's hiccupping could so disrupt the classroom that he would have to be removed. I was wrong.

When the child was brought into my office, the severity and the loudness of the hiccupping were almost more than I could stand, and I was not trying to teach thirty-five other children. The hospitalization was made necessary because of the child's constant loss of sleep and because of the intense problems the hiccupping was creating within the family. Before I could develop any incentive or positive consequence for not hiccupping and for maintaining a pattern of no hiccupping, it was necessary to stop it for a short period of time. I had been assured by the physical report that there was no medical basis for the hiccupping and it was clear to me that the explanation lay in the benefits the child had originally achieved by the hiccupping.

It is hard for us to imagine how people can be seduced into behaviors against their best interests until we think of such problems as stuttering, overeating, smoking, and related phenomena so prevalent in our culture. There are many behavior patterns which generate both positive and negative consequences. In this case, the hiccupping originally had generated the positive consequences for this child of a great deal of attention, avoidance of school, and special privileges. The negative consequences, however, were depletion of physical health through loss of sleep and an awareness that he was the cause of the gradual frustration and annoyance of all the adults around him. But by the time these negative consequences became apparent, the habit had been established. I gave the boy the conditions under which we would operate. When he stopped hiccupping and could maintain it, he would receive a pocket radio that he badly wanted. This incentive, of course, was not enough. He could not control the hiccupping. It was necessary for me to help him. A mild electric shock was used, again as a form of punishment but with his full consent. At each hiccup, he received a shock which was not intense enough to cause severe pain but was enough to make him uncomfortable. Within a matter of half an hour the hiccups had stopped and the problem was solved. It had taken a month to bring him to the point of hospitalization but half an hour was enough to solve it. Had I not used punishment in that situation it is conceivable that the problem could have gone on for months longer.

In the second case, not one of mine, a girl sneezed every two minutes. Before effective training was utilized with her, she had spent over five months either in hospitals or on visits to specialists. All medical reasons were ruled out and the case was perplexing to everyone until a psychologist utilized the technique I have just described. In her case it took about three and a half hours to suppress the sneezing long enough so that she could receive a positive outcome for not sneezing.

It seems to me that the wise family should recognize that when punishment seems necessary, expert assistance should be called in. The judgment as to whether punishment is necessary or not really requires more expertise than the average family can hope to develop. Most of the cases that I can think of which required the use of pain or severe deprivation as a method of temporarily suppressing behavior long enough to teach its alternative involved a kind of problem with which the average family is not prepared to deal.

I should like to make it clear that I am not arguing against the use of negative consequences. Later in this book we will discuss many types of negative consequences and how effective they can be in discouraging certain kinds of undesirable behaviors. The issue here is the use specifically of punishment, which is one member of the whole class of negative consequences. Because it is important to differentiate between a negative consequence and a punishment, let us examine some cases that will clarify the distinction. In one case where it was desirable to calm a young girl having tantrums, a method of negative consequences was used to discourage and decelerate the tantrums. One of her favorite dolls simply was turned upside-down and stood on its head while the child was having tantrums. The doll was placed right side up when the tantrums had ceased. This hardly could be construed as a punishment and yet it was extremely effective. It discouraged the tantrum behavior and encouraged self-control.

In another case a teacher discovered an effective method of

keeping her young students quiet and avoiding unacceptable behavior. She used the technique, familiar to many teachers, of merely writing the offending child's name on the board. There was no punishment attached to placing a child's name on the board, except that the children preferred that it not be there and so would be quiet in order to avoid having their names written on the board. She would immediately follow this technique with a positive approach by praising the children for their ability to maintain silence and appropriate behavior in the classroom. Why writing a name on the board should decelerate behavior in certain children seems strange to me. The fact that it will work with many children is, however, an established fact. One hardly can call writing the name of a child on the blackboard a punishment. It is, however, a negative consequence.

The giving of an incentive can be seen as a positive consequence and its absence can be seen as an example of a negative consequence. The absence, however, may be only temporary. A negative consequence may be seen as similar to an employer's refusal to pay a commission to a salesman who has not made any sales, in contrast with an employer's docking the pay of a worker whose performance he does not like. The real question is who owns the pay. In the first case, ownership of the paycheck remains with the employer. He dispenses it only if and when the salesman performs his task. In the second case, the employee owns the paycheck and the employer is taking back from him that which he has already been paid because the employer does not like the performance or because it fails to meet some previously determined standard.

There is a world of difference between the two types of negative consequences. In the former, we do not resent the employer's failure to pay; in the latter, great resentment is engendered at the unfairness of the technique, even when it is warranted by the agreed-upon commitments on both sides. The parent who chooses to take away from the child that which the child already possesses is engaging in punishment. "You cannot watch television any longer because you have been bad," implies that she is docking the child for misbehavior; as compared with "As long as you are behaving, you are earning the right to watch television, but if you fail to behave, you have failed to earn the television." The difference is subtle and yet profound. Children will respond differently to the two kinds of negative consequences, showing resentment in the one case, and in the other accepting it as a legitimate consequence of their behavior. In the use of punishment as a negative consequence there is no way to recover the right to watch television until the arbitrary punishment has been fulfilled. In the case of "You have failed to earn it" as a negative consequence, the child's first question is usually, "How can I earn it? What must I do?" The emphasis is on the positive.

A negative consequence is any outcome of behavior which tends to weaken that behavior. Punishment is one kind of negative consequence which has the major characteristic of pain or fixed deprivation. Punishment has limited usefulness. In a clinical setting, it can be invaluable in saving time and in helping children to acquire appropriate skills more rapidly. Its use must always be limited and carefully controlled in an over-all setting where the emphasis is on the positive. The emphasis on the positive cannot be stressed too often.

Let's look at the example of taking away or granting television viewing privileges, for this case makes clear the essential difference between a positive management system and a punishment system. In a punishment system the child avoids loss of rights by good behavior. We start with the premise that a child is entitled to many things and he has them by right. Then, we believe, the way to create discipline is to threaten him with loss of rights or, in some cases, with the receiving of actual pain (spanking). The only thing the child stands to gain is what he already has ·or is entitled to have. Punishment is supposed to loom as a major thing to be avoided, with the parent being the judge as to which things are taken away, when, and for how long. In a positive management system, the child may also fail to have something at any given time, but he never has ownership of it to begin with. The television set is granted to him as a privilege based upon his correct behavior. If he fails to earn it, it is not punishment, although it still may be a negative consequence.

The general class of negative consequence certainly includes punishment as one kind of negative outcome. But we should not equate punishment (which is time out plus pain) with a negative consequence (which may be simply the absence of a positive consequence or the presence of any other outcome which has the effect of weakening the behavior). When we turn to the section on method, a good deal of time will be spent on showing the various differences between negative consequences and punishment. At this time it is sufficient to point out the very real differences between the failure to earn something and the loss of that which is already possessed.

The primary question before us is always how to raise children who are obedient and disciplined, who learn rapidly, and yet are not fearful, guilty, or ashamed? What would control them? Perhaps the answer lies in the desire to achieve certain kinds of positive outcomes. Instead of running scared, as the saying goes, they would be behaving appropriately and striving to live a good life because they believed in it, respected it, and enjoyed it. Perhaps, if no punishment were utilized in a family, it might be possible to produce the kind of love and warmth that most of us have experienced only rarely and only occasionally with people close to us. Perhaps the desire of most people to find personal satisfaction within the family could be achieved.

The myth of punishment as the only effective method of discipline needs to be dispelled. Many people believe that seeing-eye dogs and performing seals are trained by spanking them with a rolled newspaper. This is simply not true. Most of the animals we see on the television, in the movies, or at the circus are trained by a positive method. The trainer would not want his animals to be afraid of him or scared in any way. He wants them as calm and relaxed as possible when he is working with them and he wants always to remain their friend rather than their enemy. It is possible to tame even wild animals without once making them afraid. The method the trainers use is an ancient one. They did not invent it, as has been pointed out earlier; it can be found in the Bible. It is simply to create an incentive, to obtain effective discipline patterns without using any technique that produces side effects such as we have been discussing in this chapter. Discipline without punishment—this is the ideal we shall turn to throughout this book as the prime method of managing children. But first we must develop an understanding of what behavior really is.

Part **2**

THE
WHAT of
BEHAVIOR

4

We Are What
We Do

Before you can really get down to techniques and ways to influence people's behavior, you have to know a little about behavior itself and about the different parts of behavior. I don't want to get unnecessarily complicated about this. As a matter of fact, I don't think you need to know a great deal about all of the precise, specific kinds of things that scientists are interested in or that professional psychologists want to know. Basically, as parents, what you're really interested in is what Johnny is doing, what reason he has for doing it, and on what occasions he does it. Let's look first at what he does.

ACTIONS

In terms of what he is doing, you should be concerned with the specific nature of the act itself. Is he eating his spinach, is he going to bed in the correct fashion, brushing his teeth first, buttoning up his pajamas correctly? These kinds of *public behaviors* are simple, easy to describe, and seem rather precise. There's no doubt in your mind as to whether Johnny is buttoning his pajamas or not. All you have to do is to watch his hands and see in what position they're placed on his shirt. You can tell if he is dawdling with the buttons because the button is not going into the buttonhole and his hands are not moving up or down his pajama front. There is nothing complicated about defining a public behavior in which he is engaged at any given time.

The problem gets much more difficult, however, if you're concerned with what he is thinking. Thinking is a kind of *private behavior*, and when he is engaged in thinking or imagining or remembering, it is impossible for you to know precisely what he is doing at a given moment. You can say he's daydreaming, of course. He is looking off into space, eyes not focused on anything particular in front of him, and he's obviously thinking about something. When you ask him what he is doing, the usual reply, of course, is "nothing." He himself may not be able to pin down what was flashing through his mind at that moment. The particular private behavior is not observable by the parent.

Mostly, however, parents are concerned with things that they can see the child doing (public behaviors). The parent looks at what the child is doing and usually describes it rather concretely. "He's hitting his sister." "He's doing his homework." "He's watching television." All of these are examples of bits of behavior that a parent can see. These behaviors are always characterized by having a beginning and an end. Many of these behaviors get repeated over and over again. If the child hits his sister today, he may well hit her tomorrow. If he is dragging his feet going up to bed, you can almost predict that tomorrow night on his way up to bed he will drag his feet in much the same way. If he is interrupting the conversation with your husband, you probably can observe the same kind of interruption tomorrow.

What we're talking about then is something that's observable and measurable. You can count how many times he does it or for how long he does it. These observable bits of behavior we call *actions* or *acts* (behaviorial responses). They are simply those small building blocks of a larger pattern, and as such they can be isolated and counted. Actions are what the person does, what Johnny or Jane does in the process of trying to accomplish whatever they're trying to accomplish.

It's important to isolate this component of behavior, the act itself, because people have a way of making value judgments about behavior. They will talk about their Johnny as being "lazy." The word "lazy" really is not a descriptive term of what Johnny is doing or not doing. He is simply sitting and staring at a wall. If he is not engaged in some desirable behavior, the parent often makes a value judgment about this state of affairs. Yet under some conditions it's very desirable that Johnny not do anything. For example, if he's lying in bed for his nap or about to go to sleep, we wouldn't want him doing anything but resting and we would not call him "lazy" if he were simply to lie still and stare at the ceiling.

On the other hand, if we wanted Johnny to do his homework or carry out the garbage, and he were lying on the couch and staring at the ceiling, we might be tempted to use the word "lazy." The word "lazy," however, is too vague, because it laps over into implications about the reasons for not doing anything, rather than simply describing the fact that he is lying still and not doing anything. "Lazy" implies that he is willfully doing nothing or that there is something wrong with his character so that he is unable to do differently. Many things are contained in the word "lazy" that are not contained in the simple descriptive statement, "he is lying on the couch not doing anything."

Further on, we will want to know more about why he's doing

things and what his reasons are for acting or not acting. Right now we are going to concentrate on learning to look at his act as a simple part of the whole pattern, without asking questions such as "What caused the behavior, when did he start using it, or what were his reasons for doing it." We are just going to look at children actually engaged in acting.

If we go to a playground and look through the fence at the children engaged in various activities, we will see them acting. One child will be pushing another child on a swing. We could count, for example, how many times he pushed her or how many different children he assisted by giving a push. We could watch the child's behavior as he wandered through the playground, engaged in different kinds of action for short periods of time. We could, if we wanted to, count many different behavioral actions. We could count, for example, how many times he takes a drink of water, how many times he goes close to the playground supervisor, whether he stays there for long periods of time or only briefly. If our measurement is to be based on time, we simply ask how much of the available time did he spend with the playground supervisor? How much time did he spend at the swings and how much time did he spend at the water fountain? In each case, we measure some action on his part in terms of the amount of time involved in the particular action.

If we felt that the child needed to spend more time with children, time would be an important measure for us. If we were concerned with the child's tendency to avoid playing with other children by staying near adults, we would be interested in how long he did various things. But if we were concerned with how often he spoke to another child, we would count the number of times he spoke or walked over and began a conversation. Again, we would not be asking anything about reasons. We would not be asking what started him in the behavior. We would simply be trying to observe, as clearly and as precisely as we could, what the child was doing.

One of the biggest problems that parents have in the management of children is that they really don't attend to what the child is doing. They are almost always concerned with the reasons for his doing things and not often enough concerned with an accurate description of what he is doing. Frequently a mother will tell me that her child interrupts her a great deal. I then ask her to tell me how many times an hour he interrupts her. This seems to her a strange question at first. When she goes home and actually tries to count the number of interruptions, she may discover that the actual number is very small. The problem may really be that the mother doesn't want even that small number of interruptions. Her impression was that the child was interrupting a great deal because any interruption at all would have been unacceptable. Another mother may find that her child's interruptions occur at the rate of ten or twenty per hour. In this case, we could say that the child really is interrupting too much and the problem is not with what the mother is expecting but with the fact that the child is interrupting at much too high a rate.

The idea of counting and being precise may seem strange to you at first, but the reason I emphasize it should be obvious by now. Trying to keep a record forces us to describe more accurately what it is we're trying to change.

I had one teacher tell me that she didn't like children running, screaming, and yelling. On closer questioning, I found that the problem was not screaming, running, and yelling, but their occurrence in her classroom. She didn't object to these things happening outside in the playground. In fact, I found that her problem really wasn't the running and screaming of the children at all, because she was perfectly willing to accept that kind of behavior even in the classroom if it only occurred once in a great while. The fact that it was occurring so *often* was what was behind her complaint.

The number of times a person performs the action may be the key to the problem. If a child, for example, takes a bath, we would not ordinarily object to that behavior pattern. But if he were taking three to five baths per day, any parent would become concerned. If someone tells you that her friend washes the kitchen floor, you would not be particularly concerned, unless you found out that she washes the kitchen floor twelve times a day or only once a year.

A good rule for determining whether or not you are talking about a behavior that can be changed is to ask whether you can count the behavior. If you cannot pinpoint and reduce the problem with which you are concerned to a precise description of a behavioral act that can be counted, it would probably be impossible to change the problem.

When somebody tells me that their child does not have enough "ambition," my first question is "can you count 'ambition'?" Is there any way that you can figure out how to measure "ambition"? You can count how many times he initiates a behavior. You can count whether or not he starts the behavior on his own and finishes it. You can count how many jobs he does, how many tasks he completes, and what the rate of his work performance is. Why not count these? Stop trying to change his "ambition" and start trying to change how many times a day, how often, and for how long he engages in useful activity. Focus on what you can see rather that what you are trying to infer. I don't know if somebody's working very hard reflects "ambition," but I do know that I like to see him working hard and doing lots of different and important things.

Very often parents will tell me that their children are "unhappy." Can you count "happiness?" How do you know that your child is "unhappy"? When you see him smiling, you can guess that he's "happy." When you see him with a smile on his face going to play a game and playing many different games, you infer that he's "happy." When you ask him how he feels and he tells you that he's "happy," that's another way that you infer that he's "happy." Why not count how many times he smiles, how quickly and how often he goes to play games, and how many times that he tells you that he's "happy"? If you were to change the rate of these behaviors that are observable and countable, would you not also be changing this other thing called "happiness"? You see, we cannot change the "happiness" directly because we can only infer its presence. There's no way we can observe it. We must ask the person how he feels and we must watch the person behaving before we can guess whether he is "happy" or not. All I am suggesting, then, is that you stop using inferences and instead translate the problem into counting the observable actions that you are already using to infer "happiness." Translate the problem into things you can count. Once you nail down the problem in this way, you'll find that you've cut the problem by two-thirds.

People frantically try to teach their children to "get along." But I don't know what that really means. When I ask them what it does mean to them, they usually can define it in concrete terms. "I don't want him to hit his sister. I want them to play together nicely." They may further concretize it by saying, "Well, I want them to share and to take turns in playing with toys and to encourage the other person to succeed rather than to be critical." Why not count those things? Stop talking about "getting along" and talk instead about his not hitting his sister. A mistake parents frequently make is that they tell their children what they want in terms of inferences rather than in terms of concrete things.

For example, Mommy will say to Johnny, "I'm going out

tonight and there will be a baby-sitter. I want you to be 'good.' I'll ask her whether you were 'good' or not when I come home." Then the parent leaves. Johnny, at this point, has no specified list of behaviors that he is supposed to use. He is required to guess at what Mommy means by "good." Some children can guess very well; most children, however, cannot. The wise parent talks about actions instead of vague value judgments. She says to Johnny, "I want you to do a number of things while I'm away tonight. I want you to be in bed by eight o'clock. I want you to do whatever the baby-sitter tells you to do as soon as she tells you. I want you to help your sister to go to bed, and certainly I don't want you scolding her or hitting her in any way. I want you to do nice things for her, such as I described, and if all these things are done when I come home, I'll know that you have been 'good.' " At that point, if the parent wishes to use the word "good" I would have no objections because then she is simply using the term as a label for her list of behaviors. She has been clear and specific in describing what she wants Johnny to do. The baby-sitter can measure Johnny's behavior. She can count it. She knows what time he went to bed, whether he made it by eight o'clock or whether there was a measurable lag of time. If he went to bed at eight-thirty, he was half an hour late. That's concrete. She has counted his time lag. Or the baby-sitter can say, "He was in bed early, at five of eight. He was early by five minutes." Because she can be concrete and specific, there can be no argument as to whether he was "good" or not; it becomes simply a statement as to what time he was in bed. The baby-sitter also can count how many times he obeyed her quickly and how many times he disobeyed her or failed to obey her.

At first, therefore, it's important for a parent trying to learn to manage Johnny more effectively to actually engage in the act of counting. She needs to count how many times he is late to school, how many minutes he is late in coming to supper, or how many times he uses an inappropriate word. She can even keep a simple record of these actions because she had defined what she is counting. She has described the beginning and the end of the act in such a way that anyone can count it. She knows, for example, what being late means. Being late means coming in past the five-minute leeway that she allows the child. If he's due for supper at five o'clock and he arrives at 5:04, he is not late. If he arrives at 5:06, he is late. So her observing can be very precise.

A behavioral act has a beginning and an end. It is something clear-cut that can be counted. An extreme definition of hitting his sister, for example, might define it as actually touching the sister, lightly or hard does not matter. Or it can be defined in such a way that everyone would agree on whether Johnny simply had touched his sister or had in fact engaged in the act of hitting. With such a definition the mother would have pinpointed the act even more clearly. She may have to differentiate what is hitting from what is not hitting the sister in terms like, "You can take her by the hand and lead her somewhere—that is not hitting. You can pat her on the shoulder in a loving manner and that also is not hitting. But if you engage in an act which causes some pain by hitting or by touching, then it is an act of aggression."

Describing the act itself, the basic component of behavior, is thus the first step in sorting out what the mother is actually seeing and concerned with in her attempts to teach Johnny how to want to obey. She must first describe for him and for herself what he is to do. This is because the most basic part of a behavioral pattern is the act itself. To begin to really understand a child's behavior, we must separate the action from the situation that initiates it and the reasons or motivations for doing it. We are helped in this by accepting the rule of counting: an act has to be observable (public behavior), definable (with a beginning and an end), and measurable (capable of being counted by someone) before it can be fully understood and ready for changing.

A parent must learn to be concrete and specific in describing behavioral acts to herself and to her child. It only confuses a child to be told to be "good." All people need to know what the standard is to be and how to measure themselves against it. We need to know how much, how often, or how long. Without guidelines like these, people tend to become confused, anxious, and resentful.

By concentrating on the acts a child performs, it is possible to avoid the very thorny problem of the concept of "personality." Many people use the term "personality" to refer to the attractiveness of a child to others: "She has a charming personality" or "He's got a bad personality." Some psychologists use the word to refer to the sum total of a person's behavior or speak of it as though it had an existence of its own. For example, psychologists often speak of a "disturbed personality" or of "personality problems." They are referring to an underlying structure which they believe explains a person's behavior. As you can see, the word has many meanings and uses. All of them, for the most part, are rather vague and complicated.

For our purposes, we can avoid all the complicated theories and vagueness by simply substituting the idea of a *behavior repertoire*. Each person has a set of actions available for use in a given situation. Some of these are public actions (capable of being observed, defined, and measured by someone else), and some are private actions (thinking, remembering, imagining, and feeling) which cannot be observed by anyone else. But all of them can be grouped together under the term "behavior repertoire." Now we have a clear, easy-to-understand concept. It allows us to talk about a child in concrete terms. Either he has an action in his repertoire or he has yet to learn it. The child may have the skill but fail to use it when it is appropriate to do so. He may have alternate actions in his repertoire, such as eating with his hands or eating with a fork. In later chapters I will return to this concept to help you understand your child and focus on the actions in his behavior repetoire which need changing, suppressing, or developing.

In the next chapter we will begin to examine some of the reasons a behavioral act grows stronger or weaker, continues or discontinues, occurs or does not occur. The component of a behavioral pattern called consequences is what we need to examine next.

5 🍂

Carrots and
Sticks

When I was a boy my parents and teachers were convinced that I would come to a terrible end. I seemed to have no motivation to develop desirable behaviors and my father was convinced that I was "lazy" although I filled my days with activity from early in the morning until late at night. But what activities! Football, reading, chasing girls, fixing cars, playing cards, talking on the phone, sleeping, eating, and chasing girls. The world of the adolescent was too much for a man who had weathered a revolution, a great depression, two world wars, and a lifetime of hard work. Imagine his surprise when I finished college, got married, and went to work at last.

All parents seem to be convinced that without constant pressure and guidance their children will turn out to be bums. For the most part, they are right. Since our children are not growing up under the same conditions as our parents did, we cannot rely on the motivating effects of a depression or poverty (with a different, more open economic system of opportunity) to provide the incentives.

Is motivation really something you have or don't have? Most people seem to think of motivation as a characteristic of the person which must be inspired to flower in some way. Yet common sense tells us that people are moved to act or to learn to act by something external to themselves. The donkey can be started by the carrot dangling in front or by the stick applied from behind. Children can be moved to action, likewise, by a bribe or a threat of punishment. Practical management systems have always treated motivation as a function of external rewards or punishments.

But what of character? Isn't character a factor which makes an individual do the right thing simply because it is the right thing to do? The idea that good character means that a person's actions are not related to reward or punishment is a myth that needs to be laid to rest at last. People do good deeds, work hard, and avoid misdeeds precisely because they want something very badly. But in the case of "good character" what they want is not always apparent. In most religious systems the carrot and the stick are heaven and hell. In a more subtle sense aren't we trying to achieve a feeling of pride or a sense of achievement when we do good and to avoid a sense of guilt or shame when we avoid doing bad things? Science teaches us that no behavioral action continues to occur or ceases occurring unless there is some kind of carrot or stick involved. Now let's examine in detail what the second major component of a behavioral pattern is.

CONSEQUENCES ∾

After every action there is some kind of outcome produced by that action. If we put our hand on a hot stove, we experience pain. If we take a drink of cold water on a hot day, we experience relief from thirst. If we turn the knob of the television, we get to see our favorite program. If we go to work each day, we receive a paycheck at the end of the week. If we dial the phone, we hear our friend's voice. If we make too many errors on a test, we receive a failing grade and may have to repeat the course.

Such outcomes are called the *consequences* of an act. Consequences affect the act itself. One of the greatest scientific discoveries of this century was the discovery that consequences can either increase or decrease the rate or strength of the act being performed. Isn't it marvelous how modern science is catching up with common sense? Now we can prove that a carrot or a stick can make the donkey move. But seriously, it was a very important discovery and made it possible to separate motivation as being truly a function of consequences. Now we are no longer helpless in motivating children. We can learn precisely how to create motivation and train children to be self-motivating. Once science gets moving on the correct path, it can refine and improve commonsense knowledge and techniques.

The consequence doesn't have to be relevant to the act itself to affect it. If the consequence follows immediately after the act in a consistent manner, it will affect the act regardless of whether or not it is related to the act in any other way. For example, if a piece of corn is dropped into the cage of a pigeon every fifteen seconds, whatever act the pigeon was engaged in at the time will tend to reoccur until the pigeon is turning or bowing or always hopping on one leg. It doesn't really matter that the occurrence of the corn was not really related to the actions of the pigeon.

Over the past thirty years experimenters have discovered many new facts about how consequences affect behavior and motivation. Here we are going to examine some of the most important of these findings in order to prepare for the methods of helping

Johnny want to obey and learn. Let's begin with the three possible effects of consequences.

INCREASING AN ACTION ❧ Certain kinds of consequences increase an action. By increase I mean that the child does more of the action, does it faster, more often, or more strongly. If I give Johnny a piece of candy for taking out the trash, it is more likely that he will do this chore more willingly tomorrow. If I pay Johnny to cut the grass, he'll probably cut it faster than if I don't. Praising a child will keep him working longer and harder. Success breeds success. If I succeed at a sport, I'm more likely to make it my favorite hobby than if I fail at it.

In all of these instances the key point is that some kinds of consequences affect the action in positive ways. This class of consequences is called *positive consequences*. A positive consequence is any outcome of behavioral actions which tends to strengthen those actions. We have no way to determine in advance whether a consequence will be positive or not—a fact to which we shall return later.

CONSEQUENCES WITH NO EFFECTS ❧ Many events occur just after an act is performed. The world is full of things happening, most of which we tend to ignore because they are inconsistent (unlike the corn for the pigeon) or follow no relevant pattern. Only certain events or consequences are related to the action by consistently occurring. We learn very quickly to ignore what seem to be irrelevant outcomes. They are *neutral consequences*. A neutral consequence can become either positive or negative if we discover that it is really relevant after all.

One day while teaching a class I found a way to illustrate this. Each time someone asked a question I snapped my fingers. I kept a record of the rate of question asking and found that it was at a fairly constant but low level. I then told the class that when I snapped my fingers I was adding two points to their grade on the next test. After that I was flooded with questions, but only when I was in a finger-snapping mood. If questions were asked on a day I wasn't finger-snapping, they tended to die out quickly, but if I snapped my fingers just once the rate increased markedly. The snapping of my fingers after question asking was at first a neutral consequence because it was an irrelevant event but it became a positive consequence as soon as it was made relevant to the students.

DECREASING AN ACTION ∽ Some consequences have the effect of causing an action to weaken, slow down, occur less often, or not at all. These are the *negative consequences*. In an earlier chapter I spoke about punishment as one kind of negative consequence. There are many others. The absence of any consequence is itself a kind of negative consequence that can discourage an action. If a slot machine never pays off we move to another. If a movie is boring we leave. If a lecture is dull we fall asleep. If one job pays more than the one we have, we quit and take that one. The stick doesn't have to have pain attached to it at all. Many kinds of things decrease behavior and all of them are called negative consequences.

DEPRIVATION AND SATIATION ∽ What makes a consequence positive, neutral, or negative? We can't predict in advance with certainty. We have to observe the effect on a person's actions to know for sure. Some consequences seem to change before our eyes. For example, if I were to visit your house and you were to offer me a piece of lemon meringue pie (one of my favorites), I would probably attack it eagerly. The rate of my eating (the action) would immediately be strengthened by the pie (the consequence). We could then say the pie was a positive consequence. If you offered me a second piece, I would probably take it just to be polite. But the rate of my eating would slow down considerably, to the point of barely touching it at the end. The pie is obviously becoming more of a neutral consequence since it no longer is increasing the rate of my eating. If you were then to offer me a third piece, I would probably try to refuse it and if you continued to press it upon me, I would find some excuse for leaving the table to avoid it. The pie has now become a negative consequence since it has decreased eating behavior to the point of eliminating it.

The important fact here is that the same consequence can be positive, neutral, or negative in its effect upon the action, depending on the state of deprivation or satiation in which the person finds himself. How much you need or want the consequence determines whether it will be able to affect your behavior in positive or negative ways. We know that the effect of food is dependent upon how long you have been without it. We know that a child will respond to a consequence like candy only if he needs or wants it.

Too often a parent will expect a reward to create incentive

when the child neither needs nor wants it. One father offered his son five dollars a week to do his homework every night. What he didn't realize was that the boy's grandmother has just given him a birthday gift of two thousand dollars. The boy was satiated with money and immediately retired. The father's offer of five dollars a week was like the second or third piece of pie. It had no effect on the boy's behavior. The secret of a good positive consequence is that it is based on a real need or desire.

IMMEDIACY VERSUS DELAY ∽ Most people generally don't consider the question of the optimum time-lag between an act and its consequence for the consequence to be able to affect the act. They promise Johnny a new bike for a good report card or a dollar for every A. (In my day it was only a quarter.) The time-lag here is usually about eight weeks. Many parents promise the child a weekend treat if he is good all week. Some teachers try to mark a test paper and return it the same day in order to motivate the children to work harder. Yet all studies show that the optimum time-lag is about one half second. Beyond a few moments, the consequences will no longer have any effect on the action.

In seeming contradiction to these findings, however, we all know of children who seem to be able to work hard and diligently for consequences which are long delayed in occurring. How is that possible? The paradox is explained by the fact that some children (pitifully few, by the way) can supply a self-administered consequence that serves to bridge the gap. Animals cannot do this. Many children can do it only poorly and some children cannot do it at all.

The *bridge consequence* is the anticipation of the positive or negative consequence. The child thinks about the consequence and his imagination (engaging in a private act) works as a positive consequence to strengthen all the public actions which eventually lead to the final real consequence. But most children can do this only imperfectly. In fact, most adults also have a great deal of trouble with this process. The best rule for motivating children is to make the consequence as immediate as possible, with the goal being one half second. There are practical ways to do this and in later chapters I will spend a great deal of time explaining them. For now, it is important just to understand the importance of immediate consequences.

UNIQUENESS VERSUS UNIVERSALITY OF CONSEQUENCES ∽ One man's meat is another man's poison. Consequences must be appropriate to the individual child. One child will eagerly seek a piece of candy, another child couldn't care less. One child will be terrified at the thought of losing a prized possession, another will forget the loss almost immediately or will ignore the threat of loss. Still another child will work diligently for a good report card, which by itself is a meaningless piece of paper. How do we explain these facts? Scientists have done many experiments to explore this phenomenon and have discovered some important facts about how we learn to value consequences. Some consequences seem to have the same effect on most or all people. Let's spend some time examining how consequences come to affect different people in different ways.

BIOLOGICAL CONSEQUENCES ∿ We are all born with certain biological needs for survival. These *biological consequences* are common to all living things. Food, water, protection from extremes of heat or cold, and the avoidance of pain are all examples of basic human needs. Without them we would die. Since the instinct for survival is deeply ingrained in living things, we tend to learn very quickly the actions that produce these things. We work very hard to acquire and maintain consequences that satisfy these biological needs. We avoid pain and seek to nourish and protect our bodies. No infant has to be taught the value of these consequences. Yet once biological needs are satisfied, mankind has learned to develop other values and may work just as hard to obtain consequences not necessary for survival.

ACQUIRED CONSEQUENCES ∿ Contrary to common belief and much psychological theory, we do not need love, recognition, or power to survive. The infant quickly learns, however, that Mommy is more likely to satisfy his needs if she is in a good mood. He learns to associate her smiles and cooing with the occurrence of the biological consequences of food and comfort. Very early in his development he comes to respond to such acquired consequences as though they were biological consequences. He will eventually work just as hard to make Mommy smile as he will to suck at her breast.

As he grows older he begins to discover the pleasures of certain activities and the associated rewards or positive consequences which are arbitrarily attached to them by other people. He discovers that sitting still brings praise or perhaps a treat. He

discovers that hard, unpleasant work brings later positive consequences. He discovers that giving up your piece of cake to another
child brings both a warm glow of satisfaction and special, very
positive privileges. Many things that were originally neutral or even
negative consequences come to take on a positive value as the
child slowly becomes socialized. These learned consequences are
called *acquired consequences* and it is easy to see how, as a result
of acquired consequences, one child learns to value certain things
while another child learns to value a different set of consequences.
Most of us learn to value the consequences, both negative and
positive, provided by other people. We seek approval and avoid
disapproval.

SINGLE ACQUIRED CONSEQUENCES ⌁ Some consequences are good
for satisfying only one need or desire. A golf club for the most
part, can only be used to play golf (although, at times, I have been
tempted to use one on one of my own children). A phonograph
record is usually able to satisfy only our desire for pleasant sounds
in the form of music. A piece of sculpture satisfies our aesthetic
desires only.

These *single acquired consequences* all have one thing in
common. They only satisfy one state of deprivation. Thus they
will be able to affect our actions only so long as we need or desire
that kind of consequence. In children, acquired consequences are
very unstable. Promise a child a trip to the zoo on Sunday and
chances are, by Sunday, he will no longer be interested. Promise
him a story if he cleans his room and by the time he completes the
task he may no longer be interested in hearing a story. The great
danger here is that the desired action is not followed by any
positive consequence. In that case, the action will be weakened. If
the child has stable tastes, of course, such a promise and
fulfillment will indeed serve to strengthen the actions.

EXCHANGEABLE ACQUIRED CONSEQUENCES ⌁ Fortunately, there
is another class of consequences which avoids the problem of
satiation or waning interest in a particular consequence. This type
of consequence may have no particular value of its own. That is, in
itself it fills no need or desire on the part of the child. But it can
be exchanged for a variety of need or desire filling positive
consequences. Society has developed a number of ways of utilizing
this phenomenon.

Mother goes to the supermarket, makes a purchase, and is given
some savings stamps as a reward for buying at that particular store.

When she has enough she can exchange them for a variety of tantalizing items listed in the savings stamp catalogue. Father works hard all week and receives a paycheck which he cashes for good old American dollars with which he can purchase food, shelter, entertainment, or financial security. Johnny receives a series of report cards which culminate in a diploma which provides him with entrance into college or into certain select jobs. Mary gets her mother's attention, which she exchanges for a drink of water, a cookie, or a trip to the movies.

All of these are examples of *exchangeable acquired consequences*. They all have one thing in common: they can be exchanged for some other positive consequence for which a desire is felt at the moment or can even be saved for a later time. It is no longer necessary to depend on a constant desire. At any given moment some desire will be felt by the person. All that is necessary for the exchangeable consequence to be able to provide some positive consequence that is relevant to the person receiving it is that it have a wide range of exchange possibilities.

Some people, like my smallest daughter, treat exchangeable acquired consequences as though they were merely single acquired consequences. She hoards money. At the age of three, she hasn't yet learned that the money can be exchanged. I must admit that money isn't yet very valuable to her, for she loses her pennies constantly, shows little regret when she does, and still works harder for a piece of candy than for a piece of money. I hoard saving stamps. Like my daughter, I almost never exchange them, but when offered them by the service station attendant I always take them.

NATURAL AND ARTIFICIAL CONSEQUENCES ᠊᠊᠊᠊᠊᠊᠊᠊᠊᠊ Some consequences are produced directly as a result of the act itself. They are the natural outcome of what we do. The pleasure produced by swimming or even the fear produced in some people by swimming is a direct result of the action. The tower of blocks produced by the young child piling one block on top of another is a direct consequence of the piling action. The taste of the ice cream produced by licking the cone is another example of a *natural consequence*. Nobody arbitrarily arranged that these consequences would occur if we performed the act.

Many consequences in our highly civilized world, however, are arbitrarily arranged. Someone decides, for example, that cutting the grass will lead to going to the movies. I was once paid with prizes and trophies for swimming. Others are paid to swim with paychecks. We call these people lifeguards.

Artificial positive consequences make it possible to strengthen many actions which have no natural positive consequences of their own. They even can be used to strengthen an action which has highly negative natural consequences. I would willingly lay down my life for my children in order to fulfill an artificial positive consequence called moral obligation. Many people work at dull, even unpleasant jobs in order to receive a paycheck. My wife has changed uncountable dirty diapers to fulfill her role as a loving parent and to make our children more comfortable and healthy. Without artificial consequences to motivate us, much useful social behavior would never be learned or practiced.

SOURCES OF CONSEQUENCES ∽ There are three main sources of consequences which influence our behavioral actions. These are the natural world itself, other people, and ourselves. The natural environment teaches us very basic behaviors. Walk into a wall and you will be hurt; better not walk into walls. Touch a hot stove and you will be burned; avoid hot objects. Eat a candy bar and it will taste good; spend your money on chocolate bars. Roll too close to the edge of a bed and you fall out and bump yourself; stay in the middle of the bed. Children learn to walk, hold onto things, and deal with the natural world precisely because the consequences of most actions are direct, consistent, and immediate. Even a retarded child learns many of the basic actions of survival and self-protection. But that group of actions in our behavior repetoire constitutes only a small part of the skills necessary to function in a world of people and subtle abstract rules of conduct.

Many skills which are necessary to earn exchangeable acquired consequences cannot be taught by nature since a person in a state of nature, in total isolation from other people, has no need for them. To survive in the woods all that is required is to learn to gather edible foods, find shelter, and avoid being killed. Even animals learn that. But to survive in a city one must learn to ask directions, earn money, and obey laws. These skills are required by people and must be taught by people.

People provide consequences: simple things like a smile, a conversation, or a hug and kiss, and complex things like certification, paychecks, or acceptance into a group. People are a major source of both positive and negative consequences. We come to value people in their own right and as the providers of other kinds of important consequences. People can provide negative consequences in the form of ignoring us when we want them, ridiculing or punishing us, or giving us traffic tickets. People can provide many positive consequences, particularly to a child who is dependent upon other people for most of his needs and wants.

But gradually the child becomes increasingly independent of other people and can provide himself with many external consequences. He can buy himself many desired things. He also can withhold from himself if he so chooses. In addition, he can supply himself with many internal consequences such as self-praise, self-hate, pride, guilt, shame, and love. In our society a person who mostly seeks self-consequences is highly praised, whereas in other societies, such as many eastern cultures, a person is expected to seek mostly social consequences. Some religions believe that the highest form of behavior is to deny the value of natural, social, and self-consequences and seek only supernatural satisfactions. The holy men of the east are good examples of people who march to a different drummer, who find their highest values in the absence of most of the behaviors we strive to acquire in our culture.

ACTS AS CONSEQUENCES ∿ One of the things discovered by research was that an act itself could serve as a consequence for another act. Every parent knows that Johnny will practice the piano harder and faster if he is allowed to play baseball after practicing. The acts involved in playing baseball serve as positive consequences for some children for the acts involved in practicing a musical instrument. The possibilities for creating incentives for behavior opened up by this fact are endless. It is not necessary to provide some tangible object or event to strengthen an action in a child. By merely making one action contingent upon another, you can strengthen the desired action. The action you promise must be highly desirable to the child. If he is lukewarm about baseball or if it is raining, the opportunity to play the game will have little if any effect on piano practicing. Although an act is intangible in the sense that it does not have a concrete existence in space and time, it is still quite powerful as a consequence. In addition it is always available. A child wants to do or avoid doing something at every instant of his life. By artificially arranging that the desired act is a consequence of some undesired or less desired act, a parent can help Johnny learn or practice new and important behavior.

CHAINING ACTS AS CONSEQUENCES: ᔕ Many acts, to be effective, must repeat themselves or be part of a larger chain of behaviors. Walking is made up of the same act repeated many times. Feeding oneself is made up of moving your arm through a continuous flow of similar and dissimilar units of behavioral actions. Dressing oneself is made up of many bits of action that, combined, lead to a final outcome. The existence of such chained behavioral actions is a result of the fact that acts can become consequences. Let me illustrate this point with an example from a research study which attempted to explore the problem of how to use acts as effective consequences for complex patterns of behavior.

In a certain mental hospital there was a woman who perplexed the staff because she seemed to want nothing at all out of life except to sit all day in a rocking chair. They could find no way to motivate her to resume the complex patterns of daily life. Finally the experimenter realized that she did have a very strong acquired positive consequence. She wanted to sit in her rocker and rock. Very well, the experimenter decided, she would be allowed to sit in the rocker only if she completed the act of making her bed. When this pattern of bed-making action leading to rocking-chair-sitting as a consequence was established the next step in the chain was begun. She was not allowed to make her bed unless she dressed. Then she was not allowed to dress unless she washed. In short order this woman was brought to the point where she rose each morning, washed, dressed, ate, and worked a full eight-hour day to earn the privilege (or positive acquired consequence) of sitting in her rocker at night and relaxing. Each additional act was strengthened in turn by a previously reinstated act.

In a similar study the simple biological consequence of food or candy was used in order to teach retarded children how to dress themselves. The last act in the chain was taught first and the training proceeded backward in the chain. Tying the last knot in the shoelace came first and led directly to food. Then the step in tying before that had to be learned in order to be allowed to tie the last knot in order to get the food. Putting on the shoe came next, followed by pulling up the pants, followed by stepping into the pants, and so on. You can see that each learned act served as a bridge consequence and all the acts together led to the biological, back-up consequence of food. Multiplication can be taught this way. In fact it is a good procedure for teaching many complex chains of behavior. It may seem strange at first to teach the last step in multiplication first, but for many children this is the only way they can learn the chain of skills involved.

STRENGTHENING A CONSEQUENCE ∽

One of the problems frequently faced by parents is that of the child whose list of acquired consequences is quite limited or whose acquired wants are very weak. Nothing seems to interest him for very long. When I was young, the only two things that seemed to interest me were books and the opportunity to roam the woods and beaches. At first my parents controlled this but I soon discovered libraries for books and the drain pipe for escape from the house. Like Tom Sawyer, one of my boyhood heroes, I would sneak out of the house at will, to the despair of my parents. At thirteen I discovered football and friends (the seven holy terrors of Wanamaker Street) and at fourteen I discovered girls. My list was complete until I gradually acquired a taste for many other things which finally forced me to go to work. How much grief might I have avoided if my parents had known how to motivate me better by strengthening other types of consequences earlier? How many more effective social skills might I have developed earlier if they had known how to help me want to learn them? My children will probably be spared some of the grief I experienced in growing up because I have learned how to strengthen and expand their lists of acquired consequences. Let's examine some of the ways of doing this.

CONTEXT EFFECTS ∽ It's a known fact that a puppy who seems uninterested in food will eat ravenously if placed at a food tray with other hungry puppies. Children play more in a playground than if left alone. Pleasant surroundings make everything seem more desirable. Companionship, someone with whom to share discovery, makes exploring more fun. The right equipment makes any activity more fun. Previous success makes the game more appealing. The general context of an activity can enhance or diminish the pleasure we find in it.

SAMPLING ∽ Allowing a child a small sample of the final positive consequence can make the anticipation more vivid and appealing. Requiring a child to sample an undesired consequence (neutral or even slightly negative) and then abruptly taking it away can suddenly make it more positive. For example, a child may not be interested in a toy you wish to use as an incentive. By giving it to him dramatically and then suddenly taking it away before he has a chance to really play with it, you may be able to make it highly desirable to him. It doesn't always work, but people tend to return to uncompleted tasks.

REST PERIODS ᔐ Rotating the availability of toys can keep the child interested in the opportunity to use the toy. In one school I set up, we made each toy available for play only one week out of every three. Instead of becoming bored with the toys, we found that the children eagerly awaited their reappearance and seldom seemed to grow tired of playing with them, even after many nonconsecutive weeks of play.

BACK-UP BONUSES ᔐ If one consequence is weak, such as Daddy's approval or reading, it is possible to strengthen its positive value by making that consequence lead to many other positive consequences. For example, if Daddy approves of you it can mean a surprise trip to the store for a toy, a sudden piece of candy, or an extra story at bedtime. Not only can reading be a positive consequence in its own right, but because you chose to read as a positive consequence for some other act, you receive a surprise piece of cake in addition or a special warm hug from Mommy. It's amazing how much stronger those positive consequences will become with this kind of back-up bonus system.

DEPRIVATION ᔐ Letting a child use up all his savings before using money as a positive consequence or not allowing movie-going as a positive consequence for a while can do wonders to create a strong desire for a previously weak positive consequence. Natural or artificially created deprivation, not as punishment for a misdeed but as a thoughtfully planned program of creating incentives, can do wonders.

DEVELOPMENTAL CONSIDERATIONS ᔐ Children need different kinds of things at different stages of development. Toys beyond the capabilities of the child have little positive value, but toys that suit the child's developmental stage can be very effective in motivating. Praise to a very young child has little meaning or value, but at the right age it can be very powerful. Choosing appropriate consequences for the age of the child is very important.

IMMEDIACY ᔐ Very often consequences are weak because they are too long delayed. If a child wants a story tonight, reading it to him the following night might find a very disinterested child.

Children live in the moment, they want what they want now. Later they've lost interest. A parent should always strive for immediacy in delivering a consequence because immediacy often can strengthen the positive value of the consequence for the child.

CREATING NEW CONSEQUENCES ⌢ In the school I mentioned earlier we often found children with very small lists of positive consequences. Sometimes we could not provide for their narrow interests with what we had available in the room we called "Kiddie Heaven." For these children the room was not heaven. Very often the same children also intensely disliked school. This provided us with the positive consequence we needed: we allowed them to leave school early or even miss a day of school if they played with the toys we had available. As soon as we observed an increase in their use of the play equipment, we began to allow them to use it only if they did some school work. One little boy who had cried every morning because he had to go to school ended up crying on Saturday because he couldn't go. We had to teach him to play. We had to create positive consequences by rewarding him at first with escape from school for playing in Kiddie Heaven. Then we strengthened school behavior by letting him play in Kiddie Heaven as a reward for study. We could not have done that if we hadn't increased and created the positive value of Kiddie Heaven. Often as a child acquires skill in playing the games, the games themselves become naturally appealing and we can then remove the artificial consequences.

DOUBLING UP ⌢ If one consequence of an action is weak, adding another may strengthen the first and at the very least will create a combined positive consequence that will be more effective in strengthening the desired action. Never be afraid that the consequences are too positive. You can always start requiring more behavior to earn them. But if the consequences are too weak, you are forced to lower the standard for earning them and the whole learning process is slowed down.

MOTIVATIONAL MYOPIA ⌢ Some children are born nearsighted. We accept that fact and provide them with glasses as a prosthetic device to help them function more normally. Some children cannot see long-range consequences even if they are very important to them. Graduation from school may mean a better job, more money, and a more comfortable life. Some children recognize these long-range positive consequences early in life and their anticipation of them serves to motivate them at each step along the way. They study hard, avoid misbehavior, and ultimately achieve. But many children are simply unable to see the value of long-range consequences. They are motivationally nearsighted. For a child with motivational myopia only immediate consequences, or at best short-range consequences, can affect his or her behavior.

These children need a prosthetic device. They need parents and teachers who can supply external bridge consequences, artificially arranged, to motivate them through the long process of acting that leads to final achievement of the important consequence. A parent's anger is of no help to this kind of child, nor are threats and punishment. What this kind of child needs is effective management. In the chapters on methods I will spend a great deal of time on systems to help such children.

REALITY CONSEQUENCES ∿ No matter what a parent says or promises, Johnny acts in terms of what actually happens. A mother may scold and yell at her child for a messy room, but if she always cleans it up herself Johnny learns that the real consequence of not cleaning his room is a lot of noise (which he quickly learns to ignore or screen out) and a clean room (since Mommy always cleans it anyway). If Daddy threatens punishment for a misdeed but doesn't deliver it, Johnny will respond to the real consequence and probably continue to repeat the misdeed. If Mommy encourages Johnny to talk to her confidentially and she promises to listen sympathetically but is usually highly critical and responds with a monologue lecture, Johnny will stop confiding in her. If Mommy tells Johnny to stop hitting his sister or else, and there is no "else," he'll keep hitting his sister.

Children are more attuned to reality than we adults. They react in terms of what is, rather than in terms of a fantasy of what should or might be. Parents must learn to recognize the real consequence patterns of their home and make those conform to the goals they desire.

It cannot be stated too often that consequences control our child's actions. Immediate consequences based on real needs and wants work best. Consistency is important. Recognizing the developmental age and needs of the child is important also. But recognizing the uniqueness of each child and arranging consequences specific to him is the most important thing of all. In the next chapter we shall examine the third component of a behavior pattern, *signals* that help determine which action will occur and on what occasion it will occur.

6

Signs and
Signals

One of the most common mistakes that parents make is to rely on telling Johnny what to do as a method of getting him to obey. It's easy to see why they do this. We are constantly being admonished to do things. Signs direct us. Announcers persuade us to buy the product they are advertising. Traffic policemen wave at us to move on. Teachers give us assignments to complete. Red lights tell us to stop. Father asks for the salt. Mother tells us to go to bed. After a while most people start to believe that these signals control behavior.

SIGNALS ᐯ

I define a *signal* as any event that announces the consequences of our actions. Signals do not *control* behavioral actions. They influence the occurrence of an act only if the consequences they announce are important enough to lead to the act. Let's look at a traffic signal for a moment. The red light signals "stop" and the green light signals "go." But that is not the whole message. The complete message is really "If you go when the light is red you may have an accident or receive a traffic ticket, and if you stop when the light is green you will make other drivers angry and slow your trip." To obtain the positive consequences of avoiding danger and speeding your trip, you must respond appropriately to the two signals by stopping at the red light and going if the light is green. The important point is that it is the consequence pattern that really determines your behavior.

If I reverse the consequence pattern your behavior will change. For example, if you have someone in the car who is badly injured and you are rushing him to the hospital, would you stop at a red light? You might check to see if it is clear of cross traffic, but you would probably respond to the red light by driving through it. The red light does not make you stop, it only announces the consequences of stopping or not stopping.

There are many kinds of signals that announce the same consequences. All of the following warn you to apply the brakes: a red light, a policeman's upraised hand, a policeman's whistle, a car in the intersection, a stop sign, a child running into the street, a child's ball rolling into the street, the oral instructions "stop at the corner" given by a passenger, or a mental instruction to the same effect given by you yourself. Unless there were some more important consequence for proceeding, you would probably respond to all these signals with the action of putting your foot on the brake and stopping your car.

There are four main classes of signals that you need to understand in order to help Johnny want to obey. These are *physical prompts, verbal signals, self signals,* and *natural signals.* All of these are ways of announcing the consequences of his actions to Johnny and influencing which actions he will use at any given time. Any child—or adult, too, for that matter—must select from his behavior repetoire the appropriate act to use in a given situation. It is not enough to know how to do something or to have a good reason for doing it; a person must also know *when* to do it. Signals help us to decide when to do it.

PHYSICAL PROMPTS ◠ Physical prompts are a kind of signal provided for us by someone else. They are the most basic kinds of signals because more than any other kind of signal they have the ability to force the behavior to occur. The stronger the physical prompt, the more capable it is of causing the act to occur. For example, if you want a young child to sit in a chair you may pick him up and put him there, you may strongly or gently push him into it, you may take him by the hand and tug him or lead him to it, or you may simply give him a gentle push. Whether or not he complies and actually remains sitting in the chair depends on the consequences of the act of sitting.

Very often, with young children particularly, a physical prompt may be the only way to initiate the desired action. After a period of training you may be able to graduate to a less direct kind of signal, but at the beginning and even occasionally thereafter you may find physical prompts necessary.

A golf instructor may place your hands on the club, straighten out your arm, and even hold your elbow locked with his hand as the first step in teaching you to swing a club correctly. Those are physical prompts which serve as the signal for the correct action of your arms. The consequences would be his approval, your own satisfaction at success, and one hopes, a lower golf score. A mother may place the spoon in Johnny's hand, close his fingers around it, and keep them closed by holding his hand with hers. She is signaling the correct act by using a physical prompt.

Gradual withdrawal of physical prompts is, of course, necessary. No parent wants to lead Johnny through his day's activities by dragging him out of bed, pushing his arms and legs into his clothes, holding the toothbrush in his hand, or moving his jaws up and down to chew his food. But, when necessary, a physical prompt is the best method of starting a behavior and can often be a valuable back-up for other kinds of signals.

If I tell my children to come to the dinner table and they fail to obey, I will often walk over and take them by the hand to start them in the direction of the kitchen. If my three-year-old refuses to pick up her toys when asked, I may take her hand and close it around a toy and together we'll put in into the toy box. After the action is begun, I will gradually withdraw my hand, leaving her to complete the chain of behaviors of putting away her toys.

VERBAL SIGNALS ◇ Mommy says to Johnny, "Go to bed and I'll read you a book." What is Mommy doing with this announcement? She is giving Johnny a *verbal signal.* In this case, the signal is expressed explicitly in words. She is telling him what the consequence will be if he performs the act of going to bed. Her reading the story to him is what is going to affect his behavior. If he wants to hear the story, he will engage in the behavior; but if, on the other hand, he places no value on Mommy's reading the story, or even places a negative value on it, he will probably not go to bed and Mommy's command will have no effect on his behavior whatsoever.

Contrary to the illusion that most people have, verbal signals do not control behavior. Their only power over behavior has to do with the type of consequence with which they are associated. When a sergeant says "left face" he is not really saying just "left face" in a very stern forceful voice. He is really saying "left face" as an abbreviation for the more complex signal of "left face or I'll throw you in the guardhouse or give you k.p." What many people fail to realize is that it is not the strong stern voice that the sergeant uses which promotes the behavioral action of the soldiers turning left, but the implied consequences. Some soldiers fail to understand that there is an implied consequence in the sergeant's verbal signal and fail to turn left. These men very quickly find that peeling potatoes, washing dishes, or spending time behind bars is a very undesirable negative consequence and they learn to listen for the implied consequence in the sergeant's commands.

Mommy, on the other hand, has no k.p. or guardhouse to back

her up and very often would not use it if she did. She tends to use verbal signals that have no consequences at all attached to them. She will say things like "Johnny go to bed." There is no consequence attached explicitly to that verbal signal, and in fact there is none implied. It is simply a verbal signal without consequences. It usually is without effect. Johnny will not go to bed. The average parent will repeat the command "Johnny go to bed." When this fails to produce the behavior which she is after, she will repeat it still again. "Johnny go to bed." In fact, I have often watched mothers repeating the same command as many as ten or twelve times with no more effect on the twelfth occasion than on the first.

Many a mother in despair at this point will call in the father who walks into the room, fixes Johnny with a baleful eye, and utters in a very stern voice, "Johnny go to bed!" Johnny recognizes the implied consequence by the tone of his voice and by the look on his face, two additional signals that Mommy did not use.

There are now three signals in front of Johnny. One contains no consequence, the verbal command "Johnny go to bed," and two (the tone and the look) contain the implied consequence of a spanking. Johnny hastens to run upstairs, complying with the implicit nonverbal signals that were contained in the father's command. Mommy now believes that the way to get Johnny to behave is to speak sternly to him. So she proceeds on the next occasion to speak sternly to Johnny. "Johnny go to bed!" Johnny waits for the consequence. He is testing her out, trying to learn if Mommy's new signal has any consequence attached to it. Mommy, at this point, not understanding why it worked for her husband and not for her, becomes frantic and proceeds to repeat the verbal signal, screaming and yelling it in a variety of ways, but still with no consequences attached. Johnny refuses to budge.

Her husband then walks into the room, looks at the chaos, and utters his verbal signal together with his baleful eye and his stern voice. Johnny may, at this point, hesitate. The husband's response is immediately forthcoming, a slap on the fanny or a grab at the ear. Johnny quickly responds to the negative consequences and hastens off to bed.

What Johnny has done is to give a perfect example of a natural law. Signals have no effect, consequences do. Anyone who attaches consequences to signals will get better behavioral results than someone who does not. Mommies have a tendency to rely heavily on verbal signals, Daddies have a tendency to rely heavily on negative consequences. Daddies most often get better behavior from young children than do Mommies. Children test out their Mommies much more often than they test out their Daddies and they often find that Mommy is a bag of wind. She gives the verbal signals all right, but frequently there's nothing with which she backs them up. Johnny doesn't have as many opportunities to test Daddy. Johnny is also much more likely to get consequences from Daddy than he is from Mommy since Daddy doesn't have a million other things to do that interfere with backing up his orders. When Mommy says "go to bed," she usually has a baby under each arm, the dishpan between her teeth, and her toe testing out the bathwater. It's very difficult for her to drop everything and arrange a consequence. All Daddy has to take care of is the paper, so it is much more likely that he will come forward and use a consequence.

The lesson here for Mommy is worth noting. It is better to spend a little bit of time in pretraining your child to understand your verbal signals and the fact that consequences will occur than it is constantly to repeat the signal. If the verbal signal didn't work the first time, it's not going to work the twelfth. Stop repeating yourself. All you're doing is wasting hard earned air and wearing out your lungs. Change to a physical prompt or state the consequences. The most effective thing you can do is to keep your eye on the consequence and not on the signal.

The only reason that we use verbal signals at all is that they are a shortcut. It is possible for people to communicate consequences to each other entirely by the use of nonverbal signals. Verbal signals are simply a shortcut for a trial-and-error discovery of what the consequences are to be. Mankind has come to rely on verbal signals very heavily indeed.

I once visited a colleague of mine who was demonstrating to a group of us that he could get children to look him straight in the eye by giving them little pieces of candy each time they got closer and closer to looking into his eyes. It was the old "hot and cold" game we used to play as children, except that instead of saying "hot or cold" as a consequence, he was dropping a piece of candy into a bowl. The children acquired all the candy in the bowl after the training session was over. He used no verbal signals at all. He did not tell them that he wanted eye contact. He was simply arranging to get the eye-contact by providing a positive consequence every time they looked at him. Eventually they discovered that looking him in the eye produced the greatest flow of candy. He was very proud of this accomplishment because it was an essential part of his system for the rehabilitation of disturbed children. By this method of helping them to learn eye-contact with him, he was helping them to develop better relationships with other children and adults around them.

I was amazed at his naïve procedure and I bet him the cost of lunch that I could produce the eye-contact much faster than he. Because he was so proud of his accomplishment with these children, he accepted my challenge readily. He sat down at a table with one of the children and I sat down at another table. A few minutes later he looked around and saw the the child with whom I was working was staring directly into my eyes, whereas his child had barely begun to maintain any level of eye-contact at all. He threw up his hands, walked over to my table, and said, "How did you do it?" I said that it was very simple. I had just leaned over and told the child, "If you look me in the eye and continue to look me in the eye, I'll give you this whole bag of candy at once instead of one piece at a time." The verbal signal saved time. The child immediately discovered what act I wanted and what the consequences were to be. It was an effective shortcut in this situation.

Keep in mind always that verbal signals are simply the announcement of the rule by which consequences occur. Whether you state the rule or not, children will discover what the rule is and what consequences will or will not occur. All of your verbal signals are simply shortcuts to help the child learn the consequences and the acts expected of him. If you can keep that in mind, communication with children becomes much simpler.

You need to learn that with younger children you must tell the child explicitly what you want of him and what the consequences will be. For example, with my older daughter I may say, "If you help your sister to bed, I'm sure that you'll feel very good and very proud of yourself." She has already learned to value self-consequences. When I asked her to help her sister, I pointed out explicitly to her how good she will feel if she does it. The only consequence I am promising her is one that she gives to herself—her own sense of pride and accomplishment. When she gets older I may be able to shorten the verbal signal to, "Why don't you help your sister out?" As she gets older, we hope she will come to understand the implicit consequence that she will feel very good if she helps her sister. With a still younger child of mine

I must say, "Help your sister to bed, and I'll come up and tuck you in and read you a story." There I am announcing the consequences also, but I'm using social consequences to motivate her behavior. With my youngest daughter I must say, "Get into bed and I'll come up with a special treat for you." The verbal signal for her announces biological consequences. The consequences will vary for each child, but the verbal signals must be explicit and clear. The child also must have no doubt that they will occur.

When I say to my children, "I'm sorry, but when you talk loudly I can't hear you," my signal is clear. The children have no difficulty in figuring out that every time they talk loudly they fail to get Daddy's attention, which is a negative consequence to them. They know that when they speak softly, however, Daddy will be able to hear them and will attend. The consequences are known. The signal makes it very clear. My children have no difficulty in understanding. When they test me out to find out if the consequence pattern is the way I have stated it, they find that it is always so. Daddy has a very funny set of ears. He simply doesn't hear loud noises, nor does he hear questions that are repeated too often. I will frequently say, "I'm sorry, I only heard the first time; thereafter, I didn't hear a thing." My children stop asking the extra questions then. They learn to stop when they have asked the question only once.

It may appear to many people that my children, the older ones at least, obey me without any consequences stated. Outside observers hear the verbal signal as, "Children please be quiet now," and they watch the children magically obey. What they fail to know is that previously on numerous ocassions my verbal signal was stated as, "Children be quiet and something will happen that you like. If you continue to be noisy, everything else stops." After a while it is possible to reduce the signal to the simple statement, "Please be quiet." Periodically I may have to become explicit, particularly when I notice the signal is no longer having an effect and the children do not become quiet. I then change the nature of the verbal signal from implicit to explicit and I make the statement, "Children, as long as you're being noisy we cannot go any farther." If we are in the car at the time I will even stop the car. When they are quiet I turn to them and say, "Now that you are quiet we can continue." I have restated the consequence. I have, in fact, engaged in the consequence. They now discover that noisiness stops progress. I, of course, do not care if the children are noisy in the playground because this is an appropriate place for them to be noisy. The car is not.

Verbal signals are everywhere. We learn to respond to them almost automatically without thinking. A sign simply saying "diner" is a verbal signal that tells us to enter this building and eat, for we will find food here. The sign is a written verbal signal that tells us that if we were to come in the building, were to ask for food, and were willing to pay for it, it would be forthcoming. Written signals can be found in notes, letters, books, or signs. These are all sets of communicated instructions which can call for different kinds of actions. We may drive past dozens of diners before we feel hunger pangs. Suddenly the sign announcing the next diner looks appealing and we find ourselves pulling off the road into the parking lot. All previous verbal signals of the same kind had no effect on forcing us off the road. This signal did, the reason being, of course, that now the consequences of eating food have become important. Why? Because we had been deprived for a long enough period of time for food to become an effective positive consequence. After we have eaten our fill and continued on down the road, all the subsequent signs which announce "diner" have no effect on our behavior until we again become hungry.

In the same way, the verbal signals we give our children can be more or less effective, depending on the strength of the consequence that the verbal signal promises and on the clarity of the signal. We may give such an ambiguous signal that the person is undecided as to whether or not to respond. It is not clear-cut. A mother may say, "Johnny, I want you to be independent and ask me questions." But as soon as Johnny asks the question, she snaps at him for his foolishness or his impertinence. Then she turns to him and says, "Now, Johnny, I still want you to ask questions of me." When he again tries to ask a question, she snaps at him because the question was a poor one. What does her signal really mean? In order to avoid being scolded or snapped at, and possibly to receive approval, Johnny must find out, for her signal was not clear to him. It contained two messages. The words seemed to indicate to Johnny that if he asked a question something nice would happen. "Mommy wants me to ask questions." But the minute he asked a question he discovered that the signal really was not clear. It was not just "Ask a question"; it was, "Ask the *right* kind of question." The rules for what constitutes the right kind of question are not clear. They can change from day to day and from minute to minute. Finally, Johnny may tend to ignore the verbal signal entirely. The next time Mommy asks him to ask some questions, he may look her straight in the eye and say, "I don't have any," or mumble an apology or avoid talking to her altogether.

There will come a day, of course, when Mommy complains that her son no longer communicates with her and she cannot figure out why. She feels she is the kind of a parent who encourages her child to ask questions. The verbal signals that she gives, however, are unclear, confused, and frequently mean just the opposite of what they purport. The child eventually will begin to behave in terms of the real consequence conditions, not in terms of what Mommy says they are. In fact, before too long a credibility gap may open up because the child no longer believes the verbal signals of his parent at all.

The parent may offer a signal explicitly announcing the proposed consequence of an action and then expect the action to occur. The child, however, understands reality all too well, and he knows that if he responds to that signal something will happen contrary to what the parent is promising, or, just as deplorably, that no consequence will occur. For example, the father may say to Johnny, "Anytime you have a problem, come to me and I will help you." When Johnny proceeds to come to Daddy with his first problem, Daddy is too busy to listen. "Later, son," he tells Johnny. Later never comes. That father, too, someday will complain to his son that he never talks to him anymore. Johnny's reply may be, "You never really wanted to hear me. You never really wanted to spend the time." Johnny quickly understands the reality of the relationship between his father's verbal signal and the true consequences, and after a while he will always respond to the verbal signal in terms of the real consequences.

There are many signals we choose not to respond to because the consequences announced are not very important or valuable or necessary to us, or because the price we have to pay is too high. The signal that says "Go to college" implies a great deal of effort. The efforts along the way may meet with such aversive consequences the child eventually will figure the price too high to maintain the kind of study behavior required to reach the final goal. He may even begin to ignore the signals, whether they are presented on a bulletin board, in the words of his parent, or in the advice of his counselor. He simply will refuse to engage in the actions that ultimately will lead to the promised consequences because the steps along the way are too painful or have no immediate consequences to make the effort worthwhile.

A child may have a variety of behaviors as possible responses to the same signal. Mommy may say, "Go to bed, Johnny." Johnny is quite capable of going to bed, lying down on the floor and having a tantrum, ignoring the request, running off to do something else instead, or standing there and engaging in a verbal debate with mother. The child may be responding to another set of consequences than the ones that Mommy is promising. Mommy is implicitly saying to Johnny, "Go to bed and you will feel refreshed and less tired." Johnny is saying to himself, "If I do what she asks of me, I will miss television, I will be lonely without any company, and I will have no opportunity to express my own individual desires."

It's obvious, then, that conflicting sets of consequence patterns are in operation—the ones that Mommy is offering, and the ones that Johnny is looking for on his own. The same verbal signal may announce a contradiction in consequence patterns. If Johnny were to obey his mother's verbal signal, he would experience certain very strong negative consequences in the loss of his independence, the loss of television time, and the loss of company. On the other hand, if he obeys the verbal signal, he will gain the approval of his mother and the needed rest. To which ones do you think Johnny is more likely to respond? Well, if he is like the average child, the chances are that he will respond to his own consequence pattern when his mother gives her verbal signal. It is up to the parent to find a way to outweigh Johnny's consequence patterns with the ones that she is providing. She must either make her approval more valuable, make the need for sleep more apparent to the child (depending on his age), or add some other artificial positive consequence that will be attractive enough to the child. She might offer, for example, to come up and read a story or sit with him while he falls asleep or to take him for a treat or read him a story after his nap.

There is an infinite number of possible kinds of positive consequence patterns that she can attach to the signal to make it more effective. The child's ultimate response to her verbal signal will depend on his estimation of the nature of the positive and negative consequence pattern and the likelihood of his getting them. The wise parent makes the consequence pattern clear-cut and the signals that describe the consequence pattern very unequivocal and easy for the child to understand. She may do this by stating within the verbal signal the whole pattern of actions the child is to engage in and all of the consequences that are involved. If the child has been trained well enough for a long enough period of time, it is possible for her to speak in shorthand, to give her signals with less and less of the whole action and consequence pattern described. She may ultimately end up by saying, "Johnny, please go to bed." But Johnny knows that verbal signal. From long experience he knows all of the consequences involved, he knows what all the possible actions are and what is expected of him. If he is well trained he will, in all likelihood, select the appropriate action pattern.

Now, this may seem quite a lot to expect of a young child, but remember that horses and dogs and many other animals learn quickly to select the appropriate actions at a given signal. Anyone who has ever watched a sheepdog bringing in the sheep at hand signals from his master is aware that the dog is selecting from a large possible repertoire of behavior just those actions necessary to herd the sheep into the pen. Anyone who has watched a seeing-eye dog respond to the short verbal commands of his master or avoid the danger of an open pit when he sees this nonverbal signal is aware that animals are capable of complex selection processes that enable them to respond with appropriate behavior to given signals. Is it too much to ask of a child that he also develop the skills of selecting the appropriate act to use in response to a signal provided by his parent or by the environment around him? The answer, of course, is that the animals have been thoroughly trained in very humane ways and the children, very often, have not been. It is incumbent upon a parent to learn how to train a child so that he can function in a given situation with the appropriate required behavior.

SELF SIGNALS ～ It is not always possible to see the signals that people respond to. Some signals are private. They are the secret sentences we tell ourselves, the memories, the images, the word signals that we use in the process of evaluating the world around us. Very often we provide our own signals.

Mother may leave Johnny a note telling him that she had to leave early, that dinner is on the stove, and that he is to go to bed at eight o'clock. She may add to that verbal signal by calling him at five minutes of eight to remind him to go to bed. Both the note and her call are verbal signals because they are a method of using spoken or written language to communicate what the child is to do.

The child may go one step further, however, and signal himself. He may remind himself that it is eight o'clock and say to himself, "I'd better be in bed because Mommy wants me to go to bed at eight." He is responding to the consequence pattern which she has set up, but he is supplying a self signal. This type of signal is evidence of the child's maturity.

We expect mature people to signal themselves and begin their own behavior patterns. We don't like having to physically or verbally prompt. No wife likes to turn to her husband and say, "Why don't you ask me how I feel?" She expects her husband to signal himself, to remind himself to ask her how she feels. She does not like to provide the external verbal signal. Similarly, no parents like to physically prompt or verbally signal their children to hurry up and get ready to leave for school. Most parents will accept this responsibility with very young children, but not with older children.

Self signals allow us to take in and store, independently of other people, all the information about our world that is necessary for appropriate acting. We memorize the important and relevant signals, the consequences that are announced by them, and the likelihood that these consequences will occur if we act. The process goes on endlessly and many of the signals become reduced to a verbal shorthand—"Danger" and we run, "Refrigerator" and we open the door to munch absentmindedly on leftovers, "Darling" and we run forward with open arms for a kiss. The alarm clock rings and we get ourselves out of bed, wash, and dress almost without conscious thought. We walk around obstacles without even seeming to notice them. Yet all the time we are constantly responding to a complex series of self signals. Sometimes we write ourselves notes to remind us of what we are to do. Sometimes we even tie a string around our finger.

All parents recognize the need to teach their children this system of self signals. The problem of how to do it with a minimum amount of pain for all involved will be dealt with in a later chapter.

NATURAL SIGNALS ∽ The final kind of signal which prompts behavior is called a natural signal. This is when the child says, "Mom, I feel tired, I'm going to bed." He is now responding to the fatigue within his own body, a natural and appropriate kind of signal calling for the appropriate action of going to sleep for the biological consequence of rest. When your husband notices the hang-dog look on your face and asks you how you feel, you are much more gratified than if you know he is doing his duty by reminding himself with a self signal to ask you how you feel. When he has to remind himself, it usually comes out affected and somewhat forced. When he notices your face, the behavior tends to come out much more spontaneously, much more related to your actual feelings.

Johnny can be prompted to go to bed by your taking him by the hand (a physical prompt) or by your asking him to go (a verbal signal), both of which are external signals. He can prompt himself by a self signal when he reminds himself or notices the time. Or he can respond to his own physical fatigue, which is a natural signal.

Whenever the signal is directly generated by the consequence, it is called a natural signal. The sight of a banana is a natural signal since it is generated by the banana itself. It says if you wish the taste of a banana or its nourishment, pick it up and eat it. If Mother tells Johnny to go find the banana and eat it, her instructions are a verbal signal. If she spoons it into the baby's mouth, it is physical prompt. If Johnny tells himself that a banana is just what he feels like eating, he is using a self signal. But the banana itself is a natural signal.

Natural signals occur all around us. We discover their relevance to our needs by trial and error or by somebody else's telling us about their relevance. Many natural signals are irrelevant—that is, the consequences attached to them are not the ones we are seeking. Relevant natural signals usually have important consequences attached to them and we learn which acts are required to obtain them by experimenting. A child is born able to respond to very few relevant natural signals. He has a sucking reflex, which is a complex pattern of actions ready to respond to the mother's nipple without any learning at all. But most of his behavior repertoire must be learned. He experiences pain and learns not to bump himself or touch something glowing or sharp. He learns what looks good to eat and what looks spoiled. He learns to avoid running into a street full of heavy traffic, not to pet a growling dog, and what a toilet bowl is for. Growing up is partly a matter of learning to cope with countless natural signals, sorting them out, and storing them in memory for later use.

The essential thing about natural signals is that, like all other forms of signals, they announce the consequences of acting. A red traffic light is not a natural signal since it is really a form of verbal shorthand. It is a verbal signal because it is a way of communicating between people. It is language although a nonverbal form of language. The sight of a banana is just something between you and the banana—or perhaps I should say between your stomach and the banana.

Johnny must learn to recognize that fatigue calls for the act of resting, that traffic means cautious action, and that cluttered bedrooms mean straightening up without being told each time.

SIGNALS AND CHAINING ∾ One last thing about signals. We talked about chaining before, showing that acts themselves can become consequences. Thus, signals can appear to be effective when no apparent consequence is immediately forthcoming. We may fail to perceive that the opportunity to engage in a sequence of acts that are chained as consequences can serve as a consequence. When Mommy says, "Johnny, go to bed," Johnny may go to bed without any apparent consequence present. The complex series of acts in going to bed, however, is later followed by the act of storytelling. "Going to bed" is the signal for storytelling, which then serves as the ultimate consequence for walking up the stairs, getting washed, getting undressed, putting on pajamas, and climbing into bed. The long chain of behaviors started by the one signal leads to an ultimate positive social consequence. All the acts in between serve to strengthen the ones that come before. There is nothing magical about this process. It can be taught.

Signals are the guideposts for action. But before we can proceed with our examination of action we have to examine another kind of behavior also, one to which I have not yet referred. This is the class of behavior called reflexes, or what I like to call reactions, the most important subclass of which is emotional reactions. Let's do that now.

7 🍃
Your Emotions and
You

    I have refrained from talking about emotional behavior until now for two reasons: one, because it can be confusing to deal with it before you thoroughly understand purposeful behavior (signals, actions, and consequences); and, two, because it is a form of behavior which is almost entirely private and not really the concern of parents. Let me hasten to add that all parents are concerned with the ways children express their feelings (those are actions) because they affect them and others directly. But only the child can know how he feels inside. The personal, private world of feelings is not subject to change or modification by the parent, although the ways in which the feelings are expressed can be modified and some of the events that trigger off emotions can be unlearned.

REACTIONS ᗥ

Emotional behavior is reflexive in nature in the sense that it is a reaction to an event that precedes it. We become emotional about something. We respond to the events around us with emotional arousal. There is a very real difference between an emotional behavior and the acts of behavior that we have been discussing heretofore. We do not learn our emotions in the way in which we learn our acts of behavior. We are born with the emotions with which we will die—fear, anger, or love. These emotions are really arousal states of the body. They are preparations of the body to do something, to run, fight, or relax.

Emotions don't tell us what to do and we never do anything because we are fearful or angry or loving. The things that we choose to do when under the influence of our emotions are almost invariably the kinds of things which change how we feel; they make us feel less frightened, less angry, more loving, and so on. We select from our repertoire of possible acts those most likely to work for us. We may do this deliberately, with careful planning and thought, or we may do it almost automatically because we have learned a favorite pattern of response (a way of acting) that we have used many times before.

Most of us are aware that emotional behavior is a reaction to something and we frequently talk about it in those terms. When

93

you ask someone why they are angry or why they are upset, they will invariably point to some prior event: "He, she, or it upset me"; "I am angry because of what Johnny did"; "I am scared of the consequences and what may happen." Even in the last example the speaker is referring to a prior event that is the source of his anticipatory fear. When a person is scared of what is to happen, there is always a prior event in the form of the thought (private act) that describes the future. A person is not really fearful of the future; he is fearful of what he is telling himself might happen in the future. To be an effective parent, you must understand your own emotional behavior and you must understand Johnny's.

Emotional reactions occur in many patterns of behavior. Frequently they serve as consequences. To make myself less angry is a very positive consequence. To make myself less frightened or anxious would also be a very positive consequence. You will tend to select behaviors to use while working with Johnny that make you less angry or less frightened. Very often these behaviors, while extremely effective in reducing your anger or fear, are very unproductive in terms of helping Johnny want to obey. In fact, they may be counter-productive; they may make things worse in the long run.

For example, if Johnny's room is a total mess, you may become so angry you see red. You are experiencing an arousal state of the body in which adrenaline is being released to speed things up, breathing increases to bring in more oxygen, your muscles are tensed, your blood is pumped more quickly by the heart and with greater pressure to send it more rapidly to arms, legs, and head, your capillaries dilate to help carry off heat (your face is beet red), and your palms are sweating to clutch a club more firmly. You are now ready to attack and destroy whatever is frustrating you. But what is frustrating you is Johnny's failure to keep his room neat. The arousal you are experiencing is extremely uncomfortable and has readied you for physical attack. You need an action from your repertoire to give you the positive consequence of anger reduction (relief from the unpleasant physical arousal). You can't kill Johnny, severely beat him, or destroy his room. What can you do? You can select yelling, screaming, spanking, breaking ashtrays, or gorging yourself with food, to pick a few common examples. They can all reduce anger.

Will any of those actions accomplish the purpose of teaching Johnny to be neat, to help him want to obey? Not really. At best he may become frightened of your anger and rush to clean the room in order to relieve his own fear. But the memory of the experience tends to fade in most children precisely because it is so frightening and the child still hasn't learned to self signal the act of cleaning. So the scene will repeat itself many times. Johnny may never learn either to self signal the act of cleaning or the self-consequences for doing so.

Emotional reactions can be positive as well as negative. Feelings of love, joy, sexual pleasure, peace, and tranquility are natural reactions of the body. The occurrence of these emotional reactions serves as a positive consequence. But the actions that produce them are hard to learn. We have many more actions in our repertoires to reduce emotions like anger, hate, jealousy, and fear than we do to produce feelings of joy and love.

CUES ∽

What makes us respond emotionally? I said that it was some event occurring before we became emotional. Let us call such an event a *cue*. I like to call it a cue because a cue *causes* something to occur. When an actor gives another actor a cue, he is determining what the second actor will say, for the second actor must speak the predetermined lines. There is no choice. When I give someone a signal, there is plenty of choice as to what behavior he may use. He may choose to respond or not respond. But when I give someone a cue I am determining what he will do. When we are talking about emotional behavior, cues mean just that. They *cause* the behavior to occur every time the cue occurs. There are two kinds of cues, natural cues and learned cues.

NATURAL CUES ∽ Every living thing is born into the world with a basic set of behaviors that allows it to deal with the physical world in ways that help it to survive. Human beings are no exception. Certain events cause certain reactions in all healthy and intact human beings. Intense light causes the pupils to contract to avoid burning the retina. Increases in temperature cause capillaries to dilate to help dissipate heat from the body. Decreases in temperature cause capillaries to contract to conserve body heat. A sudden change in stimulation (loud noise or sudden silence) causes an emotional arousal state called fear. Deprivation of basic biological needs (e.g., oxygen, water, food) will produce an arousal state called anger.

All of these events are called natural cues because we don't have to learn how to react to them. We are born with the ability to react appropriately. In our modern world most of the natural cues that require a state of body readiness occur quite rarely. Yet our bodies don't know that. Nature sometimes has quite an evolutionary lag and we are still equipped with the body states that help us to swing from trees and run great distances to escape an animal. When is the last time you needed an extra surge of strength to do something physically difficult?

There are very few dangerous natural cues to which we must respond. I can think of a few, of course—the sudden screech of brakes, diving too deep and being without enough air in our lungs, a bullet whining overhead, being caught in a snowstorm and suffering frostbite—but these are rare events. Most of our emotional reactions occur from learned cues.

LEARNED CUES ∾ A *learned cue* is any event which acquires the power to cause a reaction. Stick a pin in me and I will yell "ouch." The pain may bring tears to my eyes; I may find my heart beating more rapidly, my breathing rate changed, my muscles tensed up, butterflies in my stomach, and so on. The pinprick is a *natural cue;* it is the event that caused my arousal state.

There are other factors, however, around the pinprick, the things we tell ourselves about it. These are the private *learned cues.*

We can increase the reaction, decrease it, or even eliminate it, depending on what we tell ourselves about the event. Learning to look at the world and the things that happen to us in appropriate ways is an age-old problem. Philosophers have told us for centuries that if we can learn to look upon the world in a philosophical way, we can become calm and peaceful. What they have failed to tell us is how to achieve an effective way of looking at the world; that is, they have failed to tell us the kinds of private learned cues (acts of thinking) that will work in our modern world. They have also failed to provide us with a method for making sure that we will think in effective ways about the events around us.

Since this is a book about managing your children, I am not going to attempt to try to teach you all the ways in which you can learn to control the private learned cues that you give yourself, the labels, the ideas, the sentences, all of the little shorthand cues which trigger off your emotions. I simply wish to point out that these components of behavior are extremely important in understanding what Johnny does and how you react to him.

Many events by themselves cannot cause emotion. Johnny's breaking a glass is not in itself a natural cue for anger. But if we add an additional learned cue to this event by a private thought or a private sentence we may cause anger in ourselves. For example, Mommy can look at that broken glass and say, "That's awful, that's terrible. He should not have done that, that's my last glass. I can never replace it. My mother gave that to me. Isn't that awful, what will I tell my husband?" At this point Mommy is furious. When you ask her why she is angry, she may say, "Because Johnny broke the glass." She has completely forgotten all the private learned cues she gave to herself about the event.

Another mother whose child breaks a glass may look at the event quite differently. "Well, there goes the glass. I guess Johnny really doesn't know how to handle glasses yet. Here's an opportunity to teach him how. He's much more important than any object and I can always get a new set of glasses. I'll be able to explain to my mother somehow and if she doesn't understand that's too bad. My husband will understand completely." When you ask her why she didn't get upset, she may say, "Well, why should I? All Johnny did was break a glass."

This illustrates very clearly that it is not the event of the glass breaking, but the learned cues with which the mother provided herself which determines her emotional reaction. The first mother is likely to hit Johnny, punish him, yell at him, scold him, ridicule him, or do any of a variety of things that will reduce her anger. All of them will have very little effect on teaching Johnny how to handle a glass.

The second mother, who has no emotions to get rid of (because she has not generated any in herself) will be much more likely to select some teaching procedure—perhaps role-playing with a glass in which she prompts and coaches him on how to hold a glass, then provides him with a lot of love and attention and maybe even a piece of candy for learning to handle the glass well. The second Johnny will probably never break a glass again. The first one will look for every opportunity he can to drop glasses to get even with Mommy or he may seldom pick a glass up again and avoid anything else that is too daring or too new. In either of these two latter cases, Mommy will end up complaining that she doesn't like Johnny's behavior without realizing that it all began with her making herself angry about the event of the glass breaking.

We ought to be able to reduce the number of times that we get angry or fearful and the intensity of our emotional reactions. We can learn to do this best, not by sitting on our emotions or taking tranquilizers and pills, but by learning to think differently about the events around us.

No two people will have the same pattern of learned cues. We all label the world differently and we all have different values and ideas. But if we want to understand our own emotional patterns we must look to our learned cues for the source of most of our emotional arousal since, in the modern world, we seldom get stuck with pins, punched in the nose, or have our oxygen or food cut off. Most of the events to which we respond have no biological power to cause emotional reactions. We end up doing it to ourselves.

If you do become angry at a child, the best thing to do is to express it openly first. Get the anger or fear out of the way before trying to teach Johnny anything about how to act more appropriately. Do it without being insulting or destructive. You don't have to browbeat Johnny with a tongue lashing or beat him black and blue to work off your feelings. Shouting a little helps. Stick to the point, what it is you are angry about. Don't bring in all the other things he has ever done wrong. Stamp your foot and pound the table but don't select actions to use for which later you will be sorry. When you are done reducing your feelings openly, then start to teach Johnny.

How an Event Becomes a Learned Cue. The process by which a previously neutral event acquires the ability to cause a reaction has been known for a long time. In fact, it is one of the most intensively studied areas of psychology. Briefly, it happens in this way. A child ignores all events that are not natural biological cues; that is, he has no emotional arousal with respect to many important events. He may start to run out into a street full of traffic, try to pet a dog frothing at the mouth, or reach out to touch a hot stove. These events are not yet learned cues to him. Once he touches the hot stove, however, he will experience a fear reaction from the natural cue of pain. A blare of horns, a shout from his mother, or a slap in the rear end will produce fear, but the *sight* of traffic will not.

But when two events are paired, one a biological, natural cue for fear (slap) and the other a neutral cue (the sight of traffic), the neutral cue will acquire the ability to arouse the response associated with the natural cue—in this case fear. The sight of traffic *must* precede the slap or shout or they must occur simultaneously. If the shout comes before the sight of traffic learning will not take place. The child doesn't learn fear; he already knows how to be afraid. What he learns is of what to be afraid. He learns a new cue for fear. The sight of the traffic becomes a learned cue for fear. I am not recommending the slap, for the shout will work just as well.

The reason we wish to teach a certain amount of anxiety (mild fear) is that the avoidance of anxiety is a very powerful positive consequence. Since the sight of traffic is now a learned cue for fear, the sight of traffic becomes a signal for the consequence of fear reduction by the act of avoiding running into the street by waiting on the curb.

Sometimes reactions to cues are learned accidentally and unnecessarily. Phobias are a good example of such a phenomenon. With most phobias the fear arousal is unnecessary because the learned cue is not really dangerous, in others it is only minimally so. For example, if a child is playing in a closet and the door shuts and the light goes out suddenly (natural cues for fear), the child may become terrified of closets, the dark, or small closed places. The process is independent of the realness of the danger.

Unlearning Learned Cues. If a child is responding emotionally to events which are learned cues in ways which are inappropriate to the situation, his parents may wish to help him unlearn the cue. This must be done slowly and carefully. Don't throw the child into the closet and close the door. Don't throw the child who is terrified of water into the swimming pool on the theory that he will "sink or swim." At best he'll become terrified of you and at worst the fear will be deepened, almost beyond repair.

Gradually expose the child to mild forms of the learned cue by means of pictures or seeing it from a distance in perfect safety. Keep the child as relaxed and as calm as possible. Give him candy or constant words of reassurance. Gradually bring him closer or make the cue more intense (for example, by darkening the room slowly). Let him be the judge of when he's had enough or is getting frightened. Then start again at a lower level of intensity. Use many practice sessions until, gradually, the child no longer responds emotionally to the event as though it were a learned cue. It is always best to consult with a professional if the fear is extreme or if there are many such inappropriate learned cues.

SIGNALS AND CUES ∽ A signal is different from a cue in that it cannot *cause* a behavioral action or reaction. It only announces what is likely to happen if we act. The signal and the cue are both events that occur before behavior, but they are markedly different. Some events are both signals and cues—the sight of traffic, for example. But many people hardly notice traffic at all and have no fear arousal in response to it. If they avoid stepping into the street and wait for a go signal before crossing, they are doing so because of the positive consequence of survival, not because of the reduction or avoidance of fear. They have outgrown their childhood fear of traffic. Most learned cues lose their power to arouse emotions over time, if they are not occasionally paired with a natural cue. Phobias, however, rarely get the chance to be unlearned because we avoid exposure to the situation and cannot discover the lack of natural cues.

We are now ready to combine all of the components of behavioral patterns that we have been discussing into an overall framework. The thing that binds everything together is what I call the contract principle. This principle will underlie all of the methods for motivating and changing Johnny's behavior that will be presented in the rest of this book.

Part **3**
THE
HOW TO of
BEHAVIOR

8 🎋
Children for

H*ire*

CONTRACTS ⌒ Like most boys, I was more interested in sports and eating than I was in school. My father once offered me a quarter for every "A" I received on my next report card. At the moment it seemed like a very good deal and I accepted his offer. But as the weeks went by the work piled up I completely forgot about it. I followed my usual pattern of leaving everything until the last possible minute. It turned out to be one of my worst report cards.

Many patients have tried a procedure like my father's, and most find it very ineffective, as he did. In addition, they have vague feelings of guilt about using a method that they feel is a form of bribery. Bribery has a bad reputation in our society and rightly so. It has been used to corrupt people in political office and to evade the law. It is both immoral and ineffective, for as soon as you stop bribing, the person being bribed discontinues doing whatever you have bribed him to do. Bribery is also a risky business because since payment is made in advance, there isn't even a guarantee that the person being bribed will do as you ask. *Bribery is payment for something which is illegal, immoral, or fattening.* We seldom bribe people to do something in their best interest. For all these reasons I am against bribing anyone, especially children.

Now let us examine the nature of bribery with the moral question removed, since I'm assuming that we agree that bribery is morally bad. A bribe is a form of *contract* since it specifies what the person being bribed is to do (the action) and what he is to receive (the positive consequence). All forms of contracts contain the same provisions. A salary is also a form of contract. So is a commission, or the hiring of a taxicab.

The general principle of contract holds throughout our daily experiences. We do something and we receive something. There are two types of contracts: *formal* and *informal*. Formal contracts are written down and agreed to; informal contracts merely happen. An informal contract exists between man and nature or between people. For example, touch the stove and it will burn you, eat the berries and they will feed you, shake my hand and I will be your friend, marry me and I will be good to you, lend me some sugar and someday I will lend you something. All of these are forms of informal contracts. They all contain the same basic provisions of an act and a consequence.

Some contracts are *natural,* in the sense that no one has to arrange them or decide on them. The contracts between man and nature are all of this kind. Some contracts are *artificial* in the sense that someone decides and arranges that a particular consequence will occur following a particular action or chain of actions. Most contracts between people are of this kind.

Let's return to bribery as a form of contract. In a bribery situation the behavior that is called for is against the best interests of the person who is to perform the act. In addition, there are no self or natural consequences involved inasmuch as the positive consequences are provided by someone else. The bribe is paid in advance, a very poor method of strengthening behavior. The bribe is paid every time the act is to occur (although I am told some politicians are on a yearly retainer). Further, the bribe is based on a type of consequence that is inappropriate to the act (a quarter for an "A" is a less appropriate reward for studying than a personal satisfaction or the long-range goal of qualifying for college).

A salary, on the other hand, is a positive consequence paid after the work is performed. It is an acceptable form of contract since the work is neither illegal, immoral, or fattening. While the positive consequences are still provided by someone else, there are often self and natural consequences involved also. We all prefer work that we like and from which we get personal satisfaction (although it is getting increasingly difficult to find such work in our society).

It should be obvious by now that it is essential for a parent to have a basic knowledge of contracts and the principles involved if he or she is to help Johnny want to obey and learn.

THE CONTRACT PRINCIPLE ᧐

An action may occur naturally and spontaneously, but for it to become a working part of our behavior repertoire it must produce a positive consequence. No act continues to occur without some form or schedule of positive consequences. No act stops occurring without some form or schedule of negative consequences. This fundamental fact is confirmed by years of observing how living things behave and how people learn. The type of consequence, the reasons it is positive, and its source are all unique to each individual situation. But the rule holds for everyone. No act continues to occur because "it is the right thing to do." We do the right thing because of some consequence that may not be immediately apparent but is always present in one form or another.

Positive consequences cause an action to increase, negative consequences cause an action to decrease—all contracts express this fact. All contracts arrange for the appropriate action to receive a positive consequence and for inappropriate actions (even the failure to act appropriately) to receive a negative consequence. Work and you get paid, don't work and you don't get paid. Do the work correctly and you get paid, do the work incorrectly and you receive no pay.

SCHEDULES OF PAYMENT ∽

A contract has rules for providing consequences. There are different arrangements whereby the amount of work, its duration, and its quality are related to the occurrence of the positive consequence. Sometimes consequences are delivered immediately upon completion of the act, sometimes they are delayed for many years. Sometimes we receive part of the consequences now and part at a later date.

We can be paid—each time the act occurs or continues to occur—on a *continuous* basis (bribes, salaries, commissions, hourly wages, independent contracts), paid on an *irregular* basis (some types of salaries, piece work, gambling, percentage of the gross), or paid by a *combination* of the two. Sometimes we are paid on the basis of the *amount* of work performed, sometimes on the basis of *time* put in doing the work.

Each type of schedule of payment produces different effects on the actions being performed and is useful for different kinds of goals. When we want Johnny to work faster, we need one kind of schedule. When we want him to persevere at a difficult task, we need another kind of schedule. When we want him to learn rapidly we need one schedule and when we want him to maintain a new behavior we need still another. Fortunately, the average parent needs to know only a few basic types to accomplish most of what he or she wishes to teach Johnny. The general rules and effects of these types of schedules can now be presented.

TIME SCHEDULES ∽ Many contracts specify that the provision of the positive consequence (payment) will be based on how long you perform the act or series of acts. It may be payment by the hour, day, week, month, or year, just as long as the acts are being performed. Nothing is specified as to how many acts are performed or how well they are performed. In some cases not even a minimum standard of quality or productivity is specified. Teachers, government workers, and many other kinds of workers get paid this way. Johnny is expected to put an hour or two a day into study and homework. Very often no check is made as to how well he has done the work or how much he has retained from the study. He receives his privileges solely on the basis of time put in at the work.

AMOUNT PAYMENTS ∽ Some contracts specify that payment will be based on how much work is actually completed. Sometimes it is on the basis of rate (how much within a given amount of time) and sometimes solely on the basis of total amount of work completed. Requirements are sometimes made as to the quality of the work performed as well.

Johnny may be required to do so many arithmetic problems per hour or read so many pages before going out to play. If he is immature or dislikes the work he will probably work faster and more accurately under this type of payment schedule. If he likes what he is doing (self or natural consequences), a time payment schedule which is easier to administer will probably work just as well. Parents prefer time payment schedules because they take less of the parent's effort and place greater responsibility on the child, which can be a good way to teach maturity.

CONTINUOUS SCHEDULES ∽ Some contracts provide continuous payments. Each time an act is performed, or at very regular intervals while acts are occurring, a positive consequence is delivered. Commissions, daily payments, or immediate payments to a subcontractor are examples of this type. A gum machine is supposed to deliver gum every time you put money in and pull the lever. With some modern teaching machines Johnny instantly learns whether his last answer was right or wrong (a bridge acquired consequence of success). He receives it *each* time he completes an answer.

The effect of a continuous payment schedule is to produce very rapid learning and a very high rate of performance. If the child is given immediate payment (in the form of praise, encouragement, or a piece of candy) each time he performs a task, he will be eager to perform the task again. If he is performing a task (doing problems, for example) that he can repeat immediately, he has many opportunities to practice and perfect the skill.

The major problem of a continuous payment contract is that once external payment stops, the act being performed usually stops pretty quickly also. There may be an initial period of rapid acting after the cessation of positive consequence, but soon the behavior may disappear altogether. Think of a gum machine that suddenly stops delivering gum. You may pull the lever rapidly, shake it, kick it, and pull the lever some more. But if no gum is forthcoming, you will probably cease altogether. The next time you pass it you will be very hesitant to put more money in it and pull the lever. If you do and still no gum appears, you may give up on that machine forever.

Johnny is the same way. Unless there are some other consequences (self or natural) for performing the act, Johnny will give up on it once a continuous payment schedule is broken. This is why bribery is such an inefficient system for maintaining behavioral acts. Once you stop the continuous payment schedule of bribing, Johnny stops the unpleasant behavior of study or chores.

While there is no doubt that the rapid learning and high rates of acting which result from continuous payment schedules are desireable, maintaining the new action is also very important.

IRREGULAR SCHEDULES ∽ Some contracts are based on either erratic or irregular payment schedules. Digging for gold, sinking oil wells, or my kind of fishing trip are good examples of how nature doesn't always provide a continuous payment for work performed. Slot machines at Las Vegas, mother answering her child's questions, and Johnny hitting a baseball are additional examples.

One of the effects of inconsistent payment is that there are many occasions in which no positive consequence occurs to strengthen the act. The act occurs, gets stronger, then weakens, may disappear for a while, reoccurs and gets strengthened, then weakens again. It ultimately may be learned or strengthened to a high rate of occurring but the process is erratic and lengthy.

However, once the act has been learned and strengthened, if we then choose to stop providing payment (a relevant positive consequence) it may take a very long time for the act to stop occurring or it may never stop occurring at all. Thus an irregular schedule of payment turns out to be an excellent method of maintaining a child's behavior but a poor method of teaching new acts.

If the child never knows for sure just when a positive consequence may occur while he is acting, he may persist in the behavior for long periods of time. By gradually changing the payment schedule we may be able to produce amazing effects in maintaining both stable and very strong behavioral patterns. Let's look at some examples.

One contract method of irregular payment used in business is called piece work. In the early days of this country, piece work was the preferred method of payment for many employers. They would pay the worker for the number of pieces turned out, so many pieces for each unit of payment. If you turned out ten sweaters you might receive a dollar. After a while the manufacturers discovered that almost everyone in the factory could make ten sweaters for a dollar in the same amount of time. They then raised the requirement to twelve sweaters for a dollar. With much griping and complaining, everyone would begin to work a little faster, a little harder and, sure enough, they were producing twelve sweaters in the same amount of time to make their dollar. Well, you know what happened. As the employer kept raising the requirements, the workers kept working harder and producing more for the same amount of money. In some factories the worker might have to produce more than twenty-five sweaters to receive the same dollar. What had happened was that the method of payment was producing a very high rate of behavior. Unions, of course, were instituted to put an end to this practice because it was taking unfair advantage of the productivity of workers without returning to them a fair return for their increased efforts.

Paying on the basis of piece work will have the same effect on Johnny. He will behave in exactly the same way that the worker did in the factory. He may eventually increase his output of arithmetic problem solving to a degree where he will be doing the most amount of work in the least amount of time to get the same amount of consequences. The amazing thing is that even pigeons will work in this same way under the same pay-off schedule. Working under a piece work schedule gradually requiring more and more behavior from the pigeon (more and more pecks) for the same amount of corn, pigeons have been known to continue pecking for 25,000 times for a single piece of corn. Originally, of course, the contract was one peck, one piece of corn. At the end of the contract period the pigeon was pecking 25,000 times for one piece of corn. How's that for a sweat shop? The poor pigeon needs a union, I'm afraid.

In other experiments, chimpanzees have been trained to pull a lever continuously for 250,000 times before receiving their food. Every 4,000 times a light would appear in the cage similar to the light that would appear when the food occurred (a bridge acquired consequence). The light was similar to the daily time sheet a worker would fill out in anticipation of getting paid. With the system a chimpanzee could be trained to pull the lever 250,000 times before getting tangible positive consequences.

It's hard to imagine that a human being would behave in this way, but this is just how human beings behave. If you have ever gone to Las Vegas and watched the human beings pull the lever, you probably have seen some of them pulling a lever thousands of times for what is apparently very little reward. The payment schedule at Las Vegas is a random one. The contract the machine has with you is that if you keep putting money in and pulling the lever, occasionally, on a random basis, it will return money to you. Very often, the average return is only 30% of what you put in, but it's occurring in little bits and pieces in such a way as to create the illusion of large-scale pay-offs, particularly when you hit the jackpot and appear to get back much more than you put in. The irregular pay schedule the machine uses is very carefully worked out by the operators of the casino to maximize your continuous pulling of the lever and placing money into the machine.

Children are taught in similar ways to maintain behavior for long periods of time with only occasional consequences. At first, when Johnny is learning to talk, Mommy is thrilled with each new word. She immediately responds with social consequences that are quite positive to Johnny for each word that he learns. The rate of acquisition on Johnny's part is very, very high. He learns new words very quickly and is constantly practicing them and trying them out to get Mommy's attention. After a while Mommy gets bored and only occasionally responds in the same excited way to new words. The rate of Johnny's acquisition also begins to drop off, although it is maintained at a fairly high rate. Now he is being weaned to occasional social consequences instead of constant ones. But he continues to learn and acquire new words because they have two kinds of pay-offs: one, the immediate effect in controlling the world around him and getting the things he wants; and two, the occasional pay-off of Mommy's excitement and attention when he says something especially difficult or cute.

There are many kinds of irregular payment schedules. Bonuses are a very popular variety. They are all excellent for maintaining an act once it is already established in the behavior repertoire, but they are poor methods of teaching new behavior. An occasional word of praise or spontaneous treat can help the child who is already a good student but it cannot help a poor student become a good one.

COMBINATION PAYMENT SCHEDULES ◇ From previous examples, you probably have suspected already that a good strategy is to combine the effects of continuous and irregular payment schedules into one contract. If you begin by arranging that Johnny will receive immediate and continuous positive consequences for each occurrence of a new act being learned or for the constant use of a new act (time payment), he will learn it much faster. If you then change to an irregular payment schedule (random bonus, accelerating performance or increasing time requirements), you can help him maintain the new behavior until self or natural consequences take over under a new type of contract. If these never occur, you can always maintain the actions by occasionally providing some external positive consequence.

In other words, you begin with a rich (frequent or continuous payment schedule) and *gradually* thin out (irregular schedule) the occurrence of the positive consequence. Be generous at first and stingy later. Of course, it takes more of your time and effort at first, but think of the years ahead when it will take so little effort to help Johnny perform at high and productive levels of behavior. In the chapters on method we will spend a great deal of time examining practical ways of implementing this principle.

CONSEQUENCE PATTERNS ◇

Consequences seldom occur alone. While every contract has an explicity or implicity stated positive and negative consequence that the contract itself provides, there are often other outcomes which result from the child's behavior. Going to bed may lead to consequences which the parent provides under a formal or informal contract but there are other contracts present as well. There are natural contracts in which Johnny stands to gain or lose. Television time, companionship, or other pleasures are lost while rest and better health are gained. There are self contracts under which he stands to gain or lose self-respect, power, or independence. All of these form a pattern of consequences with a combined or conflicting payment pattern. Which are the strongest will ultimately determine which action Johnny performs.

Sometimes it is not easy to determine all of the consequences involved in influencing Johnny's decision to obey or not to obey. If he is not choosing to obey your requests, you can be certain that some other contract is influencing his behavior. The solution to this problem is the basis of all good management systems and will be covered later.

CONSEQUENCE CHAINS ∽ Many consequences are dependent on a chain of occurrences, each link of which provides a partial consequence, with all links combining to lead to the larger, more important ultimate consequence. Grade school leads to junior high which leads to high school which leads to college which leads to graduate or professional school which leads to better material goals, higher social status, and a more interesting career. Each promotion and graduation is a partial consequence leading to the final ultimate consequences. Studying for the test tonight instead of going to the movies in order to get a higher grade means giving up an immediate positive consequence in order to build up to a much delayed but more valuable consequence.

Learning to choose the action which maximizes the most important positive consequence not only in the immediate consequence pattern but in the total pattern, which includes long delayed, future payment, is one of the best measures of maturity which I know. Not many adults are able to do this well. Helping Johnny acquire the judgment and skill required is one of the most important jobs of a parent.

Complex life contracts almost always include long-range effects of our present actions. Although throughout the rest of the book I will be talking predominately about short-range contracts, you should never forget the importance of ultimate consequences and their effect or lack of effect on your child's behavior today. Most contracts are affected not only by the over-all situation present at the time but also by Johnny's awareness of the future.

SEQUENTIAL CONTRACTS ∽

Contracts can occur in patterns. There is no more powerful tool for teaching a new behavior than the use of sequential contracts— that is, a series of contracts with gradually increasing requirements for earning the same or gradually increasing positive consequences. The series of contracts are related because they deal with the same act which you are trying to increase in strength, rate, or likelihood of occurrence.

The first contract in the series, which may require very little of the final action, stipulates immediate payment upon completion. The next contract in the series requires still more of the final action pattern for either increased or constant payment. At each practice session (which may be immediately after the preceding one or delayed for hours or days) the contract is made more difficult but it is always possible for the child to fulfill it.

For example, if you wanted a child to strengthen his muscles, you might begin with a contract requiring him to lift five pounds five times for one piece of candy. The next day you might require him to lift ten pounds for three pieces of candy (for greater motivation). On each subsequent day you might increase the requirement of either the amount of weight to be lifted or the number of times he is to lift a specified amount of weight. Each new contract might include either a larger payment or the same amount of payment as the previous one (depending on the child's own motivation). The contracts are related because they all deal with muscle building.

We might wish the child to learn to sit still and not fidget. The first contract might require him to sit still for only five seconds in order to receive a word of praise from his father. The instant he has completed a five-second period of sitting still, he would receive both the word of praise and a new contract. His father might say "that was very good, now let's try to sit still a little longer." This time, however, the father might wait anywhere from six to sixty seconds (until Johnny appeared to be about to fidget) and then praise him again, immediately beginning a new contract with an irregular payment schedule. Each contract has an unspecified time period, except that it is longer than the one before. He may get dozens of contracts completed before ending the practice session. The time schedule and irregular payment schedule in the contract were chosen in this case because they are the best methods of teaching the child to maintain an act which he has already demonstrated he can do (sitting still). The series of contracts began at a point where the child could succeed and each contract in the series was possible for the child to fulfill because the father only gradually increased the requirements.

IMPOSSIBLE CONTRACTS ∽

Many contracts which parents set for children are impossible for the child to fulfill. Sometimes it is because the child is too young to perform the act satisfactorily. Sometimes it is because the consequences the parent is providing are neutral or negative to the child. Sometimes the child cannot recognize the signals which call for an act he is capable of doing.

"A two-year-old should be toilet trained." "At six she should be able to keep her room neater." "Stop talking in line, you're in second grade now." "At fourteen, you should know how to budget your money." "Why don't you ever do your homework without my nagging you?" "Fifty cents a week for an allowance is more than I ever got." The complaints of parents are endless. All of the ones quoted above reflect a poor understanding of contracts and the real abilities of children.

Sometimes the contract is so poorly stated the child has only the vaguest notion of what he is to do. "Be good and you can stay up late." "Take care of your sister." "Get all your work done before you go to the movies." Sometimes there are no explicit consequences, sometimes there are no clearly stated requirements. Small wonder children get confused, uncooperative, and rebellious.

Some parents are expert in the setting of contradictory contracts. "Talk to me," the mother says, but whenever Johnny tries to talk to her he finds she prefers silence. "Ask before you take," says father, but when Johnny complies, his father seldom grants the request. "Go out and play and enjoy yourself but don't get dirty," admonished Mommy. Have you ever seen a four-year-old who can play and have fun and still remain clean?

The list of impossible contracts is endless. The results of such contracts are a frustrated parent and an insecure child. The constant appearance of willful disobedience in some children often began with a willing child who failed to fulfill impossible contracts. The constant appearance of an angry and punitive parent often began with a loving parent's unrealistic expectations or profound ignorance of the ability of children at different ages.

PREPAYMENT CONTRACTS ∾

Have you ever said to yourself, "I'll make the beds after I have another cup of coffee?" How often did you then end up killing the morning with the beds still unmade? A good contract always makes payment after the act is performed. Otherwise you tend to strengthen the wrong act. In the case of the coffee before making the bed, you are really strengthening reading the morning paper or listening to the radio instead of productive work.

When Johnny asks you for the payment now and promises to do the work later, you end up strengthening begging, conning, or manipulation rather than productive effort. He'll promise you the moon in order to get an advance on his allowance, permission to go to the movies, stay up later, or see his favorite television program "first." But he seldom delivers even a piece of green cheese.

Partial prepayment, however, can serve to strengthen the positive consequence by acting as an incentive for agreeing to the contract. But it is a less desirable method than payment upon completion. Whenever possible, a good contract provides payment at completion because you are then strengthening only the act you wish to strengthen and not some undesirable one.

SELF CONTRACTS ⌒

While both nature and other people are constantly setting up formal and informal contracts in both natural and artificial ways, the most important source of contract in our culture should be the ones you set for yourself. Johnny must learn to arrange his life so that he is constantly earning what he allows himself to do or have as a positive consequence. This is the basis of feelings of self-respect, pride, and true self-confidence. He must learn to watch television *after* his work is done and *because* his work is done. He must learn to set realistic standards for himself so that he is not living under self-imposed contracts impossible to fulfill. He must learn how to set a series of contracts for himself so that he gradually strengthens actions that bring delayed but important positive consequences. He must learn to set his contracts with full awareness of the complex consequence patterns, both immediate and delayed, that realistically should control his behavior.

You must teach him how to do this in order to fulfill your role as parents in our society. Independence is our society's goal for our children, and we have an obligation to teach them how to accomplish the only meaningful form of independence, effective self-contracting. During the time they are children, under our care and supervision, we must train them to function without us. The earlier we teach self-contracting, the better.

In the next chapter we begin the methodology of how to accomplish some of the things I have been talking about. We shall start with an overview of the general approach, the problem of how to decide what needs changing and how to formulate an effective strategy for change.

9 🦋

Beginning at the
B*eginning*

You need a plan. In order to help Johnny want to obey and to help him learn effective behavior, you must approach the problem systematically. I don't mean mechanically. There is no magic technique that will work on all children or solve any problem. Each child is different, each technique is different, but the strategy you use will be essentially the same. Let me explain.

Positive consequences strengthen actions. That is the general principle. But every child requires a unique positive consequence, a unique amount, and unique timing in the giving of the consequence. You may have to begin at a different point with each child. Some will already know how to perform the action but not be sure of when to do it. Others will know how and when but have no motivation for doing so.

What steps do you follow? Where do you begin? how do you know for sure that the change in behavior is going to last? Who should be in charge of the teaching procedure? Who should provide the consequences? All of these are important questions that need to be determined in advance. It is not a good policy to plunge ahead in anything without having thought about the problem carefully first.

Unfortunately, many parents do just that. They are disturbed about Johnny's lack of appropriate behavior or by the presence of some inappropriate behavior. They want it to change. Immediately. So they demand change by using a technique. They punish. They cajole. They threaten. They plead. They ignore. They try anything and everything they have ever heard about or had used on them. More often than not, they fail. If they are lucky, Johnny outgrows the problem or grows into new behavior. The accidental change, brought about by maturity, the intervention of teachers, friends, or other significant people in Johnny's life, gives them confidence in the effectiveness of many irrelevant techniques.

I don't mean to imply that parents do everything wrong. They do much that is right. Often they apply effective procedures without realizing it. A good deal of Johnny's appropriate behavior can be directly traced to the loving, concerned, and effective care of his parents. It's just that they haven't been trained to distinguish an effective approach from an ineffective one. The average parent's handling of Johnny, therefore, is a hodge-podge of good and bad techniques.

What I would like to do now is to provide you with an approach which I call the *strategy of change.* Its purpose is to organize your thinking in such a way as to answer many of the questions I raised earlier and to prepare you to select and modify the appropriate technique for your child. Later chapters will discuss a variety of techniques to change Johnny's behavior once you have selected where to begin.

STRATEGY OF CHANGE ⌒

The strategy of change may sound ominous at first but it really isn't. It's simply an orderly procedure to help you decide what to do first, what you do after that, and what you can reasonably expect in terms of a child's ability to change or to add new behaviors. Remember that we're concerned with the three main parts of behavior: the act itself, the consequences of that act, and the signals. These three components can be seen as points of intervention or as places to effect change. ·

For example, we may not be concerned with the child's actions of running, screaming, and yelling, or his reasons for doing so since he's having fun in the activity; but, we may be very much concerned with what signals begin the running, screaming, and yelling. We prefer those signals to be the playground or recess time, not the classroom, the living room, or the kitchen. The child must learn when it is appropriate and where it is appropriate to use the action. The problem for the parent, then, would be to teach the right signal, to teach the child when it is appropriate to act and when it is not.

On the other hand, the child may be trying to use social skills in appropriate situations and for the right reasons, but might be very ineffective in the social skills she is using. She may run up to a new friend and throw her arms around the friend and begin to kiss wildly, as my daughter did when she first went to dancing class as a little girl. She was certainly doing it for the right reason—she wanted to make friends. It was certainly appropriate to show warmth since this was a potential new friend. However, the way she went about it was very inappropriate and needed to be modified. It tended to overwhelm the other children who were not as free and demonstrative as she was. We had to teach her a little more restraint in the behavior itself. We did not wish to eliminate the action; we simply wanted to tone it down a little bit.

Sometimes parents find that children will act correctly to the appropriate signal but for the wrong reasons. They will cut the grass only when somebody either threatens them or bribes them. In this situation, if the child is about sixteen years of age, most parents would expect him to be cutting the grass for his pride in participating in the family or his sense of achievement in maintaining the chores and contributing to the needs of the family. Parents do not wish to have to offer praise, money, or punishment to motivate the action. Parents who find that only this external system of consequences will get the child to perform the behavior are frequently disappointed and angry. They desire a different kind of consequence system to motivate the child.

There are seven steps in the overall sequence of successful change technique. You can begin anywhere in the sequence but the best strategy is always to maintain the correct order of steps. Let's examine these seven steps.

1. *Setting the goal*

The very first thing that a parent should do in determining a change of behavior in a child is to decide what they want the final action to be. Most people concern themselves very little with what it is they're trying to teach. They're mostly concerned with what they're trying to get rid of. Very few people clearly set a goal that they are going to strive for with their child. The goal might be effective care of his own room, good social skills, effective study habits, or a variety of other kinds of behavior. The wise parent will sit down and carefully think through (on occasion writing it out, if necessary) what she finally expects of the child. Then she will know when the child has achieved the goal.

She also will try to formulate this final goal in terms she can easily communicate to the child. The older the child, of course, the more necessary it is to formulate the final goal or the act in ways that the child can understand. If Johnny is only two, she does not really have to specify the act for him. She simply has to have it fixed in her own thinking and clearly specified. If Johnny is sixteen, on the other hand, including him in planning the final act is a very effective technique. Johnny himself can contribute to the design of what the final behavior will be, offering suggestions and corrections to the final pattern. If Johnny is allowed to participate in the design of the final act, the whole process will be easier. In any case, with two-year-olds and sixteen-year-olds, the first step in the strategy of change is to determine where you are going.

2. *Assessing Current Behavior*

The second step is to assess the child's current behavior. How much of the final action you have chosen as a goal is the child doing now? If you want him, for example, to be polite, how often is he polite now? Is it one out of a hundred times when he has the opportunity to show politeness? Is it fifty out of a hundred times? Or is it ninety-five out of a hundred? Perhaps the goal you are setting is much too high. It is important to determine what he is doing now because you might find, for example, that not only is his rate of polite behavior low, but there is a high rate of sarcasm, insults, rudeness, and impoliteness. These incompatible actions must first be gotten rid of or reduced to a very low frequency before he can even begin to become polite. So in assessing the child's present state of behavior we are looking at two things: how much of the new act is present now; and how much of some other act is present that must first be eliminated before we can teach the new act?

Remember, that by eliminating I do not mean gotten rid of forever, but simply put on the shelf and not used again. There is a real difference between permanent elimination and suppression of an action. The only way to eliminate an act permanently is by surgery. By replacing it with another act, however, we can permanently suppress it, which is just as good in the long run.

This second step is the planning stage, the time when you think the problem through. You should not be engaged in this at the moment of crisis, when the child is misbehaving or failing to behave and you are in the middle of cooking dinner or trying to get him to bed. Any golf pro will tell you not to stop and think through your golf game in the middle of a tournament; if you stop to think about what you're doing while you're playing, you're going to louse up the game so badly that you'll never even get close to winning. The time to think things through is in the quiet of the evening when the children are asleep or at some peaceful moment in the day while they are at school. You plan what you are going to do. You plan where you're going and you assess where you are.

3. *Starting the New Action*

The third step for the parent is to prompt the first beginnings of the behavior she is after and the first deceleration of the behaviors that she is trying to get rid of. It is a two-pronged attack. She is going to help the child to begin the new behavior and she is going to help him to refrain from the incompatible or the inappropriate behavior.

If her children are fighting, for example, she must step in and prompt the end of the fighting. She does not have to do this by yelling, hitting, or threatening, or even by using a negative consequence; she can come in and use a prompt to reduce the behavior. She can simply separate them and hold them tightly against her. She can enlist her husband's aid so that he takes one child and she takes the other. She can use all kinds of physical prompts without even touching the child, such as walking in the room and suddenly turning off the light and turning it on again. The sudden darkness will startle her children and will probably prompt them into ending the fighting. She can suddenly turn off the television set and then snap it on again.

Anything which will attract the children's attention will usually stop the fighting. I know one mother who worked out a very effective technique for doing this. She would simply walk into the playroom with a glass of water and proceed to slowly pour it on the floor. The children would become so startled by the behavior and convulse with laughter at the silly sight of Mommy pouring water on the floor that they would forget that they were fighting. She would have physically prompted, by her own action, the end of the incompatible behavior.

Her next step should begin to teach them how to cooperate and how to solve the disagreement. She might have to teach them how to discuss their differences. She might even have to take their hands and put them together as a way of shaking hands to make up. She must encourage and prompt until the first signs of cooperative and compromise behavior occurs. It is her obligation to do so because she is the person who wants to see the behavior changed, not the children. So she must take the responsibility for prompting the beginning of new ways of acting. Sometimes she can do this with a verbal prompt by simply telling them what she wants. Very often she will have to do it physically.

If you want a young child to go to bed, you can try a verbal prompt, but you would be much wiser to walk over, take him by the hand, and lead him to bed. When you're beginning to teach a new behavior to a young child you should usually physically prompt the behavior to start it. If the child is older, initiating new behaviors often can be accomplished by verbally signaling them. You can tell Johnny what the new action is to be. However, if he fails to respond by at least making some effort to act in the new way, don't hesitate to use some kind of physical prompt.

4. *Providing the Consequences*

The fourth step now takes into account the contract principle. You have started the new action going or you have weakened the inappropriate act (the one that you're trying to replace). Now it is up to you as the parent to provide the reason. Don't expect the child to perform the new act or stop the old act because he wants to, because it's the right thing to do, or because it feels good. On all three counts you are probably wrong. It does not feel good to stop fighting in the midst of your anger and it does not please a child to give up anything. But giving things up (even actions) can become a positive consequence if giving up something can get you more of something else.

Most children are quite selfish, quite hooked into the immediate consequences of what is going on around them, and oblivious to the future. They are near-sighted. This is what differentiates the child from the adult. The ability of the child to see his present actions in terms of future consequences is quite limited.

It is now up to you to provide the reason for him to stop fighting and to be cooperative. The external consequences which you provide are the reasons. These consequences may be in the form of a simple word of thanks or praise, merely paying attention to the new behavior, giving the child a treat—either something tangible or the opportunity to do something that he wishes to do. But regardless of what consequence you choose, it must be related to what the child wants and it must happen quickly, within a few seconds. As rapidly as possible you need to provide the effective positive consequence for the child's new way of acting, no matter how imperfect it is.

Now you have decided on the goal, you have assessed where the child is, you have prompted the new way of acting, and you have provided a relevant consequence. You are now ready to begin moving toward the final goal.

5. *Strengthening Actions*

You are ready to require more and more of the new action. Johnny should be required to be more polite than he was yesterday, to do more things that are helpful, to put more of his room into order than he did yesterday, to spend longer amounts of time at his study—in short, to do more of the desired action.

He is also required to do less of the old, undesirable action. If he was hitting his brother thirty times yesterday, then today it should only be twenty-nine and tomorrow only twenty-eight. You need to prompt continuous improvement in either direction—reduction of the undesirable behavior and/or the addition of the desirable behavior.

In each case, your process will be similar. You should be raising the standard by changing the contract and asking more of the child each time while continuing to provide the external consequences. When we discuss the process of shaping new behavior, which is what this really is, we'll talk more specifically about the techniques to be used and some of the problems to watch out for. For now, we are simply discussing the whole overall process of change and the strategy that the parent should use. Remember, the child is continuously prompted and helped to begin the action. He is never expected to initiate it on his own and he is never expected at this stage of the game to be doing it for his own reasons. You need to supply the reasons and you need to supply the prompts during the fifth phase.

6. *Changing Consequences*

Now Johnny has acquired the final behavior; the action is performed well according to whatever standards you have set up or he has helped you set up. He is doing it right, but he still is doing it because you are supplying the positive consequences. It is now time to wean him, to change the consequence structure that maintains his new action. You need to be concerned at this stage of the game with changing from the external and artificial positive consequences you have established for him to the kinds of consequences that he will supply for himself or that can be found in the natural consequences of the act itself.

If you have been teaching him how to play, he may have very rapidly weaned himself from your praise and approval and he may now be playing because it is fun. In one short step he will have gone from your external, artificial positive consequences to the natural positive consequences of the play itself.

Sometimes you will have taught him a new action which has no natural pleasurable consequences. He must perform the task because there are valid and justifiable reasons for his doing it in terms of his contribution to the rest of the family. He has to take out the garbage, for example. He has now learned to do this without spilling the garbage, has learned to do it quickly and effectively, and has learned to put the garbage in the right place for the person who is to pick it up. However, you still must prompt by telling him when to do it (verbal signal). You still must supply the positive consequences, either in the form of a word of praise, a special privilege that he has earned, or a treat.

We can never really expect Johnny to *like* taking out the garbage, to find the act pleasant, rewarding, and pleasurable in itself. Then what motivation can he have for taking out the garbage, other than your external positive consequences? The answer is that he can be taught to develop a sense of pride in maintaining the chore and doing it correctly. He can feel a sense of achievement when he has completed it. He can avoid the feeling of guilt he will have if he fails to do the chore. There is a positive and negative motivational system that he can establish for himself.

The establishment of such a motivational system does not occur without a parent's help. The parent must wean the child in almost every case. It is true that the process for many children happens so easily that the parents are unaware that they have taught some of their children this process and have failed to teach it to others. Parents tend to assume that it happened naturally with one child because he has a good character and did not happen with the other child because he does not have a good character. One child is lazy and the other is not. This is simply not true. The only truth here is that one child was able to learn by your method of teaching and the other child was not. The so-called lazy child is simply the kind of child who cannot learn by your casual method of teaching. He must be systematically weaned and the weaning must be done carefully and under the direction of the parent.

Too many parents leave the process of learning self-motivation to the child himself because they assume or desire that it will happen naturally as the child gets older. They end up spending most of their time complaining that their child has not acquired self-motivation at all. They are frustrated in their attempts to try to teach it because they do not understand the principles, the procedures, or the fact that developmentally the ability to acquire it takes place at a much later age than most people would imagine. We'll come back to how to do it in a later chapter.

7. *Changing Signals*

The last step in the sequence is the change of signal control—that is, a change in who will prompt the action. Initially the action should have been prompted by the parent. The parent has the obligation of prompting the child's actions during the process of learning and frequently even after the behavior has been learned. But no parent wishes to go on prompting the actions of his children indefinitely—at least, not in our country.

Under a patriarchal or matriarchal system, the oldest member of the family reserved the right to tell people what to do, when to do it, and how to do it. In our country we follow a different concept that says that a child is to prompt himself in order to become independent of external control and direction in many areas as soon as possible. Some parents are torn between the old system and the new. Never quite sure whether they want the child to prompt himself or not, they vacillate back and forth, further confusing the child. They may say that they want the child to prompt himself, and yet by their actual behavior toward the child, the child learns very quickly that they really do not intend to give up the control of prompting to him. They always want to be the ones to tell the child what he is to do, when he is to do it, and how he is to do it.

But let us assume that your goal is in keeping with the stated goals of our society. Your desire is to teach your child independence, to teach him to respond to his own signals, or the natural signals that the environment provides for him. You now must gradually change the type of signal that controls Johnny's actions. You should, if necessary, start by taking Johnny by the hand and pulling him up to bed. You then begin to switch to verbal commands, because it is usually too difficult to leave what you are doing to take him upstairs. You want to be able to tell him when to go upstairs as the next step in changing signals. But as soon as Johnny gets a little bit older, you should expect him to do it on his own. You want him to notice what time it is and to tell himself that it is time to go to bed. So you must teach him to signal himself at eight o'clock and not wait for your reminder.

Eventually, you should expect that Johnny will develop adult, mature judgment and will ignore the clock and go to bed when he is tired, at seven o'clock if necessary. An adult ignores the clock for the most part and responds to his body needs, the natural prompts of sleep.

The change of signals is accomplished by gradual steps which will be covered in the chapter on methods. At what level of signal control you stop depends on many factors. Some situations require that we continue to listen to the signals provided by others, such as when we come to an intersection and wait for the officer to tell us whether to go, stop, turn, or wait. The type of signal that he responds to should be determined by the situation itself and by the age of the child.

REALISTIC EXPECTATIONS ∽

I expect my own children to be able to do certain things at a very early age. For example, I find that my daughters are quite capable of picking up their room and making it neat at the age of three. So I teach them the actions necessary to clean their rooms at that age. Developmentally, at three most children have sufficient coordination and muscular ability to do this.

On the other hand, I expect to supply the positive consequences until they are about eighteen, because I am a realist. I am aware that developmentally they will have little reason to keep their room neat for any other reason than the ones I supply. At about eighteen I would expect them to have self-consequences and maybe even find some pleasure in the activity of cleaning up the room. I am told that some people do enjoy housekeeping, although I frankly have never done so.

I expect that they will notice that the room is dirty and respond to the natural signals at about the age of twenty-two. Therefore, I will take the responsibility of prompting them or verbally signalling them to clean their room until they are twenty-two.

These expectations, on my part, make life much easier for myself and my children. By expecting little, I am seldom frustrated or angry. Of course, I try to achieve things much earlier—but I don't *expect* success. If we learn to look upon the three aspects of a behavior pattern in this way, many of the problems that we have with children can be avoided. My younger children are capable of performing the act of coming to the dinner table but they are not capable of telling themselves to do so by self signals. I must supply those signals.

They will have very little reason for coming to the dinner table unless they are quite hungry. They must leave their play activities in order to come to the dinner table. To expect them to be motivated by either pride or a sense of achievement at an early age is very unrealistic. Therefore it is up to me, as a parent, to make the dinner table fun, to make my approval important, and to make other kinds of incentives available to the child as the motivation for coming to the dinner table.

Different behaviors will have different developmental sequences in terms of self-motivation or self-prompting. It is easier in some areas than in others for a child to learn to signal himself, and it is easier to develop intrinsic or self-motivation in some areas than it is in others. Wise parents accept reality and never ask the impossible. If the child appears to be unmotivated by the natural situation, they do not chastise the child for his failure to value what the parent values. No child that I have met really values the act of study as we have decided the act of study shall be. The child likes learning, of course, and the acquisition of new knowledge is fun, but the way we make a child do it in our education system is, frankly, simply not fun.

The parent who insists that the child motivate himself to study is banking on the fact that a few selected children can develop self-consequating patterns very early in life to keep themselves studying. The parent who has this kind of child is lucky. Only one of my five children developed this kind of motivation early. The rest of them had to be externally motivated, and frankly I think the one who developed the self-motivating system is a little nuts. I really can't see the fun of study as the schools require it. The fact that she takes a sense of pride and achievement in such behavior at this early age has me a little worried, since I don't approve of the assign, lecture, and test system. I would be much more comfortable if, like most children, she had to be externally motivated.

SUMMARY ᴄ

The seven steps in the strategy of change are: 1. decide on the goal; 2. assess the current action repertoire; 3. begin to prompt the first approximation of the final action; 4. supply the initial consequences; 5. require more of the action a little bit at a time; 6. gradually wean the child from the types of consequences with which you began to the types of consequences you wish ultimately to maintain the behavior; 7. and finally, change the nature of the original signal you used to the kind of signal that you ultimately want to control the child's actions.

Although it is systematic, this strategy of change can be done in a spontaneous manner, without being mechanical. Even though this system may be hard to learn at first, we must learn to do it as correctly and systematically as we do any of the other things we choose to do in life. There is no shortcut to effective management. It is as difficult to be systematic in managing children as it is to play the piano, play golf, or learn any of the other skills that we spend so much of our spare time in acquiring. Yet we are perfectly willing to practice bridge playing, bowling, golf, or piano playing. We also must be willing to continuously practice how to manage our children.

In the next chapter we will turn to some of the basic approaches to child management that I have referred to in previous chapters.

10 🌿
Choosing the
*R*ight Tool *I*

What, exactly, is wrong with Johnny's behavior? What am I really trying to accomplish? As a parent, you must ask yourself these basic questions. Are you trying to teach him a new action? Are you trying to eliminate one that is already in his repertoire of actions? Are you trying to modify some action because of how he is using it, when he is using it, or why he is using it?

Once you have decided what the problem is to be, then you must select an appropriate technique to bring about the change. All techniques are based on the contract principle but they can be grouped into a few general classes. Each of the groups of techniques works best on a specific kind of problem (adding, eliminating, or modifying an action) and is best suited for a particular age level.

Within each class, there are literally, thousands of techniques possible. By techniques I mean the specific procedures and tools that you design to fit *your* child. Whether you use a piece of candy or praise, whether you break the teaching into steps or teach the whole task in one step, or whether or not you use special devices to aid you are all determined by the problem and by the needs of the individual child.

Rather than list and describe a sample of hundreds of problems and techniques for solving them, none of which may fit your particular situation, I am going to discuss each class (group of methods) and give you some examples of how parents have used that general approach to solve a particular problem. Even if you feel your problem is quite similar to the one I describe, you must still change the technique I describe slightly to fit *your* situation and *your* child. Too many books, written to help parents raise children, offer techniques which do not work when tried by the parents. The techniques are sound enough, but without understanding the principles upon which they are based, the parents cannot properly adjust them to fit their situation.

ADDING OR MODIFYING ACTIONS ✑

Let's first look at the classes that deal with helping Johnny acquire a new action, one that is not in his repertoire. Remember that nature makes it possible for a child to learn directly from his

127

environment. The processes that I will be discussing underlie the acquisition of most new skills or the improving or modifying of imperfectly learned skills. There is nothing theoretical about the methods by which a child learns. What you can do to become a more effective teacher is to use those natural principles in systematic ways called techniques.

MODELING ⤳Parents are always wanting to show a child how to do something. Frequently, they are quite enamored with their own ability to do it. They proudly demonstrate with great skill the final complicated behavior pattern, rapidly passing over the different parts, and then turn to the child with the admonition, "Now you do it." The child may make a half-hearted attempt, forgetting many of the different steps along the way, and making a horrendous mess out of the new behavior pattern. Parents may then try to break the complicated skill down into smaller parts and model step-by-step what the child is to do. Again the child watches passively, and when he begins he is still required to perform the final task all at once. There is no step-by-step approximation in this learning system, which I will call modeling. You are usually expected to go from zero to the final goal in one step.

Amazingly, many children can do this, and most people pick up a great deal of behavior in many areas by modeling. It is, however, seriously damaging to a child to attempt to model and to fail. Few of us can tolerate failure because our culture tends to make failure a basis for rejection. Rejection is a serious threat in early childhood because being rejected by his parents can mean death (real or symbolic) to a tiny child. Later on, of course, being rejected will no longer be any significant danger to an individual, and yet the emotional response to rejection will continue to be just as intense. Since failure is a major reason for being rejected, the child being taught by modeling is constantly being exposed to the dangers of failure, the fear of rejection, and the intense emotional anxiety connected with it.

Thus many children will avoid modeling by saying, "I can't," or "I don't want to" or will avoid the situation entirely. Much of the school dropout problem can be explained on this basis. There are many other reasons for dropping out, of course, but often the dropout from life is an individual who has found that modeling is a terrible way for him to learn new behavior and knows of no other way.

The ability to learn by modeling presupposes a good deal of previous ability and learned skills which may or may not be present in a child's repertoire. For example, one psychologist found that some children didn't know how to imitate, that imitation is not a universally well-developed process in children. It may be that it is a learned skill which can be imperfectly learned. Children who have never fully developed the ability to imitate will be very seriously handicapped by any method of teaching that is based on modeling. Very young children, retarded, brain-damaged, and even normal older children who have imperfectly developed imitative ability may appear unable to learn if modeling is the technique being used.

I don't wish to discourage parents from modeling, because for many behaviors it is a useful shortcut to the acquisition of blocks of behavior all at one time. When the child is capable of it, it is the method of choice. The wise parent may try modeling when she is sure that the child can do it, and where the child has demonstrated in the past the ability to use modeling. But as soon as modeling fails, the parent should reassure the child that failure is permissible and that it does not lead to rejection. It is also a good idea to teach your child that rejection is not a terrible thing.

There are many training techniques based on modeling. You can show a child how to do something by actually demonstrating the action and pointing out the appropriate signals that should initiate it. You can show him slides or films and instruct him to copy what he sees. With older children and adults it is possible simply to describe the action and its signals using spoken or printed words (verbal instructions).

A good modeling technique is always built on the principles of the strategy of behavior change. The first step is to decide on the final goal, the action to be acquired by the child. You must decide what it is the child is to do and whether or not he is really capable of doing it. Then look carefully at what he is now able to do. If he is already able to do some of the parts of the final pattern, these will not have to be taught. For example, a child may already know how to hold a spoon properly but not how to balance it when there is food in it. You should then concentrate your modeling on the skill of balancing. Later you can put all the parts together. Sometimes parents make the mistake of trying to teach the entire pattern of skills involved in feeding oneself to a young child all at once.

The third step, that of prompting the action, can now begin.

Instead of a physical prompt or a verbal signal, however, you present the child with a "picture" of what he is to do. You can execute the action, letting him watch. You can sing the song, letting him hear the musical pattern. In each case, he has a "picture" before him to copy. It is important to give him verbal instructions that tell him that he is to copy what you have modeled as closely as he can. Warn him that you don't expect him to do it as well as you at first and that he must practice the action many times in order to master it. Reassure him that even total failure is acceptable to you and that you yourself have failed many times whenever you first tried to learn something new. Make sure that he tries. Don't hesitate to use a physical prompt to begin his practice session.

As soon as he has begun and continuously thereafter, provide him with the positive consequences of your praise, admiration for his attempts, and any other relevant consequences you may have chosen. Do not criticize him. You should even avoid telling him what he has done wrong. Keep the emphasis solely on what he is doing right. You don't have to point out his errors. You can correct them at the next attempt by putting more emphasis on modeling the correct form of the part of the action he has missed.

At each practice session model more and more of the final pattern. Doing so will require him to make continuous progress in order to get the positive consequences. In some cases natural consequences will come into play; so much the better if your child is a self-motivator, but don't count on it. Be prepared to provide the external consequences throughout the training and thereafter, if it should prove necessary.

If he begins to show excessive errors at any point in his progress, stop and reexamine your modeling technique or the complexity of the task. Go back and give him more practice on just the part he is failing to perform correctly. Go more slowly. Praise more profusely. Reassure him that failure is acceptable to you and that perhaps the task is more difficult than you realized. This is the most critical point in his developing the attitudes of trust in you, self-confidence, and stick-to-itiveness.

Once he has mastered the skill, you can become concerned with the reasons (consequences) for which he does it and the signals that initiate it for him. You must wean him to the appropriate consequences. This process will be covered later in the chapter in the section devoted to effective techniques for weaning. Teaching the appropriate signals will also be covered in a separate section dealing with how to change signals.

SHAPING (SEQUENTIAL CONTRACTS) ⌒ In modeling, the child is given a "picture" of what he is to do. This allows you to shortcut a longer process, called shaping, because larger units of behavior can be learned at one time. But, as I pointed out earlier, modeling is not always possible. You need a technique that will always work to teach new actions. Shaping is that technique. It is based on the principle of sequential contracting.

Sequential contracting simply means that the complex final action is broken down into simple steps, one following the other. The child may be prompted to begin the first step (first approximation of the final action) and when he does he receives a positive consequence. Then the standard is raised and the child must complete the second step in the sequence of contracts to receive a positive consequence, and so on until the final step is mastered.

In some cases it is not necessary to physically prompt or verbally signal the first approximation. All you have to do is wait until the child accidentally performs the act and then provide a positive consequence. For example, if you are trying to teach a child to share with another child, you can wait until you observe him accidentally drop a toy near the other child. Without saying anything, give him a piece of candy. Wait again. Soon he will drop another toy somewhere in the vicinity of the other child. Again say nothing and give him a piece of candy. Before long he will leave something else near the other child and you repeat the process. When you observe that dropping toys near the other child is occurring more often than chance would dictate, you change the contract (but still without telling him anything).

Now you will provide the positive consequence only if the object is dropped next to the other child. It will happen eventually, by accident probably, but that doesn't matter. You still give him a piece of candy. After a while, when the child is habitually dropping objects he has tired of next to the other child, you change the contract again, this time requiring that he actually give it to the other child in some manner—even throwing it at him would be acceptable at this point. Later you can require that the object be handed over before providing the consequence. The final contract might require his giving the other child a toy with which he is not quite finished playing.

Nowhere in the sequence of contracts is it necessary to tell the child what you expect. Animals are trained this way quite successfully. It is the most basic technique for changing behavior that science has discovered so far. But it is time-consuming and, since even young children (unlike animals) can understand language, it is unnecessary in most instances. Special education teachers are now learning to fall back on this approach if a child is diagnosed as having a serious learning disability (retarded, brain-damaged, or similar problems). If your child can understand instructions, the process of shaping a new action can go much faster if you explain each new contract in the sequence. Let's take an example of this approach.

You have decided that your child must be able to sit still for at least an hour because he will be required to do so in many situations, such as in church, in school, while traveling on a trip, at a dinner party, or in various other places. You examine your child's present behavior pattern and you discover (by timing him) that he can sit still for about 10 seconds. He's a very fidgety child; every few minutes he jumps up and dashes off somewhere. He also grabs for things impulsively. You must eliminate his grabbing for things and his fidgeting in order to teach him to sit still.

You begin the process by asking yourself what approximation of the final behavior you can prompt. The answer may be simply a few additional seconds of sitting still. I have seen children with whom you must begin to teach this skill by getting them to hesitate for only a fraction of a second. This would be the first approximation of sitting still for an hour. You can physically prompt this type of child into hesitation by a sudden noise such as a clap of the hands, which will startle him and cause him to hesitate for a fraction of a second. Or you may be able to use a verbal request with your child, such as, "Please sit on this chair and sit still for a moment." In this case you have used a verbal signal instead of a physical prompt to prompt the first act in the sequence.

Once your child has sat still for the first ten seconds, you then can provide a positive consequence and begin the sequence of contracts. The positive consequence can be a pat on the back or a piece of candy or a point on a chart. It can be almost anything that the child responds to as a positive consequence and on which he will not satiate very quickly, since you do not want to weaken the positive consequence by giving too much, too often.

He has now succeeded. Notice that you have provided an errorless learning situation. You have guaranteed the first success of your child. You are also going to be building his self-confidence, since he will experience nothing but success. Anytime he does fail it will be only momentarily, and you should apologize since you have created the failure by an ineffective setting of the standard. You could say, for example, "I guess I made that a little too hard. Let's try it again, and I'll make it a little easier." You know, for example, that if you go to a coach to learn to lift weights and he asks you to lift more weight than you can lift, it is *his* failure, not yours. He set the standard inappropriately. In the same way, if you ask Johnny to sit still for a longer period of time than he is able to, it is *your* failure, not his. If he does fail you cannot give him the positive reward since you do not want to teach him that failure pays off. But you can apologize for setting the standard too high.

After apologizing for asking too much of him, you should set another shorter contract with him, telling him, in effect, to try again, reassuring him that he can succeed this time. You encourage him by offering him the consequence and promising him as many opportunities to try as he needs until he gets it. See to it that he succeeds even if you finally must set a contract at one second.

What you are doing in the shaping process is beginning where he can succeed and increasing the requirements so slowly that he should, ideally, never fail. Of course, this is really impossible. You will have to reset contracts many times. No one is perfect in their ability to guess what a child can do. You may think that he can increase his ability in ten-second intervals. Some children can. In fact, with many children, once the process has begun, you can require them to increase their ability to sit still at each trial by minutes. With other children you must go very slowly as you change contracts.

You change the contracts in the following way. At some point, you realize that he's getting just a little bit restless. You know he's about to reach the limit of his ability and so you give him the positive consequence (the word of praise, the piece of candy, or the point). You then say "Keep it up now, let's see how long you can sit still this time." Now you stretch the requirement still further. You watch and see that he's passed ten seconds. He's up to fifteen, twenty, thirty seconds. At thirty-five seconds he starts to get restless. At this point you give him another positive consequence and point out that he has increased his ability to sit still. As you continue to do this, increasing the amount of time he has to sit still before he gets the consequence, you are shaping and increasing his ability to sit still.

You must teach him all the things he needs to know to sit still effectively. You may have to tell him, "Keep your hands in your lap, look straight ahead, breathe deeply, think of things that will keep you amused while you're waiting." Many things are involved in the process of sitting still and you may have to teach them all to him. You must show him how to relax, how to occupy his thinking, what to do with his hands, and so on.

As you do this, you are gradually increasing the amount of time that he is required to sit still. You may jump from thirty seconds to a minute-and-a-half on the next trial (which follows right in line). Johnny is still sitting on the chair. But now you notice that he can sit still for a minute-and-a-half before getting restless. Wait and then give him the consequence after that length of time. You may find that Johnny cannot sit still for four minutes before you have to give another positive consequence after a number of trials. On the other hand, you may find that Johnny starts to get restless at the three minute mark, or even at a minute and thirty-five seconds after the first few trials. You must time him closely, using a watch.

Johnny will tell you how he is doing, whether he's getting tired, restless, or going beyond his ability to sit still. Watch carefully and always let Johnny determine what he can or cannot do.

In any shaping procedure you always rely on the child to tell you how much of the new behavior he can acquire and how fast. When he fails a contract you have set with him, he is telling you that it was a bad contract, not that he's a rebellious child, not that he's resistive, not that he's uncooperative, and not that he's inadequate. He is simply telling you that your contract was inappropriate. Don't feel guilty, just set the next contract a little bit lower.

The process of shaping involves setting a series of sequential contracts. You teach the new behavior a little bit at a time, arranging a positive consequence at each successful step, requiring more and more of the behavior at each new trial, until finally he has achieved the ability to sit still for an hour. Some children can learn this in a single long practice session with their parent. Some children may take a number of months with hundreds of practice trials before they arrive at this ability. You may have to increase the requirements slowly and patiently with many days between each increase. The average three-year-old can be trained to do it in a matter of weeks.

If the child is young, the first practice sessions should be short. Gradually you can let each practice session go for longer and longer periods of time. No matter what the behavior is that you are trying to teach—whether it's staying in bed for naptime, sitting quietly at the dinner table, using more polite behavior with other children, or studying for longer periods of time—you have to think of the process as requiring a *series* of practice sessions.

You should choose times for the practice sessions when both you and the child are relaxed and not likely to be bothered by a thousand other chores. Nobody tries to practice their golf in a middle of a tournament or in the middle of doing thirteen other things. We like to set aside a time for practicing our bowling, our bridge, or our golf when nothing will distract us. In the same way, when you are systematically teaching a child a necessary skill, you should set aside practice sessions.

I know that many parents have more than one child and that the other children are all clamoring for attention. You may not have help in the house and may be required to manage it all by yourself. But there is no shortcut to success. There is no magic way to teach children behavior. You cannot accomplish effective teaching and do all those other things at the same time. Something has to give. I can only suggest to you that if you do not spend the time initially in training your child in effective behavior for living with his family, you will spend more time in the long run arguing, fighting, or worrying. Johnny's poor skills will interfere with your general style of living much more in the long run if you fail to make the initial investment of time in training him properly. As each child is born, you should be concerned with training him to fit into the family.

One method of finding time for practice sessions is by training the other children to wait their turn. You can do this simultaneously with training the child with whom you are immediately concerned. You simply ask the others to sit around and watch. You shape their ability to wait patiently at the same time that you are teaching Johnny how to handle his knife and fork or how to refrain from touching objects in the room that he is incapable of handling effectively. The other children can be trained to sit still and watch during Johnny's practice session. I have frequently demonstrated this technique of shaping more than one child at a time to teachers who always use the argument, "I have thirty children in a classroom; how can I give attention to one child?" The answer is that you teach the other twenty-nine to wait patiently while you're working with one, and you do both simultaneously. It simply takes a little bit more effort on your part, a little bit more planning. But it can be done.

Shaping, then, is a basic process for helping a child acquire many new kinds of behaviors or improving old ones. It should be considered whenever modeling is likely to be ineffective. With young children shaping is the method ʔf choice. With older children modeling is the method of choice because they are being required to learn much more complex patterns of behavior and have already acquired many of the basic prerequisite skills. Shaping is an effective method for everyone, but it takes longer than modeling. Modeling represents a shortcut, and where shortcuts are possible, they are, of course, desirable. But we should never sacrifice a saving in time for a saving in effective teaching.

Shaping is always the most effective technique for difficult and basic skills in new areas. Actively practicing the behavior with someone encouraging you and providing the motivation for it is a non-failure situation; it is a situation in which the parts of the new task can be broken down into basic steps and in which the process of learning is kept active and involved. Children under shaping methods of teaching never appear bored, never stare off into space, their eyeballs never glaze over, and they never appear to have learned, only to demonstrate that they have not learned when they are checked later. You know at each step along the way how competent he really is because he is performing the behavior in front of you.

SUBSTITUTING OR ELIMINATING ACTIONS ↶

In these next classes of methods the problem is not that of teaching a new action but of eliminating the use of an undesirable one. Sometimes the problem is the failure to use an action which has been learned previously; sometimes it is one of motivation, and sometimes that of a very strong habit difficult for the child to give up.

POSITIVE CONTRACTS ↶ When a child has already acquired the ability to do something and is simply failing to use the action, it is possible to use a single positive contract rather than sequential contracts. A *positive contract* states that when the child performs the task, the consequence will occur. You know that the child can study, so you simply set a contract for study time. You pay him by the hour or allow him certain privileges when he is done studying, such as watching television or playing sports. Whatever the contract is, it simply calls for a behavior which is not presently being used but which is *already there* in the repertoire. You know the child can do it. You are really concerned only with the problem of motivation. You must supply the motivation. You are not teaching the child.

If your child is misbehaving and you know that he can refrain from that behavior, you can set a contract to get him to stop the undesirable behavior. It is still a positive contract. It says, "If you don't yell at your sister all day, you will have earned the right to watch television tonight."

On the other hand, if you know that he does not have the ability to control himself you cannot use a positive contract. You must first teach him the acts of self-control. You can do it by shaping *out* the undesirable act. For example, you might use the following kind of sequential contract: "You usually yell at your sister thirty times a day. If you can beat that, I will allow you to watch television." If he only yells at his sister twenty-nine times, he has beaten his record and he has earned the right to watch television. You would set the next contract as, "You've got to beat twenty-nine today." You are gradually decelerating his undesirable behavior. It is still a series of positive contracts, but it is called shaping. Each day he must hit less until you can change the contract to require positive acts toward his sister on a gradually *increasing* basis.

If you know that he does have effective skills in self-control which he is not using, for whatever reasons, it is possible to set a positive contract at the final goal and say, "Being nice to your sister most of the day and at no time yelling at her will lead to the privilege of watching television tonight." A positive contract states that you know he can do it because he has done it in the past and you believe that the problem is one of motivation only.

NEGATIVE CONTRACTS ⌁ On occasion we use *negative con-tracts*. In the chapter on punishment and discipline I pointed out that a negative consequence is sometimes necessary to weaken or suppress an action. This is different from strengthening an act to *replace* the undesirable act. If positive contracts fail to work and it is impossible to find a starting place to begin the shaping process, it may be because another action is too strong. This competing action may be receiving such positive consequences that it is being maintained at a very high rate. For example, the sister may be very subtly encouraging the brother to yell at her. No matter what the parent tries to do with Johnny's actions, his sister provokes him into yelling at her. In addition, Johnny may have such a high state of irritability that yelling feels good, much better than any kind of self-control you are trying to teach him. Mother tries shaping, father tries various forms of positive contracts, but nothing seems to work. At this point you must set a negative contract for Johnny (and also his sister).

The negative contract would say, "When you begin to yell, you must leave the room." Each time he yells, he is forced to lose the positive consequences of yelling. There is no punishment since the negative consequence is simply a time out (one half of the components of punishment). Another example may further clarify the difference between negative contracts and punishment.

If a child is biting her nails and you wish to help her give up this action, you may try offering her a positive contract, some desirable consequence for not biting her nails. If that fails, you may try using a series of positive contracts for decelerating the rate of nail biting. Each time she bites less she gets the positive consequences. If this procedure fails, what can you do? One way is to require her to wear a white cotton glove for a five-minute period after each act of nail biting. You can hardly call this punishment, yet it can be an amazingly effective negative consequence. The rate of nail biting will certainly decrease for most children if the procedure is followed carefully. Having to wear a glove after nail biting would be an example of a negative contract.

The purpose of a negative contract is to clear the field for the teaching of a desirable behavior. Thus a negative contract should almost never be used alone. If you do use it alone, you are allowing any other action to replace it and the new action may be even more undesirable than the one it replaces. Left on his own, Johnny may change from yelling at his sister to tearing her down verbally with sarcasm, teasing, and insults. It is up to you, as Johnny's parent, to help him learn a desirable behavior in place of the act being suppressed by the negative contract. In order to do this effectively, you need to combine negative contracts with positive contracts and sometimes include shaping or modeling as teaching procedures.

COMBINATION CONTRACTS ➤ The negative contract with Johnny, which was designed to suppress his yelling at his sister, required him to leave the room for a time out each time he yelled at his sister. To avoid the possibility of a drift to another undesirable action, you can add, "You can return when you feel you can control yourself." This is a very subtle and very important point. The emphasis is really on a positive contract. You are saying to him that if he wishes to be in your presence, he must earn it by appropriate behavior. If he uses inappropriate behavior, he will temporarily lose your presence. You stated a negative contract but you included a positive contract.

I often say to my children, "If you cannot behave appropriately at the table, you must leave the table. When you are ready to behave appropriately you can come back." That is a negative contract. I am cutting off the source of food, pleasure, and what-have-you that goes on at our table. But I leave it to the children as to when they can return. I encourage them to return by saying that as soon as they can control themselves they may.

This principle I have called the *"No-no, yes-yes" principle.* It simply means *never end with a no.* If you end with a no or with a negative contract, you are not teaching anything. If I were to send my child to bed without supper, it would be strictly a negative contract with no positive contract built into it. It would be extremely ineffective. Going to bed without supper would mean that even after the undesirable behavior has stopped, she is still receiving negative consequences. There is no encouragement for new, appropriate behavior and so it is very unlikely that any will be learned. If anything is learned, it is resentment and anger at the unfair, arbitrary outcome of the child's behavior.

When you take television away from a child for a week, you are using only the negative contract principle. It is a "no-no," of course, but there is no "yes-yes." The "yes-yes" must begin almost immediately if possible. Your goal is to teach the child how to behave. When you take television away for a week, you are giving up the opportunity to teach the child how to behave. You are hoping that in the future he will remember the deprivation of no television and will refrain from the old behavior. Somehow, magically, he will become a good child. It just doesn't work very well with most children. A much more effective technique is the "no-no, yes-yes" system.

According to this technique, if the child misbehaves the television is turned off as rapidly as possible. As soon as the child begins to behave appropriately the television is turned on again. It may be in a matter of seconds or minutes. When he is behaving badly the television is off. The environment is very responsive because the parent has arranged it that way. It takes more time on the parent's part, of course, to stay in there turning on and off the television set or ushering Johnny in and out of the room depending on how he's behaving. But each time he comes back into the room and behaves appropriately he is receiving a positive consequence. He is getting to watch the television. This is the procedure that will actually allow you to teach acts that will replace the bad behavior.

Yes, you are using a negative contract by taking something away, but because Johnny decides when he can come back, you are teaching him self-management. When beginning this approach with young children or with children who have established long histories of bad habits, you may have to send them from the room thirty or forty times in the same evening. The television set may go on and off like a traffic light every few seconds. But each time you have ended with a "yes-yes," you have strengthened the likelihood that the appropriate behavior will reoccur. Each time you have withheld the television set or sent the child from the room, you have decreased the likelihood of the inappropriate behavior.

The parent who is able to do this consistently has to win. The laws of behavior are immutable. Given enough time, the child will become discouraged with the inappropriate behavior and encouraged toward the appropriate behavior so that the appropriate behavior will eventually control the situation. The technique I have just outlined is a combination of positive contract, negative contract, and shaping, in which all three principles are being implemented.

Let's take another example of a "no-no, yes-yes" type of combination contract, this time involving a very young child. The untrained and inexperienced parent seeing a two-year-old child reaching for a fragile, easily breakable ashtray is very likely to let out a shriek of horror and then run over and slap the child's hand. Usually the child will immediately grab again for the ashtray. As I have said repeatedly, all punishment can do is suppress the behavior temporarily. The child is still being tempted by the ashtray, still wants to manipulate objects, and the ashtray is still sitting there. The parent may continue to slap the child's hand, suppressing the behavior. The child may grow increasingly aggressive in grabbing for the ashtray until finally, in despair, the mother will really spank the child, put him in his crib, and put the ashtray away until he grows older. The child has learned nothing except that Mommy doesn't like him very much and is completely bewildered and confused by the whole experience. He has not learned to not touch ashtrays; he has simply learned to stay away from ashtrays when Mommy is around (if he has learned anything at all).

We now have a child who will grab at ashtrays when Mommy is out of the room and, of course, he ends up breaking them. Mommy, in using what she felt was an effective negative contract, is deluding herself. She ends up angry and frustrated and guilt-ridden, and she accomplished nothing. There was a "no-no," of course, but it was a badly chosen "no-no" because it involved pain and punishment. Punishment has bad side-effects and really doesn't accomplish very much. What is more, there was no "yes-yes" to follow up the "no-no" by teaching a new behavior.

Let's look at a trained parent using a combination contract with her two-year-old child in the same situation. She sees the child reach for the ashtray and immediately resigns herself to the fact that she is now about to engage in a long training session with her child. She puts down the magazine she is reading or the dishes she is washing and decides that she will invest enough time now to give her greater freedom for the next two years. She is going to train her child not to touch things.

She walks over to the child and she prompts the end of the behavior. She does not slap the child's hands. She first says "no, no" as a verbal signal, but the child does not respond to "no, no" because he really doesn't understand it. Now she could teach what "no, no" means by slapping him, or she can teach "no, no" by taking his hand and physically prompting the end of the behavior. She holds his hand a few inches away from the ashtray, saying "no, no" at the same time. The "no, no" will serve both as a signal and as a consequence. Later she will be able to use the words "no, no" to indicate that she will come over and restrain the child. But right now she is using the physical restraint as a prompt. She is holding him from engaging in the behavior of touching the ashtray.

At the same time she is holding him into a new behavior. The new behavior is self-restraint. He cannot touch the ashtray so now she gives him a "yes, yes." She says "no, no, don't touch, " then "good boy, you're not touching." She begins to praise him and perhaps provides a treat as an additional positive consequence. Remember, she's still holding his hand. However, she does have the first approximation of the new behavior, for he is not touching the ashtray.

Now it is up to her to change the nature of the prompt. She is going to gradually withdraw the physical prompt, leaving only the verbal prompt, "No, no, don't touch." A little at a time, she takes away the physical prompt. She holds him less and less firmly, and pretty soon her hand is resting just slightly above the child's hand. She is still saying "no, no, don't touch" and always ending with "good boy, you're not touching." She is now putting the emphasis on teaching self-restraint.

She may teach him a substitute action also. "If you feel like playing, come over here and touch your toy." Many parents keep touchable kinds of things around. In our kitchen we have the bottom drawer of the cabinet full of toys. Any time a child wants to touch something, she is led gently away from the pot and pan drawer or the bread drawer or the silverware drawer and taken to *her* drawer. It is "no, no" for the pots and "yes, yes" for her special drawer.

Sometimes there is no alternative act possible and you must simply teach self-restraint by itself. It is simply "no, no" for touching and "yes, yes" for restraining. You can see how this would apply even with older children. The constant emphasis is on what you are to do, not on what you are not to do.

In a strictly positive contract you never even mention the negative alternative. You simply say, "If you don't touch anything in the room for the day, you may have so-and-so." When you're using a negative contract, you may say, "Touching anything in this room leads to leaving the room." In a combination contract you say, "Leave the room if you touch anything, but when you think you can control yourself you may come back in the room and practice not touching things again. You may stay in here as long as you are not touching things."

In the combination contract you need to get rid of the incompatible behavior first and so some form of negative consequence must be used. In very rare instances the parent may have to say, "Leave the room for five minutes," which now becomes a time out consequence rather than simply a temporary withholding of the positive. When you designate how long there will be an end to positive consequences, there is no way for the child to get them back during the time out. This is the strongest kind of negative consequence that the average parent will ever need.

On extremely rare occasions—and this was discussed in the earlier chapter—it is necessary to use pain or deprivation as part of the negative contract, but remember that punishment can never be used alone. No kind of negative consequence should ever be used alone. You are not trying to suppress a behavior temporarily, you are trying to eliminate it. The only method of elimination (permanent suppression) is to teach a new act to replace the old one. In the next chapter the problems and methods relating to changing signals and consequences will be discussed.

11 🍃
Choosing the
R*ight Tool II*

ADDING, ELIMINATING, OR MODIFYING SIG-
NALS ⌁ Until this point, we have been concentrating on the methods for changing the action component of
behavior. That is the most frequent problem parents face. But
often the problem the parent faces in dealing with Johnny's
misbehavior has to do with where or when he is using the correct
action. He runs and yells in the house instead of in the yard. He
wants to do his homework just when it is time for bed instead of
after dinner. He forgets to say "please" and "thank you."

Sometimes the problem has to do with the kind of signal that
initiates his actions. "I have to tell him to do everything, he never
thinks for himself," is a frequent complaint of parents. "He
doesn't know enough to come in out of the rain," is another.
Johnny has to be taught which signals are and which are not
relevant for the action of which he is already capable. Let's look at
the class of methods which deals with this problem.

CHANGING SIGNALS ⌁ A signal is made relevant to an action by
the process of association. You associate the signal with a
consequence. Sometimes this happens naturally and sometimes
you arrange it artificially. It happens naturally because the natural
consequence of an act always has some kind of signal attached to
it. Poison ivy has three reddish green waxy leaves in a cluster. The
first time I saw some I picked a bunch of them to take home. The
second time I saw them I can assure you I recognized the
consequences of that signal and brought into play every avoidance
act in my repertoire. By the process of trial and consequence, the
young child learns to avoid or to perform an act in the presence of
a relevant signal.

As a child gets older, you can shortcut this process by
instructing him as to the relationships between signals and the
consequences following certain acts. "Be careful crossing that
street. There's a lot of traffic and if you don't look carefully, you
might get hit by a car," mother tells Johnny. Sometimes he listens
(learns), sometimes he doesn't (fails to learn). A near miss by a car
will be much more effective than all the good advice in the world.
"Let him learn for himself what life is like," says father about
other less dangerous situations. He means that Johnny must try

different actions in his repertoire when certain signal conditions occur. Once he tastes the various consequences, his parents hope, he will learn to choose the appropriate actions to keep the consequences positive.

Often you can spare Johnny a lot of grief and make learning the relevant signals easier by using a special method psychologists have developed. The principle behind it is that you can create a relevant signal artificially, and then gradually substitute the actual real-life signals to which Johnny must learn to respond. This method of substitution is called *fading.*

The term originally came from experiments with pigeons. The experimenter wanted to establish whether or not pigeons could discriminate colors. He created two signals, a green disk and a red disk. If the pigeon pecked on the green disk he received corn. If he pecked on the red disk he received either no corn or a mild electric shock. The signals had different consequences for the same act (pecking). If the pigeons could tell colors apart, the experimenter reasoned, they could avoid the shock and obtain the corn. The pigeons learned the correct signal for pecking very quickly.

Next the experimenter wanted to determine whether or not pigeons could discriminate shapes. He arranged two signals which had very similar shapes but which human beings could distinguish. He repeated the experiment with the new signals based on shape. The poor pigeons did miserably on this task. But he did not stop here. He went a step farther. He colored the relevant shape signal green and the one which led to shock red. As soon as the pigeons established the action appropriate to the shape signal which was colored green (in this case, pecking), he began to slowly *fade out* the colors of both signals. Within just a few practice sessions the pigeons were able to discriminate the correct shape without any color at all to help them.

Then he began to teach them to recognize words by this method. That's right, words. Some pigeons have been able to demonstrate correct actions to over fifty written words. They peck when the sign says peck, bow or turn when the sign tells them to do so.

The importance of this principle for modern techniques of education is immense. Programmed instruction, computer assisted instruction, and many other new approaches in special education for teaching disabled children are all partly based on this principle. A child can learn to read much faster, much earlier, and with less difficulty than was ever believed possible.

For example, most children can say the word "cat" when they see a live cat or a picture of one. They fail to do so when they see the letters "C-A-T." By writing the word "cat" over the picture of a cat, two signals are presented together. If the picture of the cat is made to fade out slowly until even the grin is gone, the child is left with only the letters "C-A-T" as the signal for saying the word "cat." It's amazing how quickly and effortlessly it happens. If you are interested in all the details of teaching by this method, any book on programmed instruction will provide it.

But our problem is Johnny and how to get him to respond to the appropriate signal with the appropriate action. Let's take an example of a technique for teaching Johnny to go to bed when he is tired and to avoid the problems arising from overtiredness.

The world is full of interesting things for children and they hate to go to bed at night. Getting them to bed is one of the most frequent problems of managing children. Here is how fading can help. Remember the types of signals I discussed in an earlier chapter? They were physical prompts, verbal signals, self signals, and natural signals. The appropriate signals for going to bed are either the natural signal of being tired or the self signal of "I guess it's time for me to go to sleep." How often in your home does your child rely on the verbal signal of your telling him to go to bed or the physical prompt of your dragging him off to bed, kicking and screaming?

Let's assume you have used the strategy of change correctly. You have planned the goal actions carefully, assessed present behavior, selected the appropriate consequence, and you have a good shaping procedure all ready. You begin with a physical prompt, taking him by the hand and leading him (dragging him?) up to bed. You then provide the positive consequence.

Soon you find him going through all the correct actions and receiving the positive consequences you are providing. Next you change the consequences so that he is going to bed for the appropriate reasons. By now the kicking and screaming have disappeared, but you are still leading him there. You are now ready to change the signals.

Once you are more skillful you can actually begin this process along with the shaping and weaning. The very first time you use the physical prompt you can imbed a verbal signal into it. As you take him by the hand you can say, "Johnny, it's time for bed." Then gradually, over a number of practice sessions, release his hand earlier and earlier in the process. Eventually you will find that he gets up and goes to bed when you give the verbal signal, "Johnny, it's time to go to bed."

You may be willing to stop there for a while, at least until he's much older. At some point you will probably want him to go to bed at the signal of the clock reaching bedtime. Now change your signal to "Johnny, look at the clock. It's eight o'clock, time to go to bed." You are imbedding a new signal into the old, already effective one. You then repeat the process of fading by reducing your signal slightly each time. "Johnny, look at the clock. It's eight o'clock." You may even set a contract with him that states "If you can get to bed at eight o'clock *without* my telling, you can have an extra treat (or bonus)." He still gets a positive consequence, however, if you have to remind him. But he gets more if he does it on a self signal.

Eventually your signal can be reduced to "Johnny, do you know what time it is?" or "Johnny, it's eight o'clock." As he gets into the habit of looking at the clock without your reminding him, he is ready to graduate to reliance on self signaling. You complete the process by setting a new contract. You state the contract as "Johnny, you only get your points (or your treat) if you get yourself to bed at eight o'clock. If I have to remind you, you don't get any."

If he makes too many errors and you have to remind him, set a new and easier contract and go back to a smaller positive consequence. Then work back up more gradually. Once he demonstrates that he can maintain the habit of going to bed at the appropriate time you are ready for the last step in the fading process, natural signal control.

Wait until some evening when he appears tired at seven o'clock. Then suggest a contract to him such as, "Johnny, if you feel tired, why not go to bed early tonight? If you do, I'll give you some extra points for being so grown up." Bargain with him, if necessary, until he does go. Make a point the next day of showing him how much you respect his new mature behavior. Wait for other opportunities and repeat the process. Eventually, he will become the kind of child who is tuned in to his own body signals and responds appropriately to them.

There are many techniques which can be developed to change signals. Mnemonics, the art of using aids to help memory, is a good example. To remember a long list of answers to questions (test signals), you associate the answers with a catchy rhyme or an easily remembered word as a key. Eventually the correct answer (action) can be associated to the question (signal) without the need for the mnemonic (temporary signal). When a child is learning to pronounce a word you may read aloud with him until he gains mastery and confidence. Then you gradually lower your voice and fade out the physical prompt so that he is no longer imitating you but reading the words directly.

All fading techniques are based on the use of a temporary signal which is easy to learn and is helpful in making the transfer to the appropriate signal.

ADDING, ELIMINATING, OR MODIFYING CONSEQUENCES

A good character is taught. No one is born with morality, ethics, or compassion for people. No one is born with a good set of values. No one is born doing the right thing for the right reason. It is the parents' job to teach Johnny values. When he is older, other people will assist you (teachers, ministers, and policemen). Eventually Johnny must take over the responsibility for adding, eliminating, or modifying the consequences which control his life. Self-management is the goal of our society. But so long as Johnny is in your care, you are responsible for his conduct and character. This responsibility weighs heavily on most parents and it leads to some of the most vexing problems in child-rearing. "Johnny doesn't like to learn." "My son is running with a bad crowd." "He's only interested in sports, sports, and more sports." "I wish she would read more and watch television less." The list is endless.

Because of the importance of this area, parents become anxious and frustrated more easily here than in almost any other area of raising children. This explains why threats, punishment, and eternal lecturing are the most common methods of change that many parents use. Let's examine some better ways.

WEANING ✧ When you become concerned with the reasons or the lack of reasons for Johnny's behavior, you are really dealing with what I call his *consequence field*. The group of consequences that he finds positive or negative constitute this field. When you examine them closely by watching what kinds of events he seeks to obtain and what kinds he avoids, you may be dissatisfied with what you see.

There may be too few or too many. There may be some that he may find very positive that you wish were negative, and vice versa. He may be responding to external artificial consequences in an area where you preferred the motivation to come from self or natural consequences (learning actions, for example).

As in all methods of behavior change, you need to follow the strategy of change with its emphasis on careful planning, assessment, and systematic approach. Whatever Johnny values now is where you must begin. It does no good to become angry at him, lecture him, or punish him for having the wrong kinds of values. He must be taught new ones, not scolded for the ones he has learned.

The process of weaning involves the gradual change of positive or negative consequences by three main methods. These are: (1) the strengthening of a weak need or desire through deprivation, exposure, or sampling; (2) the pairing of two consequences, one which already has value and one which is to acquire value; and (3) the artificial creation of exchange value for the ineffective consequence.

The use of deprivation works best with biological consequences which have become weakened in positive effect because of continuous satiation. It can also work with satiated acquired consequences, but its effects are somewhat less certain. When an experimenter wished to use recreation to motivate delinquents in a reformatory, he first had them placed in solitary confinement for two and a half days in order to make recreation with other boys and the stimulation of pinball machines and games more effective. In this case, putting them in solitary confinement was in no way done to punish them.

Waiting until a child has used up all his money or candy can make money or candy much more positive as consequences. Increasing his interest in a consequence by making it seem more appealing and necessary is another example of using subtle forms of deprivation. Television advertising of children's toys works in this way by attempting to convince the child of their great fun, status value, and necessity to him. It is designed to make him run to Mommy and plead for her to buy it for him.

Another experimenter paid boys hanging around on street corners to talk into a tape recorder. At first they came only because of the money and spoke haltingly into the microphone. They were told to talk about anything at all. They began with foul language, silliness, and gripes. Before long they began showing up early and asking to stay later. Even when pay was stopped, they expressed a strong interest in continuing to talk to the experimenter, an activity they had never sought before. Talking to someone about their feelings and ideas had become a positive consequence through exposure to the activity, artificially maintained.

In the section on strengthening consequences I mentioned the use of sampling to make a consequence positive. Taking a child to the opera and making him endure it until the end is a good way to make it a negative consequence forever. But letting him sample opera on records in small doses, letting him leave when he gets bored, or preparing him for it by reading the story can serve to make it a positive consequence eventually.

One of the most effective techniques in the weaning process is that of pairing. By giving a valuable consequence at the same time as you give one with little or no value you can strengthen the weak or neutral one. The process of withdrawal of the originally more positive one must be done gradually.

Children begin responding to biological consequences at birth. They want food, water, relief from pain, and so on. Mommy's attention, her smile, her cooing, and her cuddling are all paired with the basic biological necessities. Gradually these formerly neutral consequences come to have acquired value to the child so that he seeks them out as eagerly as he seeks out biological consequences. Many people have been fooled by the early appearance of these acquired values into believing that they are *inherited needs* rather than *acquired wants*.

One experimenter who wished to motivate delinquents to engage in academic learning found that the only consequences that had positive value for them were such things as black leather jackets, pinball machines, cigarettes, and *Playboy* type pictures. Since he understood the principle that you must use relevant consequences, these were the things with which he paid them for working at their studies. Later he began slowly introducing into the recreation room such things as educational games, books, and magazines, mail order catalogues (from which they could purchase items), and other more acceptable consequences. Little by little he withdrew or deemphasized the original types of consequences so that there was a gradual progression toward more middle-class consequences. Ultimately these formerly delinquent boys were doing such things as paying for their own tutors and for the privilege of doing homework and giving up to 60 percent of their weekly incomes for private study rooms. He had weaned them from one type of consequence field (value system) to another. The future of these boys is now much brighter, not only because they can read and write and have graduated from high school, but also because their value system has been expanded. Now that they appreciate consequences of which society approves, their chances of returning to lives of crime and violence are diminished considerably.

The artificial creation of exchange value can serve to facilitate the process of weaning. No one, except a collector, wants Confederate dollars, but if the South should rise again those dollars could be exchanged for other consequences. This important principle of economics is just as important in the management of children. A poker chip has little if any value to a young child. But if you give him one and then immediately *exchange* it for a toy, a piece of candy, or a cookie, you will find him much more interested in gaining poker chips. If you repeat it a few times, then gradually require him to obtain several before the exchange is made, you will find that poker chips (or tokens, or points, or gold stars) have become a strong positive consequence. Let me show you how we have used this principle to solve a problem with one of our children.

The problem arose out of my daughter's first experience with kindergarten. Her reaction to kindergarten was that it was a total bore After three days she announced she was not going back again because it was no fun. We asked her, "Why not?" We found that she had a pretty accurate assessment of what happens in kindergarten. When she was engaged in activities that she enjoyed, the teacher would call her to drop what she was doing and go over to something that she did not like doing. She was willing to go along with this up to a point, but she soon found that the routine repeated itself every day. She had grasped the basic pattern of kindergarten, which involved the same repetitive activities over and over again. She much preferred new things, creative things, each day. She did not enjoy the process of sitting with the group and singing since she did not like to sing. She much preferred to play with her dolls or draw pictures. She also found that she was supposed to draw certain kinds of pictures even when she wanted to do her own kind. She was required to color between lines when she wanted to try different drawings on the page regardless of whether there were lines there or not.

To the school authorities the problem appeared to be one of immaturity. Well, immaturity is a very vague term. We assessed the problem differently. We saw it as a problem of the kinds of consequences that controlled her behavior. We knew our daughter to be quite capable of obeying orders, cooperating, and engaging in many kinds of activities that were not intrinsically fun for her. We asked ourselves why she did it for us and not for the teacher.

The answer was that we gave her things on a contract basis. Because our approval meant something, it was a consequence that would control her behavior. On the other hand, the teacher's approval or disapproval did not mean anything. She still got to go out to recess even when the teacher disapproved of her. She still got to play with dolls even though the teacher disapproved. The teacher's approval had no *exchange* value for her. Therefore she was not going to acquire the behaviors that the teacher required of her.

To solve this problem we set up a contract at home in which we provided artificial consequences for her by giving her a point every time she did what we asked her to do quickly and obediently. At the end of the week, the twenty-five points she had earned were exchanged for a special treat. After the first week we told her that this way of getting points was too easy. We were going to change the nature of the game we were playing with her. She would have to listen to the teacher and do what the teacher asked of her immediately. This would earn her points toward her special treat at the end of the week. We would call the teacher and find out how she was doing and the teacher would report to us as to whether she was earning her special treat or not. We knew that we could use such a point system because our daughter could delay getting a positive consequence until the end of the week.

We knew also that we could wean her from our consequences to the teacher's by this procedure. We were now making the teacher's approval valuable to our daughter because she would be earning something she wanted on the basis of the teacher's approval. Since the teacher was not using such consequences in the classroom, we were going to do it for the teacher at home.

We called the teacher at the end of the week and asked, "How did Linda do?" The teacher told us that Linda had suddenly become very obedient, very cooperative, and very happy about her cooperation. She had developed a great deal of maturity overnight. What really had happened, of course, was that Linda had acquired a new motivational system. We had weaned her from responding only to the natural consequences of the environment around her; she now responded also to the external social consequences of the teacher. We had given the teacher an assist without the teacher's even knowing it. We had weaned Linda from our approval to the teacher's approval very carefully and systematically. Within a few weeks Linda said to us, "I don't need the points anymore. I like when my teacher likes me and I'm working hard to please her." The weaning process was complete at that point.

We hope some day that Linda will get into a learning environment where she will work because of the work itself. But even more importantly, we hope that she will develop a self-motivating system. We plan to systematically teach her a sense of pride and achievement, the desire to do well for her own sake, not for the teacher's, so that she will no longer be dependent on external consequences to maintain good school performance.

If we leave her at this point, under the control of the teacher's approval only, and fail to wean her further, she will be in danger if she gets into a situation where a teacher is very poor at giving approval. Linda might then stop behaving appropriately. This would be a very bad situation for Linda and one that we must prevent. To do that we are going to teach her that self-approval is as valuable as other people's approval because you yourself can earn certain kinds of things by your own self-approval. Let me give an example of how we do this with our children and perhaps you may choose to do it with yours.

When a child is old enough to evaluate and monitor his own behavior, we begin to ask her to do so. We say to her, "How do you think you did at what you just did?" This begins to establish the habit of evaluating herself, of watching what she does. We require her to be accurate in this process. We don't want her to inflate or deflate herself. We don't want her to overvalue or undervalue what she's done either. When she is accurate, we let her know it. We say, "I agree with you, that's right. Very good. Since you have behaved as well as you just said (or you've done the task as well), here's what the consequence will be." We may give her some points, we may give her a treat, we may give her simply our approval and love, or we may give her extra affection and attention. There are a variety of different consequences that we can administer.

Now the process has begun. We are teaching her to watch her own behavior, to evaluate it, and to monitor it. We are also teaching her, by this process, that when she evaluates herself as having done a better job, she receives more positive consequences than when she does a poor job.

We try to avoid the use of ridicule or any criticism of failure. Very often we don't appear even to notice the mistake the child has made. When one of my daughters brings home a paper that has errors on it from school, I will ignore the errors and praise the successful part of the paper. I ask her, "What do *you* think of the paper?" I try gently to encourage and prompt her to focus on what she did right and to take pride in it. Her pride becomes valuable to her because I am pairing it with my approval. Remember that a consequence takes on value when it is paired with another consequence which already has value. Later in the evening, I may ask her to participate in a practice session at which I will teach her the deficient skills; the mistakes that she made are then presented to her as new problems to be learned or solved. I may never even mention to her that she added incorrectly on her original test paper.

On rare occasions, I will give her negative feedback (criticism) in order to teach her that negative feedback is as valuable as positive feedback (praise). Criticism can be useful information to help us alter our behavior. But the essential thing I am trying to teach our children is to value their own appraisal of themselves. My wife and I try to back up their appraisal of themselves by giving them our approval and by letting it lead to some kind of positive consequence. As they get older, we are teaching them to set contracts for themselves. "When you feel you've done a good job, then you may turn on the television set. When you feel you have been effective, then you may go to the kitchen and get yourself a treat. When you feel you have been effective, you may stop for the night." We are teaching them to appraise their own behavior and to give themselves back-up consequences for their own approval because we wish to maintain their own self-approval at a very strong level also. Most people who have good characters are people who first of all evaluate their behavior carefully and accurately and then permit themselves luxuries, privileges, or positive consequences on the basis of what they have earned by their hard efforts. This is what keeps their self-approval high.

Confidence comes from a "shaping" approach to life. "This is only my first approximation. I didn't do well. I can try again and I can keep trying until I succeed." Isn't this what we really mean by self-confidence? Shouldn't it be taught early to children, instead of the method we now use, in which we are continuously pointing out what they do wrong, showing them how much better we are than they are, and proving to them over and over again that they are doomed to failure because of their basic inadequacies?

The method of teaching that I have described using fading, shaping, and weaning leads the child toward self-motivation and self-management that will ultimately free him from the terrors of anxiety, low self-confidence, lack of a sense of self-worth, and all of the other ills that plague our society today. Maybe many of the problems we experience today are really products of how we've raised our children and how our schools have managed their learning experiences.

COMBINING METHODS: THE FOUR-STEP METHOD ∽

It is seldom that you use one class of methods alone. More often than not the problem lends itself to the use of shaping, weaning, fading, contracting, and modeling all at once or at different stages. After you have practiced the various classes of methods on simple problems, you will find yourself able to handle several aspects of one problem or several problems at once. Before going on to more specific overall management systems for the home, I want to spend some time on a systematic method that was developed to deal with problems involving a child's doing too much or too little of some action. Such problems account for about seventy-five percent of all the problems encountered with children. Your primary concern is with changing the *rate* (how many times Johnny does something in a given period of time) of an action. This method incorporates much of what we have discussed so far; and consists of four steps.

ASSESSMENT ∽ The first step is to define the problem in terms of some action that can be counted. It is not that Johnny has too much aggression in him but that he hits his sister too often, slams doors too often, and says nasty things too often. Those are three observable and countable actions. Once the problem has been reduced to the rate of countable actions, you select just one of these as the target for change. Usually the problem involves just one action, such as thumb sucking, dawdling in the morning, or eating too few vegetables. If there is more than one action, you can deal with the others at a later time.

COUNTING ∽ Before you do anything else, you must establish exactly how often the action is occurring. Don't trust your memory or your subjective impressions of the rate of occurrence. People make too many errors at this point. My favorite story about this concerns a husband and wife who came to see me quarreling about the way to handle their children. I noticed that the wife interrupted the husband every time he attempted to tell his side of the story. I quietly slipped on a counter and began to press it every time she interrupted him so that I could keep an accurate record of her interruptions of his statements. After a half-hour I asked them if they were aware that the wife was interrupting the husband. The husband quickly jumped on this and said, "There, doc, that's exactly what I've been trying to tell you. She never lets me get a word in edgewise. She's always interrupting me." I turned to the wife and asked, "How many times did you interrupt your husband in the last half-hour?" She said, "Well, I guess it was about twice." The husband in great anger exclaimed, "What do you mean twice? It was at least six times. You see how she's always minimizing it, doc?" I looked down at my counter and the numbers were clear and large—twenty-seven times in a half-hour. Neither of them had been very accurate in counting the behavior, even though they were both aware of the problem and had argued about it frequently.

Very often a mother will tell me that her Johnny is *always* refusing to do things when he is asked. I will send her home with a simple counter (a golf score recorder which can be purchased in any sporting goods store and worn on the wrist). I ask her to press the counter every time Johnny refuses to obey. At the end of the week we sometimes find that there are as few as twelve disobedient occasions recorded on the counter—very different from *always* disobeying. For this kind of mother any act of disobedience is so emotionally charged that she remembers it as *always* occurring instead of as occurring rather rarely for a child like her Johnny.

On the other hand, many mothers have come back and shown me the counter and pointed out that there was an average of ten or twelve disobediences a night, or even an hour. On these occasions I will ask the parent, "How come you're giving so many orders? Perhaps you are really repeating the same order fourteen times and counting it as fourteen disobediences. Maybe we have to define the problem even further."

Sometimes I'll find that Johnny is disobedient four or five times a night and that the parent is not being unreasonable in the number of requests being made to Johnny. We now have a basis on which to begin. We have pinned down what action is to be counted and the parent actually has kept a rough running record of what he does. The more precise she can be, the better, but she need not devote her life to keeping elaborate charts and graphs. Although this is desirable for an experiment, it is simply not practical for a household. It is enough if she just gets a fairly accurate picture by counting the number of actions the child is performing during a given space of time. The counting may involve nothing more than keeping a time record such as: how long he usually sulks, how long he sits at his homework, how much time a night he winds up watching television, or what time he actually goes to bed. These are all counting procedures.

CHANGING THE CONSEQUENCE ᵒ⁄ You now know just what Johnny is doing and how often he is doing it. In the third step you must change something that happens *after* Johnny's action occurs. If the rate is too high (for example, hitting his sister) you must arrange a negative consequence to help reduce how often he does it *and* include a positive consequence for the reduced rate. If the rate of the action is too low (bath-taking, for example), you must arrange a positive consequence after he performs the action.

Keep counting and recording the counting. You need to know if you have selected the right consequence for Johnny. The only way you can tell for sure is to see if the trend of the change in his action is going the way you want it to go. Records can be kept in a very simple way, but if you don't record the count each day you are very likely to forget.

In some cases you may not be able to think of an appropriate concrete consequence. Research has shown that if you change the consequences of his behavioral action in any way at all, the chances are good that his behavior will change. For example, if you have been scolding him each time he hits his sister, the mere act of not scolding him may be sufficient to change his rate downward. Don't worry about whether or not you have chosen exactly the right change to make. The next step will take care of that.

REPEAT ᵒ⁄ Thousands of parents have used the method described here and a major university is keeping careful tabs on the results. It has been found that no more than four attempts are necessary to bring about the desired change in the rate of a single action. That means that very often the first change the parent makes may not be the most effective one. The rate may stay the same or go in the opposite direction from the one desired. Don't worry. If your records reveal that Johnny is not changing, simply *repeat* the process with the full knowledge that by the fourth attempt you probably will succeed. Let's take some examples.

What is the consequence of Johnny's not eating his spinach? You yell at him. Okay, do something else besides yelling at him. Why don't you try turning your chair to the wall and staring at the wall for three minutes when he won't eat his spinach? At least it's something different from yelling at him. Try changing something.

As you become better trained you will tend to select consequences that will have a greater chance of working or being effective. If you have already assessed and pinned down the problem in the way that I have been talking about, you are probably going to be pretty accurate in your first choice. But remember, all you're doing is trying it out. You're going to continue to count.

Let's say that what you are counting is the number of times that Johnny hits his sister. What is the consequence of Johnny's hitting his sister? Being sent to his room. Okay, don't send him to his room when he hits his sister. Do something else instead. Every time he hits his sister have him stand on one foot for thirty seconds; on the other hand, if he does not hit his sister for an entire hour give him five points toward a model airplane he is trying to win. Thus you will have set up a combined contract, a "no-no, yes-yes" system. The thirty seconds on one foot is a negative consequence. You just as easily could have suggested that he put on a white glove for five minutes if he hits his sister. These are not punishments in the sense that they are painful, aversive, or depriving; they are negative consequences in that during the time of being on one foot or wearing the glove nothing positive can happen. The positive aspect of what you're doing is setting an incentive for not hitting. You have begun by making a change in the consequences of his behavior. You continue to count the number of times he hits his sister. Most often there will be a rapid change. Sometimes there will be no change at all, and sometimes there will even be an increase. Do not become discouraged. Remember, step four is to repeat the first three steps as often as necessary. Next time you may give your daughter a privilege each time he hits her. If that doesn't work, you can put his favorite toy in the refrigerator. The list is endless. Just remember that it is extremely unlikely that more than four *systematic* tries will be necessary.

Assess, count, change, and repeat. These four steps are a method for changing single behaviors. You now have the overall, general approach to behavior change, but you are not done yet. We still want to explore specific systems that can be built up to manage a household, systems that can be so concretized that they can be used almost like a cookbook. The next chapter will go into such specific methods.

12 🎋
Simple
Systems for Simple

Problems

The other night I had a family in my office concerned with the problem of their seventeen-year-old son who had very poor study habits and showed very little desire to put out the effort required to raise his grades and work for the future. The father, who could not understand the boy's problem, kept repeating, "He's seventeen. He should understand how important an education is." He kept saying over and over again that the boy should be able to do certain things. He insisted that any attempts to create incentives for him was a waste of time—was, in fact, wrong. When I asked why was it wrong, he answered in angry tones, "Because he should be able to see how important an education is and how important it will be for his future life." The word *should* rang out in my office a dozen times before the father was finished.

He kept asking me, "Why can't he do this, what's wrong with him, doctor?" I looked at the father, who was wearing glasses and who was obviously near-sighted, and I quietly said to him, "You should be able to see without glasses. Take them off and throw them away. You're just not trying hard enough." He was quite annoyed at my statement until he began to realize what I meant. I was making his eyesight a moral issue. I was saying to him that if he wanted to, he could see without the glasses, that it was his own moral weakness that he was unable to do it, and that he was simply not being cooperative. He angrily blurted out, "But my eyes are bad. I'm near-sighted, I can't see without the glasses. It's unfair to ask me to put them down." I replied to him, "But your son is near-sighted with regard to future consequences. It's unfair to ask him to work without a prosthetic device or a prosthetic system. If I ask you to take your glasses off, I have to be prepared to write very large on the blackboard, to ask you to come closer, or to give you a new set of glasses. In your son's case the problem is that he can see the consequences right in front of him, the fun of watching television, sleeping late, or playing with his friends; but somehow he just can't see the future consequences, no matter how hard he tries. No matter how hard we try to inspire him and urge him to look ahead, he really can't do it. He has motivational myopia. Your own problem is a structural deficit," I told him;

"your eyes are the problem. The structure of your body in some way is not quite perfect. We have learned to recognize that fact and to build devices that make it possible for you to see as well as someone whose structure is intact. We have yet to learn about functional deficits, the near-sightedness of being unable to see the future, or the inability to delay a consequence more than the biological limits of a half-second. Some people can anticipate the future, some cannot. Some people have their own built-in prosthetic system of being able to anticipate the future by their memories, by their imagination, by the things they tell themselves. Other people have poor consequence sight. It is unfair to ask the child to squint, to struggle. It is much more humane to give him a prosthetic device."

The prosthetic systems that we are going to talk about are based on the contract principle. The contract principle is the rule by which consequences occur. It can be called the differential rule, the idea being that a positive consequence always follows the appropriate behavior and a negative consequence never does. If the environment can be made consistent and precise, appropriate behavior can be learned by almost any child, no matter what his functional or structural deficit. Even a brain-damaged or retarded child can function well under a contract system which is precise and consistent.

Unfortunately, however, many parents immediately equate any type of prosthetic system with bribery. The first thought that comes to their minds is that children ought not to be paid for what they do; for the most part they are expected to perform with no external consequences at all. Whenever the parent feels like giving external consequences, he does so as an "expression of love." The child is expected to recognize that the positive consequences are coming out of the goodness of heart of the parent. The child should acknowledge and appreciate this fact and, in turn, perform in exactly the ways the parents wish.

This is a very poor contract system. We will discuss later, in detail, exactly why it is poor. For now, let me say simply that it doesn't work very well. How do I know that? Because it is the most common kind of home management system, and if I just look around I can see all the kids who are floundering.

Some children raised under this system are not near-sighted, are able to look ahead, are able to relate the parents' giving to the chores and obligations that they, the children, are expected to perform. Such children generally complete the unstated contract;

they fulfill the requirements seemingly with little effort and with very little dissension. Parents with such children are thrice blessed. The average parent may have only one child like this, usually the oldest. The rest of their children (or for many people, their only child) tend to develop many kinds of problems under such a system.

A corollary to this type of unstated consequence system is the implicit belief that, by reason of his birth, the child is entitled to all the privileges of childhood. I see this as almost like going on welfare from the day you are born. You don't have to do anything except exist in order to get the necessities and the good things of life. You are entitled to them by virtue of the fact that your parents brought you into the world. On the one hand we complain that the child is spoiled and not doing his work or carrying his load; and on the other hand we continue to ply him with all of the goodies that he wants, including our love and attention. We have undying faith in the miracle of his someday recognizing what we are doing for him; our fervent prayer is that he will one day appreciate us.

The father I mentioned earlier was following this type of mythology. He felt that his seventeen-year-old son was entitled to the privilege of driving the family car because, "after all, he is a teen-ager." He believed the boy was entitled to his allowance. He was entitled to a good room (large and airy with a television set, hi-fi, and bookcase). He was entitled to the free privileges of the refrigerator any time he desired a snack. On the other hand he asked, "Why won't the boy work? Why won't he put out any effort in school? Why won't he help around the house? There must be something wrong with the boy." The father and mother both were denying their poor management of the boy and were trying to blame their problems with him entirely on him. In reality they had a very poor contract system in use with him. Let's examine the nature of a contract system.

HOME CONTRACT SYSTEMS

THE REQUIREMENTS The home management system that most families use can be analyzed into a small number of components. The first component is that the requirements for the child's actions must be specified in some way. They should be stated clearly and objectively so that the child can understand what he is to do and know when he has achieved it. Too often the requirements for the actions of the child are left vague and the standards are completely subjective, fluctuating according to the mood of the mother, the baby-sitter, or the teacher.

When Mommy leaves the house she tells Johnny to be "good." He really doesn't know what she means. He thinks he does, but when he discovers that Mommy had a different idea he becomes discouraged, resentful, and angry. After all, he really didn't hit his sister very hard and he was only a half-hour late in getting to bed, and he did listen to most of what the baby-sitter asked him to do. Why can't Mommy appreciate that? But Mommy wants him to obey all the orders the baby-sitter gives, and wants no hitting of his sister at all, and wants no delay whatsoever in his going to bed. She evaluates his performance as quite bad and refuses any acknowledgement or any positive consequence. It is easy to see that the fault lay in poorly specifying to the child what he was to do.

Similarly, teachers frequently tell children that their essays are not really very good, but they don't always tell them why. The wise teacher says, "I'm going to count the number of different thoughts that you express in your essay and that's how we'll tell how rich it is or how impoverished." The child now, by a simple method of counting how many thoughts he had in a paragraph, can objectively evaluate his performance, even by himself. If we tell him that every paragraph must contain a certain amount of thoughts, the child now clearly understands what is expected of him.

The next time you are in someone's home listening to them give orders to their child, listen to how vaguely the requirements are stated. In some homes the requirements for actions are not even stated at all. The child is expected to know them almost from birth. He is constantly being admonished for not having done the "right" thing, although he didn't know what the "right" thing was.

Some families have an almost unlimited number of require-ments for children and each of the requirements for an action has so many precise specifications that the child spends most of his time trying to live up to them. You can easily see that this can become a very burdensome and overwhelming task for the child. He may eventually give up entirely.

THE RECORD SYSTEM ❧ The second major component of con-tract systems which relates closely to the requirement component is that of the record system.

At the heart of any good management system, in any factory or office, you will find a record system. Somebody keeps track of how many hours people work, how many pieces are produced, and how many things are done to specifications. This is the basis upon which workers are paid. Without an accurate record system business and industry would be in serious trouble, simply because there would be no way of arranging adequate consequences that would be related to both the work performed and the requirements set. The record system is the heart of any effective management system.

In most homes, on the other hand, record-keeping is done by relying on the subjective memory of the parents, who say to themselves when the child asks for the car on Saturday night, "Let me see, have you been good this week?" In this type of home "good" is some unspecified set of requirements for actions and Mommy or Daddy is the final judge of how well the actions were performed. What is more, they are also the record-keepers. They record how often, how much, or how good. The child may dispute their judgment and there may be frequent arguments as to what was done, how much, when, where, and to whom.

The record system is most often vague, poorly constructed, or totally ignored. Very few homes keep an accurate record of how much time was spent in study, how many tasks or chores were done each day, or how quickly.

Very often parents ask their children to keep their own records, to evaluate themselves. Sometimes they try to establish such a system before the child has the maturely developed set of behaviors that could make it work. Very few employers would ask their employees how much work they did and pay them on that basis. Most employers recognize that people are fallible, that their memories may be imperfect, and that they can be tempted. The memory error on the employee's part usually tends to be in his favor. The errors in the employer's memory, of course, tend to be in the employer's favor. The same thing is true in many homes. Children remember their performance as better than do their teachers or their mothers. Parents, much too often, remember the performance as poor. If a child has been good for five and a half days and does something wrong on the last half of the sixth day, the parent frequently will refuse privileges that evening because the child has been bad "all week."

Parents have a tendency to use words like "never," "always" and other absolute terms that put the child in a defensive position almost immediately, "You *never* make your bed," "You are *always* contradicting me," can be heard throughout the households of the land, with children answering almost immediately, "But just yesterday I did," or "I didn't." The child, of course, is right. He did do at least one of the things that he claims he did, and the parent ends up wrong because of the use of the absolute terms "never" and "always." Sometimes the children can be heard saying to a parent, "You *never* understand. You *always* forget to keep your half of the bargain." The "always" and "never" are just as wrong when a child uses them.

To avoid this entire hassle of subjective record-keeping, a good management system should include some method by which the amount of work performed by the child and the requirements set for that work are recorded—that is, counted in some objective fashion and written down somewhere. One of the reasons that I recommend objective recording is that it forces the parent to be concrete. You can't tell a child to be "good" because it is impossible to count goodness. If you are going to count something, you have to break it down into a description of a countable act of behavior. Once the parent has done that, it is usually possible to figure out some objective way of measuring the amount of work.

The wise parent, wishing to avoid unnecessary hassles, arguments, and tantrums, manages to define the action and requirements for the child in such a way that her record-keeping ends all arguments in advance. A child merely has to look at the objective record of what he has done. He began studying at 8 o'clock and it is now 10 o'clock. He has put in two hours. There is no question of "Is that enough?" By designating in advance that two hours is the proper amount for a boy his age with his specific problems in school, there can be no argument either way. If he has done only one hour, it is obvious that only half the amount of time was put in. If, on the other hand, he puts in two-and-one-half hours, it is obvious that he has exceeded what was required of him. The parent who says "You have not studied enough," when the child is putting in two-and-one-half hours is being unfair to the child. If there were no countable requirement set up, the parent could get away with failing to value what the child has done. But when the record system is such that counting is possible and objective recording methods are used, the parent now knows that the amount of effort put forth calls for some kind of recognition.

All homes use a record system. It is impossible not to. Some, however, are so sloppy that we can hardly even rank them on a scale of desirability. They are, as I said earlier, vague, confused, subjective, and even inconsistent. A child under such a vague record system is confused and frequently responds with anger, tantrums, or withdrawal. It is just too hard to function under a system where nobody ever remembers what you have done, or where they only remember the bad things and forever throw them up to you.

That's another kind of record system seen fairly often, the parents who only count what the child does wrong. That kind of parent can tell you chapter-and-verse for the last 15 years every single act the child performed incorrectly. But when you ask them to name five things the child has done right, they are almost totally unable to remember a single positive thing.

The purpose of the record system which is made objective is to allow the child and the parent to notice both the pluses and minuses, the correctly done behavior and the occasions when the behavior failed to occur correctly.

THE CONSEQUENCE SYSTEM ∽ The third and final component in contract systems of child-management, one which exists in all homes, is the consequence system for the child. This includes the actual consequences that are present, the manner in which they are delivered, the frequency of providing them, and the rules by which they are given. The consequence system and the way in which it operates is, of course, the key component of any home management system; because behavior is largely a function of consequences, the type of consequence system has a great deal to do with your child's behavior.

There are many kinds of delivery systems for consequences in homes. Payments occur for children all the time. The payment may be simply a smile, a pat on the head, or a word of praise. Sometimes the only systematic pay-off for the child is the one he discovers for himself, the natural consequences of the environment. Sometimes the only important consequences he can find are the ones he gives to himself; he grits his teeth and takes pride in surviving. No home exists without some kind of consequence system for the children. They can be ranked, however, from most desirable to least desirable.

The most desirable home consequence systems supply consequences to a child that are appropriate for his stage of development and are based on his earning them by performing appropriate actions. For the young child, consequences tend to be biological, with the addition of a certain amount of social consequences such as fondling, hugging, kissing, and swinging in the air. As the child gets older and his development and learning continue, the consequences may begin to move subtly from mostly biological to some kind of acquired consequence pattern: his favorite toys, his blanket, the stories he likes to hear, and the television program he likes to watch. These may still be external kinds of tangible or intangible consequences supplied by the parent. As the child develops even further in this kind of consequence system, the consequences being used again alter to fit the requirements of the child. There tends to be increasing emphasis on pride and self-respect as the major consequences for the child's actions.

The child should always be striving to achieve a standard which previously had been set at a level at which he can succeed. The child should be encouraged to sort out consequences in terms of those which not only are available but are appropriate for him. The addition of awareness of and attention to future consequences should be included as the child becomes mature enough to handle them. The final complete consequence system should include long-range consequences as well as immediate consequences. There should be a broad selection of consequences from personal, social, and natural sources, and the child should be able to select from the pattern those which are in his own best interest. For example, he should choose to please his parents when learning a behavior in his own best interest, but he might refuse to work for their praise and approval if the behavior that he was attempting to learn was not in his best interest. He should learn to differentiate wisely between the two. He should learn to accept the approval of some strangers and not of others. He should learn when it is appropriate to conform and when it is appropriate to work only for self-consequences that help him maintain a set of standards that he had helped to shape.

The bribery type of contract system falls much further down the scale of desirability. It is an attempt to try to get the child to do things that have no intrinsic or self consequences for him. Very often the things he's being forced to do are not in his own best interest and he resists and resents them strongly. Offering a positive consequence to help the child improve his own behavior is really not a bribe. A bribe, as I have said earlier, is a payment for something not in one's own best interest. Many parents, unfortunately, attempt to get their children to do things which are not in their own best interests, like obeying 100 percent of the time, overeating or even undereating, because the parent thinks they are desirable for the child. The parent may even attempt to promote behavior in the child which may cause the child serious difficulty as he tries to deal with other people. For example, the parent may want the child to be guarded and withdrawn because he imagines that is the "right" way to be. But the child may be living among peers who are open, friendly, and giving. Thus he will find that if he accepts the standards of the parents he will be in constant turmoil with his friends.

Going further down the scale of desirable consequence systems in homes, we find homes where the pay-offs are completely arbitrary and unrelated to the behavior of the child, but are given according to the whim of the parent. If the parent is feeling generous that day, the allowance is given. Sometimes extra allowance, extra hugs, and extra kisses are given when the parent is in a good mood. The effect of this is to leave the child confused and uncertain, with a great deal of lowered confidence. He has no way of dealing with his world. He has no way of producing the outcomes he wants. No matter what he does, Daddy's wrath will fall if Daddy has been drinking, fighting with mother, or being chastised by his boss. It will have very little to do with what Johnny does. Mommy will love Johnny no matter what Johnny does. He has no way of finding out what produces love in people. The love is either constant or capricious. After a while he begins to believe that other people's giving to him is related to how they wish to give, not to how he acts. This becomes a serious problem for Johnny for the rest of his life. He is always suspicious and distrustful of people because "you never know how they're going to treat you." He is always guarded and defensive because they can become arbitrary anytime they wish to. There is nothing he can do about it. The world is seen as a frightening place, a place full of capricious outcomes.

It is easy to see, then, why so many people in our society develop continuous social anxiety and continuous problems in dealing with the world. It is hard to convince them that they can produce consequences by their own efforts. Constant consequences (either being given or withheld) or capricious consequences (occurring at the whim of the parent) can destroy a child. Maybe he will survive, maybe he will be able to function to a limited extent in the world, but he will never quite be a whole human being. Relating the consequences children experience to their own acts is essential for their full development. Parents who do not take the time to recognize this are failing to fulfill their roles as parents in the most effective way possible.

These three components of any management system—the requirements set for the child's actions, the record system kept, and the consequence system—are now going to be examined in the light of the types of system I have most often recommended. There are two types of systems that I recommend—the informal and the formal. Let's look at the informal systems first and see if you can recognize families you have known who have used any of them.

INFORMAL CONTRACT SYSTEMS ᔦ

BARTER SYSTEM ᔦ A barter system is a trading arrangement that requires an appropriate action from the child for which he receives a particular positive consequence. There is no overall organization to this system; each transaction is separate and distinct. In a barter system you would say to your child, "If you do this, then I will do that."

Barter systems are as old as man. We have been using them ever since the first cave man offered to trade his axe for a piece of meat that the other person already had. These trades or exchanges go on continuously. The explicit type states openly what the exchange is to be. The conditions are set for the swap. The parent says to the child, "If you do your homework tonight, you can watch television." "If you eat your spinach, I'll give you some ice cream." "If you stay home and watch your sister, I'll let you go to the party tomorrow night." In each case the transaction is a barter. Any good management system will always have a certain amount of such outright horse-trading.

The horse-trade is a very useful kind of thing for the parent because it is a clear signal. It tells the child what he is to do under what conditions, what will be acceptable in terms of the adequacy of performance, and what he is to get in exchange. But it has severe limitations. It requires that you, as a parent, always have available something to barter. It is cumbersome. It leads to continuous negotiations at almost every turn of the situation. The child very quickly learns to barter and to measure every task he performs in terms of its value and worth to you. If you fail to have available something to barter, the child probably will turn you down. Why should he put forth effort if you do not have something to exchange for it? Why should he give you something if you give him nothing? If we are to consider children as people, we must, of course, give them the right of refusal, particularly if what we have to trade is not worth very much.

There is an additional problem in this type of barter system in that the child usually gets to be better at it than the parent and so wins most of the horse-trades. You find yourself with horses that are swayback and old and whose teeth are falling out, while he is forever riding off on thoroughbreds or walking off into the distance with your bag of gold. Children are quick and sharp. They have to live under this system. If the only way they can get what they want out of life is to swap you, they'll become experts. They'll constantly be holding out for better and better goods of more and more worth for larger and larger privileges until you finally realize that you have been had. Many a parent has set up a barter with his child only to realize that it was a bad bargain for him; then he reverts to his patriarchal rights and reneges.

Under this type of a system the child becomes angry, and rightfully so, I think, because unfair advantage was taken of him. For example, a parent may say, "If you do your homework, I'll give you something." The child says, "What will you give me?" The parent may offer a movie. The child says, "That's not enough. I want to go to New York for the weekend." After much haggling, the parent in desperation promises anything. "Yes, you can go to New York for the weekend with your friends. Just finish your homework." The child gleefully goes off, completes his homework in five minutes, comes back, and says, "Here it is." The father realizes he's been had again. He had to promise an entire weekend away for only five minutes of effort. He had forgotten to ask the child how much homework he really had. At this point many a father will renege on the contract. Even though bartering is an informal system, it is still a contract. When the father says, "I changed my mind, you cannot go for the weekend," the child has every right to be annoyed. After all, he hadn't lied to his father; he just failed to mention how much homework there really was. In a good horse-trade it's perfectly acceptable not to point out that the horse has lost a few teeth. The boy cannot understand why the father will not accept the rules of horse-trading. His anger, resentment, and rebellion will show up very shortly when he starts to refuse future opportunities to barter and will not participate in any more horse-trading with people who are so unfair.

Even when the bartering system works well, it is cumbersome.

When it works badly, it is dangerous for the child and bad for the parent. At the very best, an informal barter system should be kept to a minimum and used only as a part of a larger system. Used alone, it quickly generates more problems than people can handle. This is one of the reasons that mankind in general has gone away from barter systems as society has grown more complex and as the requirements for behavior have become more precise. We no longer offer someone a bushel of potatoes for a job. We much prefer to pay him in money. Money is always available, cheap, easy to print, and convenient to carry. Can you imagine what it would be like if you were paid in goods instead of money? You would come trotting home every day with food or a load of potatoes on your back for your family. In addition, you would work only for people who had the goods and services that you wanted and if you got tired of what your boss was bartering for your labor, you would no longer work for him. In short, the system would be totally unworkable. A horse-trading type of barter system really doesn't work and is not recommended as a total system. It should be used only for emergencies and only as a supplement to a larger system.

UNSTATED CONTRACT SYSTEM ∽ The best and the worst type of contract system is the kind in which the contract is implicit. There is an unstated "If . . . then" relationship which is completely non-specific. The child knows that as long as he is performing as required the goodies will keep coming but as soon as he stops the goodies will stop. There is no attempt to relate these two occurrences precisely, for such a system is an ongoing process whereby the child is expected to do his work, carry his share of the load, and use the kinds of social skills acceptable to his family. In exchange, he will be provided with room and board, a certain amount of luxuries, and the tender loving care of his parents.

This is the best of all systems because, when it works, it is the easiest, has the greatest generality, and is the most humanistic kind of approach. That is, it shows tremendous respect for the needs and wishes of both parties. There is an assumption of responsibility on the part of both parties, parent and child. The general relationship is one of loving acceptance and eagerness to contribute. When it works it's beautiful. It is a goal of mankind that is seldom reached.

The problem with such a system is that it requires great skill, great maturity, and great compassion. Few homes meet these qualifications. What most often happens instead is that the parents set up such a system. They decide what they will provide for the child without really consulting the child about his needs and wishes. They are prepared to give and they expect from the child certain kinds of behavior in return. They even may specify the requirements for the child to the child himself. But poor Johnny may not have the maturity, the experience, the wisdom, or the ability to function under such a system and he quickly subverts it for his own purposes and to his own ends. He manipulates the system very quickly into a situation of all taking and no giving. He does as little as is humanly possible and takes as much as he can get.

In desperation the parents may even raise the ante, giving more and more to Johnny in order not to lose his love or approval, which is the only thing they are getting from him. They're not getting much effort or much work, but at least Johnny likes them. The child quickly grasps this and proceeds to threaten them with the withdrawal of his love unless they continue to up the ante and give him more and more.

The typical spoiled brat syndrome occurs because the parents engage in the process of *vacuum-filling*. When there is an absence of action on the part of the child (a vacuum), the parents believe they must do the action for him (fill it). If the child doesn't clean up the room, you can't really leave it dirty. You've got to pick up after him. If the child doesn't communicate very well, then you have to speak for him, because, after all, there is a vacuum and it must be filled. The parents begin to do more and more of what is rightfully the child's to do, under the mistaken impression that they really have tried to get him to do it, but it is impossible. Their method of trying is usually a method of signal control; they implore, they plead, they beg, they cajole, they inspire, they lecture, or they reason. Over and over again, they send out the signals. But Johnny knows the facts of life. The facts of life are that in this kind of unstated contract system all he has to do is sit tight and the noise will gradually abate. His parents will continue to give, particularly if he manipulates them a little by making them feel guilty. All he has to do is look sad or unhappy, withdraw or sulk a little bit, and they'll work ten times harder to give him more and more. If he will just look interested he can ignore their signals. Thus most children under this system manage to look interested during the lecture even though they intend to forget it as soon as they leave the room. Some adolescents, however, do not even have to pay their parents the courtesy of seeming to be listening to them.

It is easy to see, then, that the unstated contract system depends upon individuals able to handle it. In spite of its dangers, I think that this approach should be the final goal of most families. Even in my own family we don't use it yet because my children are too young, too inexperienced, and too restricted in their skills to be able to handle such a system. I hope some day to graduate to this type of system. I think that over time we will. Yet I see many families attempting to begin with this system, even with young children. You can almost always recognize this system by the plaintive whining of the parents about how much they give to a child and how little the child appreciates it. They're right, but it was they who trained him to be that way. They set up the system that led to his developing manipulation as an approach to life.

TOKEN SYSTEMS–TASK-ORIENTED ∽ Another kind of informal system that can be used effectively in child management is a token system. A *token system* is a method of providing delayed consequences by using bridge consequences (tokens or points) between work performed and things desired. There are several kinds of token systems and the ones we will consider first are those which are *task-oriented.* Such systems specify the requirements for the actions which the child contracts in advance to perform. In exchange he receives some kind of token which in turn can be exchanged at a later time for more concrete positive consequences. The use of tokens is also a good method of counting the number of times an action occurs, recording them almost automatically by the number of tokens given. An accumulation of tokens can be exchanged for any available tangible or intangible consequence the child finds positive at any given moment.

With young children the tokens may be checker pieces, brass tokens, pieces of paper, paper clips, toothpicks, or even pennies; a variety of such objects is available to the average parent. It is desirable to pick the type of concrete token that the child cannot get anyplace but from his parents. This type of bridge consequence is usually used with young children, who need something concrete as a token.

Older children, however, would resent being handed poker chips or pieces of paper as a method of tokens. They much prefer to have check marks or gold stars on a chart, marks put into a book, or simply numbers accumulated on a counter. They are able to deal with what I call *symbolic* tokens. A symbolic token takes no concrete form; it is simply a point or a number, a way of counting and recording.

Sometimes the token is exchangeable for only one thing; you save all your points to get candy bars and the only thing you can get with them is candy bars. Or you save up all your points to play golf, because the only thing you can use them for is the privilege of playing golf. Or you save all your points for the privilege of watching television because these are television points. Sometimes the points are exchangeable for a variety of things. When you have twenty-five points saved, you can go to the store and buy anything you want, up to whatever value has been set for the points by the parents. You could set the purchasing power of twenty-five points at ten cents or two dollars, depending on the wealth of the parent and the sophistication of the child.

Now let's examine some other task-oriented point systems. They all have one thing in common: a specific task is required, such as being polite, not hitting your sister, encouraging another child, or being in bed on time. This is the requirement component of the system. The points can be given for a single task or for a group of tasks, any one of which can earn the points. It can be as simple or as complex as the child can handle and as the mother desires to use.

A second feature of the point system is that, instead of direct payment with objects or opportunities to act which the child wants, there is an in-between step. The in-between step is the giving of points, which serve as the counting system, as the record-keeping system, and as a part of the consequence system. Each point has value because it is exchangeable and each point is a method of counting. If you give a child a point for being at the table on time, not only have you counted the fact that he was at the table on time, but you also have given him a *part* of the final positive consequence.

The next aspect of token systems is the consequences which are exchangeable for the points accumulated. The consequences can be a single item or multiple items. It is always better to allow the points to be exchanged for a variety of things than for a single thing. The child may grow tired of what you are offering because he is satiated with it or he may lose his interest in it because something else is more tempting at that moment. The points themselves will begin to lose value very quickly if they cannot be exchanged for something of value or if the something of value waivers, vacillates, or has very little real influence on the child. Promising a young child a treat on Saturday for accumulating twenty-five points may fail utterly for two reasons. In the first place, he really cannot see that far into the future and the points are insufficiently valuable in their own right; and in the second place, when he gets to Saturday he may no longer want the treat that you offered because his tastes may have changed. Children are quite inconsistent.

Let's attack the first problem first. In itself a point has no value whatsoever to a child, be it a poker chip, a mark on a piece of paper, or a number on a dial. It cannot influence behavior in any way. It is a neutral consequence. However, if you give your child a point for the task he has performed and immediately take it back and exchange it for something of value, he quickly will grasp that the point is exchangeable. The younger the child, the more explicit this must be and the more you must act out the process. With a very young child of four or five, you must hand him a concrete token (poker chip, paper clip, or penny) and as soon as he has it in his hand you say, "Give it back and I'll give you something for it." Take back the token and give the child a piece of candy, a peanut, a cracker, an apple, a swing in the air, or a hug. The child quickly grasps that this one token can be exchanged for something else. How quickly, varies from child to child. Some children learn it almost immediately and some take days to learn this simple exchange potential of the token.

Once he grasps that one token will buy something, you teach him that two tokens will buy more. Refuse to exchange a single token and make him accumulate two before you exchange. This should happen soon after he has mastered the first step. Sometimes you can teach him by giving the two tokens at once, then taking them back and giving them one at a time until two are accumulated. Even with young children you can gradually work your way up to five, ten, or even twenty-five tokens before they are exchanged. What you watch for is whether or not the tokens continue to influence his behavior. Will the child work to get them? If he stops working to get them, you know you are going too fast or the exchange rate is too low. Some children have to have concrete positive consequences exchanged every five or ten tokens. Some accumulate hundreds before they wish to, or need to, exchange them. A good rule of thumb is that children under five should not be expected to accumulate more than five or ten, children under seven more than twenty-five. Over seven, you can make the system even more complicated. Frequently older children will ask to save up to hundreds of points to get something of real value that they wish.

Another rule of thumb for the parent is never to give your child anything that you would not ordinarily give him. No matter how he pleads or begs, the point system should be no substitute for a parent's judgment. In arranging a contract with the parent the child can ask only for consequences of which the parent approves.

The decisions on the tasks that the child is required to perform as he gets older should be subject to the child's participation. The older the child, the more right he has to question, modify, or even veto the task requirement. Children are people, and as they become competent they should be given the right to negotiate and refuse tasks that are not appropriate for them. With young children this is rarely a problem because what you ask of them is usually some simple action, necessary for the child or for the family. You wish him to stop having tantrums, to be in bed on time so he has sufficient rest, to eat his food to prevent illness and maintain his health, and to refrain from bullying other children in order for him to have more friends and for you to be able to turn your back on his interaction with other children. All of these tasks as well as the actions necessary for acquiring a basic education are easily seen as being in the child's best interests. Parents are usually to be trusted in their judgment as to which task is appropriate.

With a teen-ager, however, the issue may not be as clear-cut as to the rights, participation, and veto power of the child when, for example, the parent requires hair-cutting in order for him to earn the points which are spendable for a driver's license or for the rental of the family car. Does he, in fact, have the right to say, "It is an unfair contract, I will not cut my hair simply because you are offering me points." Will you, as a parent, truly accept his right to veto that task or to modify it in terms of a trimming rather than a complete shearing?

These are questions that this book can only raise. We are concerned primarily with the management of children, although effective design and humanistic goals are, of course, an essential part of good management. Of course, our society gives parents the right to specify the task requirements for their child. I am simply pointing out that it is much more effective and much more humanistic management policy to allow the child to participate in the setting of that task and ultimately to have the same right as we would accord to any competent adult in our society to decide as to whether a task is desirable or whether a skill that is to be added to his repertoire is worth acquiring. The real issue, of course, is how much self-management a child is to be permitted.

Under a point system, these issues become clear-cut. Very often tasks the child does not wish to perform will be performed because you are now adding a positive consequence that changes the outcome for the child. Although he doesn't want his hair cut, does not wish to study, or does not wish to take out the garbage, he may do so with no feeling of rebellion or resentment and no attempt to subvert the activity, because he is receiving a fair pay-off in terms of the positive consequences afforded him by the point system which he could get in no other way perhaps. The justification the parent can use, then, for why he wishes him to cut his hair is, "I am paying you to do so. If you wish the points, do it." Very often this will completely sidestep the problem of who determines what. The child can say to himself, "I am doing it for the pay," and the parent can say, "He is doing it for the points but I am happy with his hair cut short. I don't require him to *want* to do so because he likes short hair too."

A cooperatively managed point system is a solution, but only a partial one, to the typical conflict between the generations as to how a child will behave and how he will look. Very often the child who does not wish to work or do his homework will accept as an explanation of why he has to the answer, "In order to get points," when he will not accept the answer, "Because at some time in the future it will be better for you." He can see the immediate consequences but he cannot always see the future ones. The points make sense to him, the future does not.

This type of a point system, then, is a more precise step up the ladder from informal barter systems. There is now a more precise relationship between consequences and tasks and there is a better, more objective method of record-keeping. This system also allows the parent to take the final consequence and break it up into many parts. In a barter system you give the child a bike for a certain performance. In this type of point system you can divide the bike into five thousand, five hundred, or even fifty different parts, depending on the age of the child.

Let's assume you pick five hundred points to get a bike. You now have five hundred opportunities to contract with your child. You have complete flexibility in arranging his motivational and incentive system in a way that you cannot possibly have with a barter system. By being able to break the bike into so many different units, you are able to relate the worth of the consequence to the amount of the task. If he does five times the amount of the task, you can give him five times as many points. If he only does part of the task, you can give him part of the points for which he has contracted. This gives greater flexibility and greater possibilities for shaping the behavior of the child. The points are always available, they seldom satiate if properly handled, and they can be given easily and quickly without disrupting the practice session. As each part of a task is completed, partial points can be given to create additional incentive for children who are especially nearsighted with respect to final outcome. How much better this system is for a parent than the simple barter system of "I will give you a bike in eight weeks if you get a good report card." The child who is nearsighted can't see that far anyhow and the promise of a bike will have very little effect on him. The child who is not nearsighted is probably not in trouble to begin with.

In addition, the parent has only one opportunity to give a positive consequence (the bike) and there are hundreds and perhaps thousands of tasks involved in getting the final report card—which is also, by the way, subject to the whims of the teacher and the vagaries of chance. It is not a very fair contract system to leave the pay-off entirely to chance, the mood of the teacher the day she marked the papers, or the types of questions she chose to make up at the last moment. It is much fairer to arrange to pay a child for the actual *effort* he puts into earning those grades. This makes a great deal more sense in terms of teaching him that the true values of life do not lie in simply beating the system by passing the grade; after all, you can cheat to do that or you can just get lucky. The real pay-off ought to come for the hard effort and the work output provided by the child on the way to the final evaluation.

Using a point system makes it possible for the parent to notice the effort, the hundreds and thousands of little tasks that are required, and to pay the child with consequences that are meaningful to him. Because points are exchangeable and have meaning they allow you to contract with the child for just the amount of work he can do at any given moment. You can adjust the contract continuously for the days he is ill, the days that he wishes to do more work, or the days that he is just too tired to put forth much effort. You can arrange that he always succeeds at the task, helping to build self-confidence. You have five hundred opportunities to do so, as compared to the one opportunity you get if you barter for the bike. There is a world of difference, then, between a barter system and even a simple task-oriented point system.

BONUS POINTS ◇

There is another kind of informal contract system which needs to be mentioned because it also is extremely effective with young children and can be used with older children as well. The *bonus point* system does the same thing as the task-oriented point system except that it is non-task-oriented. This system is concerned with strengthening the action that occurs spontaneously, whereas in the task-oriented point system you are specifying in advance to a child what action he is to do in order to earn points. With a bonus point system you are doing no preplanning, you are not specifying for the child in advance what he is to do and how he is to do it. Instead, you are observing the child and giving points when you notice an appropriate action occurring.

The bonus point system uses either concrete or symbolic tokens. The token, by the way, can also be a word of praise. So many words of praise can be exchanged for a special treat from Daddy or a special hug. You can say to a child, "You know, I told you how good you were so many times today that I just feel like hugging you." The child will come to know that the words of praise are also exchangeable. However, with young children the symbolic or concrete tokens are even more meaningful.

The bonus point, as I have already said, is not task-oriented. No previous goals are set. You simply watch the child's behavior and spontaneously step forward and say, "You did that right, you deserve an extra-special bonus," or "That was really very nice, I wish I would see more of that behavior. Here is a bonus." You can give a single point or you can give a number of points. The essential thing is that it must happen after the act. The bonus still exemplifies the contract principle because it arranges for a positive consequence to occur after the correct action appears in order to strengthen it. Bonuses will strengthen acts even though the act was not contracted for in advance. They also will increase the likelihood of the act's reoccurring.

The bonus system is not a fixed system. There is no pre-determined consequence for any predetermined act and no predetermined amount of the consequence. It is random on the parent's part and it is deliberately kept that way. The child is never allowed to plead, beg, cajole, or use any other kind of manipulation for a bonus. If you inadvertently give in to the child and give bonuses because you were asked, you will teach your child to beg. If you give bonuses because your child becomes tearful, you will teach him to whine and cry. If you give some extra bonuses because the child has become aggressive and threatens a tantrum or a withdrawal of love toward you unless you give them, you will be teaching your child to use these kinds of techniques in order to get the bonus points. No one other than the parent can determine what is worth a bonus point. Even the same activity repeated a few minutes later may not get a bonus point. The wise parent keeps this system random and occasional.

The purpose of a bonus system is twofold; it strengthens the child's desirable actions and it teaches you to put the accent on the positive. The parent who is looking to give bonuses is not very likely to be excessively critical by constantly noticing the child's inappropriate actions. In all likelihood you will find it much easier to ignore his errors when you are thinking in terms of giving bonuses. Many parents notice the child only when he is doing something inappropriate and call only that to his attention. Without realizing it, in many many cases, they are inadvertently increasing the likelihood that the child will repeat the inappropriate behavior because that is what they are giving attention to. Very few parents continuously notice their children when they are behaving appropriately.

How many teachers do you know who walk up to a child and thank him for being quiet? Not very many, I'm afraid. Most teachers continuously scold children to be quiet and to stop talking, and then they can't understand why the more they scold the worse some kids get. The answer is obvious to anyone studying the principles of behavior. What the teacher is doing is arranging a positive consequence for misbehavior. She may think the scolding is negative, but it is obvious that it is not since it is increasing the acts of misbehavior.

Besides increasing what she wants to decrease, the parent who constantly notices and criticizes the inappropriate behavior of the child will tend to teach the child to be fearful of trying new things because it may lead to criticism, ridicule, or punishment. She will teach the child that the standards expected of him are much higher than he can reach, but he will assume that other children somehow can reach it or else why would Mommy set such a standard? When you notice errors, you are teaching your child that you expect perfection.

In addition, the child will feel rejected and unloved because most of the feedback from Mommy and Daddy tends to be in terms of negatives rather than positives. No matter how much a parent may profess her love for a child, the end effect of constant criticism is that the child will feel unloved, will lose his sense of worth, and very often will tend to develop extremely inappropriate behavior, either giving up the search for love or striving to get it by whatever means possible from whomever he can get it. Either way, the end result is devastating for the child. He may recover, but he may remain scarred and damaged for life.

DEMERITS VERSUS BONUSES ∽ An informal bonus system can be misused only if it becomes a *demerit* system. A demerit is a negative bonus used if a child misbehaves to take things away as punishment. We have already seen why punishment is undesirable, and the same arguments explain why no demerits should ever be given. Punishment can hurt a child. The bonus system, on the other hand, cannot hurt a child. It is impossible to spoil a child with a bonus system because you provide the love, attention, notice, tokens, or tangible consequences only when a child has *earned* them by behaving well. The only behavior you can increase with a positive bonus system is good behavior; the only thing you can do with respect to a child's self-confidence is to build it.

A child soon begins to realize that people notice what he does right and that they're not watching to tear him down. In addition, the child learns that goals are achievable and that his parents are not using standards of perfection. When he makes a mistake it is obvious to him that even though he did something inappropriate, Mommy is concentrating on the appropriate part. She is willing to accept a certain level of imperfection depending on how he is doing. There is the constant feeling of love and affection being given, since Mommy's major interaction pattern with him is to give love and affection, not to scold, criticize, yell, or lecture. Under this type of care, the child gravitates very quickly to that part of the behavior in his repertoire most acceptable to Mommy and most reinforced by the positive consequence system.

COMBINING SYSTEMS ∽ A bonus system can be attached to other systems. It can become a part of a larger system. You can add it to a barter system or to an unstated contract system. You can have a task-oriented point system with bonuses for special occasions. You most certainly can have bonus systems built into any total contract system of child management. Implementing the contract principle in this way can only enhance a home.

Bonus systems are used in industry and business as a way of creating more effort and contentment on the part of workers. People who receive frequent bonuses along with their salaries, but on a "work earned" basis rather than as routine Christmas bonuses, constantly strive by working harder to keep the bonuses coming and to increase them. If a bonus is given routinely every Christmas, it comes to be considered a part of the salary and does not lead to increased work output. Similarly, the parent who gives bonuses routinely and mechanically at predictable times is defeating the purpose of the bonus system. The bonus system must be related to effort and must be random so that it never gets to be accepted as routine. The child is not entitled to bonuses; he must earn them. If your child is the type of child who hangs her coat up every day when she comes home from school, a bonus should not be given every day. The bonuses should be very rare and very occasional for hanging up coats. Otherwise it will lose its meaning and come to be expected or it will become a task-oriented point system rather than a bonus point system. For a bonus to strengthen behavior it must occur by surprise. It must occur only when a correct behavior is occurring, of course, so that the child will know that if he is performing appropriately something nice occasionally will happen. But he never knows exactly when. When he's contracted for a task to be performed he can always predict the points will be given when he's finished. But he can never predict bonuses. He never knows when he will get extra points for doing the task especially well. He never knows when he'll get points for doing something that Mommy never even told him about. The bonus system will keep him working very hard all the time because he knows that he gets bonuses only when he's working hard and never when he's goofing off. The likelihood is increased, then, that he will become a much more efficient and diligent child with respect to the tasks required of him and he may even look for things to do because he wants to maximize his chances of getting bonuses.

Remember that bonuses and task-oriented points are effective only if they are exchangeable for something that the child wants. It is most desirable that they be exchangeable for a variety of the things the child wants and the easiest way to assure this is to let the child pick out what consequence he wants to exchange the points for. There are a variety of ways of doing this and I will discuss them as we get into more formal contract systems for the home in the next chapter.

13 🦋

Your Home as an Economic
S*ystem*

Just recently I was asked to help convert a school for deaf children to a motivational system that would increase the effectiveness of the teaching approach and reduce the number of problems the school had to deal with in the behavior of the children. When I looked over the system that was being used I found that it was an unstated contract system. With those children who could function under it there was no problem at all, but the great majority of the children were floundering and developing ineffective behaviors ranging from sullen withdrawal to overt rebellion. In many ways I feel more sorry for the child who is passing through the educational system and slowly being destroyed in his life of quiet desperation than I do for the child who is actively rebelling, fighting, and although suffering his lumps, still alive and kicking. In looking over this school's motivational system the first proposal I made was to suggest that the school system conform to reality. They were supposed to be preparing these children to go out into the real world. They were attempting to pattern their vocational training on real factory and business employment, and yet the motivational system they were using was totally unrealistic. The children were not paid for their work and did not have to pay for their privileges. They were given no training to prepare them for the outside world. In fact, this system was a discontinuous one.

According to some anthropologists, we have a child-rearing system that is discontinuous in our culture. We prepare children for a way of life that does not exist and then suddenly dump them on the real world and expect them to quickly grasp the subtle implications and requirements needed to succeed. For example, we teach our children to be dependent and to take orders from us until they are twenty-one. At twenty-one we say, "You are an adult; make decisions for yourself and give other people orders." In the motivational system that we use in rearing children we give a child everything he wants without any effort or earning of it; and then suddenly we throw him into the outside world and say, "Okay kid, it's over now. Go work for a living." We expect him to be able to make this adjustment quickly and easily. He very seldom does. It takes a long period of difficult adjustment before most adolescents settle down and are able to accomodate themselves to the pay-as-you-go-and-earn-your-way type of world in which we live.

What I am suggesting is that your home be brought into more continuity with the way things really are. A formal home contract system, then, is an attempt to prepare your child for the real world at the earliest possible age. You should run your home the way the world is run. The child then will have a continuous upbringing which fully prepares him to take his place in a democratic society. The principle behind this philosophy is that you must respect the child. You do not want to put him on welfare and teach him sloth and other kinds of bad habits. What you should want to do is to teach him as quickly as possible to become competent and to develop an attitude toward life which is consistent with the overall philosophy of our culture.

To do this you need to look at the management system within your home. You have to make allowances for the ability of your child, for the level at which he can function. You need to have a record system that suits your needs. There are many different ways to keep records. You also have to build a consequence pattern that is workable and desirable within your own home. All members of your family need to be accounted for. To be effective, a formal home contract system should be neither too burdensome nor too restrictive. It should take into account all of the needs of your child and should allow for change and growth as he grows older. It should be possible to arrange different management systems for each child within your family so that proper attention can be paid to individual differences.

Let's discuss some practical steps for setting up such a home management system. The overall system I'll be discussing will have certain essential features which I'll cover one by one. These will include such things as the contracts themselves, the menus and catalogs, bank books, savings books, scorecards, and other necessary tools. I also will discuss various procedures to be used, such as the negotiation sessions with the children, and the use of additional outside sources, such as mediators to help resolve differences. But let's begin with the components of the home contract system. The first of these is the contract itself.

THE CONTRACT ⌒

The contract is actually a very simple document. It is written, of course, so that it can be referred to all during the week by both the child and the parent. On the left-hand side it should list the the tasks to be performed, specifically and concretely. On the right-hand side it should contain a designation of how many points are to be given for the performance of that task.

TASKS ⌒ The task may be a single task which can be performed only once during the week, such as cutting the grass. It may be a task which can be repeated many times—a half-hour of study, for example, or, for a child who has difficulty in concentrating, five minutes of study which can be repeated six times in a half-hour if the child becomes skillful enough to do so. The task may be the offering of a word of encouragement to a brother or sister; each occasion of offering encouragement can be counted and a point or more can be given. Depending on the age of the child, there can be two or three things listed as tasks, or twenty or more. The more tasks, the more complicated the system becomes.

Sometimes it is desirable to have only one task or one kind of task listed in the contract for a given week. For example, one boy may earn all of his points by study if you especially desire to increase the rate of his study. You are not necessarily interested for the moment in his outside social behaviors, how he gets along with his brothers and sisters, or how good any other personal habits may be. You wish him to put his major effort into improving his study skills. So the only task listed on his contract might be the time he spends on studying in units of five minutes, a half-hour, or an hour, depending on his ability to concentrate. You need to make it possible for him to earn. If you set the unit of time for study at a half-hour and he can only study fifteen minutes at a time, he will fail to earn anything for that task. But if you make the units five minutes apiece he would have succeeded at three five-minute units and thus would have earned something for his efforts. Since you do not desire for him to fail and your object is not to make things too difficult for him, choose a unit of time that he is able to complete. Some children have to be paid by the minute. In some studies done in classrooms, children were paid every ten *seconds* for attending to the teacher. It is not necessary in a home contract system to be as precise as that, but it is necessary to be realistic in terms of what your child is able to do.

In addition to giving credit for the amount of time to be spent at a task (since this in itself is not all that you are trying to teach your child), pay him for the number of problems he completes, the number of subjects that he does in an evening, or the number of pages he has read and can successfully answer questions about, and so on. If you don't include number of tasks as well as time spent, many children will just sit and stare at their books without putting forth much effort. The goal is to increase the output of work, the active part of studying. You must set the tasks according to what you wish to see changed in your child in terms of his study behaviors.

Each family will write a different contract for each of their children. No two contracts should ever look exactly alike. I once ran a learning environment for a year-and-a-half in which every child in the environment had a different contract from that of every other child. In addition, most children had different contracts each hour during the day. Some of them were given new contracts every ten or fifteen minutes, since they could work only in short spurts of time. We would change what was required of them in keeping with their interests and abilities. If they liked mathematics and disliked reading, we would have them read so many units of reading material before we would let them do so many problems in math in order to receive their points. We called this process of completing the least desirable together with the most desirable task in that order before points could be earned *yoking* a task.

Our task system was complicated. A child could choose one basic unit of a task and receive a certain number of points for it. In order to encourage him to work harder and longer, we would make two times the basic task unit pay three or four times as much as one unit. If he chose three times the basic task unit, the pay-off was increased proportionately, and if he chose to do five units of math in which there were five or six problems each, he would receive as much as ten or fifteen times as many points as if he chose a single unit containing only the basic five or six problems. By this method a child was free to determine how hard he wanted to work at any given time. The harder he worked, of course, the more points he earned.

I have seen contract systems where the parent had a large variety of behaviors listed down the task side of the contract. The list included such things as: homework time, the amount of homework done, remedial work, enrichment work, current assignments (listed separately), social skills such as time spent away from the house with friends, solitary activities such as going for a walk, activities spent with other children in the family, keeping his room neat, and helping to clean the kitchen and the living room. The child was paid different amounts of points for each of these activities. He was paid points for courtesy to other members of the family, for engaging in weight-reduction activities, and, in addition, for refraining from second helpings. Every time he completed a meal with only one helping he received a very large number of points. This was a very complicated system for a teen-ager, because the parents had chosen to try to modify many behaviors all at once. The essential thing was that the tasks were all clearly spelled out and they all had points attached to them in different amounts depending on what the parents thought the task was worth. The child had agreed to all the prices on the list.

TASK POINTS ∽ The total amount of points that a child can accumulate in any given week by completing tasks should amount to approximately 80 percent of his total weekly income in points. That is, if you're using a point system where each point is worth a penny, you might choose a system based on a thousand points. The thousand points on a penny system would give him the equivalent of ten dollars' worth of buying power a week. He would earn up to eight hundred of these points by successfully performing task-designated activities. That would still leave a deficit of two hundred points or 20 percent of his weekly point income.

BONUS POINTS ∽ This 20 percent should be given by you in the form of bonuses. Remember that the purpose of bonuses is to encourage you to pay attention to the positive behavior of your child and to teach your child that maintaining good behavior and exerting himself even in areas not designated as tasks might lead to positive consequences. The bonus points also allow you to strengthen actions which occur spontaneously in your child and which are not task-determined. Any spontaneously occurring desirable action in your child that you note during a given week can be strengthened in this way.

THE NEGOTIATING SESSION ∽

You and your child sit down together in a private negotiating session once a week. For most home management systems I have found one week to be the most practical unit of time between such sessions. In most schoolrooms I find that a daily contract is much more effective, whereas in a precise learning environment, as mentioned earlier, the contracts can be renegotiated every few minutes. If one-to-one teaching is being done, where there is one teacher per child, contracts can be renegotiated every few seconds since you usually are working on one behavior at a time and can increase or decrease the amount of the task required for the consequence and even can shift to other tasks rapidly and easily. It is not practical, however, for parents to devote their entire day, minute by minute, to their children. Furthermore, extending the contract time is desirable in home situations since this is a closer approximation of the kinds of experiences the child would be having in regular school or real life situations.

By changing the contract frequently it is possible to undo any mistakes that are made if the contract is set in such a way that the tasks are too hard or the prices too low, or vice versa. In once-weekly sessions the child and the parent have the maximum practical opportunity to interact, negotiate, discuss, bargain, specify, and clarify whatever confusions exist.

At these bargaining sessions you are management and your child is labor. Management specifies the terms of the contract, what is required of the worker, and what management is willing to pay. Labor has a right to make counter-offers, to insist that the pay be higher or that other things be paid for as well. By this method you, the parent, attempt to teach your child the realities of life—the fact that tasks are paid for, that pay is received only for work performed, that there is a fair relationship between the two, and that the child has some say in this outcome. Bargaining should be dominated neither by management nor by labor, neither by parent nor by child.

In reality, parents still have most of the weapons. They can refuse to negotiate further and they can wait it out an awful lot longer than the child can in terms of the resources they control. The child has no other home to go to. He is forced to deal with his parents. He cannot take up residence somewhere else—although in extreme cases foster home placement, boarding schools, and institutions are used as an alternative for the child and parent who cannot resolve their differences. The use of contracts, however, makes it easier to resolve the differences since in almost all cases you are talking about objective, concrete, and specific tasks that can be counted objectively and for which fair payment can probably be agreed upon. On occasion outside help is necessary, and I will discuss this topic under special problems.

The amount of points given for a task can change from week to week. It depends on how badly you want Johnny to do something or feel that he needs to do it. There are no fixed amounts. Each family must work out for itself what a fair wage for an activity is to be. It takes a little trial and error to set wages properly. The use of the 80-20 ratio between task-earned and bonus points should help as an overall guide. These percentages have been fixed arbitrarily as a working guideline for putting the emphasis on task-oriented activities while still allowing the parent the flexibility for strengthening spontaneous actions and for learning to pay attention to the positive behaviors of their child. In the section on special problems I will discuss some reasons for altering these percentages under unusual circumstances.

MENUS AND CATALOGS ⌒

A catalog is simply a tangible list of what consequences the parents are willing to offer the child and the prices they are charging for them. It is modeled on the saving stamp catalog or the mail order catalogs that we are familiar with in our culture. It follows the same types of principles.

I have seen families who made up elaborate loose-leaf catalogs picturing a variety of items and using an elaborate descriptive terminology that would make your mouth water. (The prices were written very small so that the emphasis was on the desirability of the items.) It was beautifully designed and executed in the best traditions of Madison Avenue. Of course, most families do not go to that much trouble. They simply make up a list of catalog items. All catalogs are built in similar ways. They have items which the child usually can buy with very few points. These I call *minor items*. Most catalogs also include items which are much more expensive and which require a long delay before the child can achieve gratification. These I call *major items.*

The minor items in the catalog, which are listed first, are the daily and weekly desires of your child. They may include such things as television time, special privileges such as staying up late or a day off from school, using the family car, necessary items like money (at so many points per penny), clothing, and so on. Whatever your child wishes or needs in the course of a given week is listed under the minor items. The prices charged should be reasonable and total no more than 80 percent of his weekly total income. That is, if he were to purchase each item in the minor list or to use the repeatable items such as television time or staying up later, he would have to spend only about 80 percent of his total weekly earnings. Try to include the most attractive and desirable items in his catalog.

Put nothing in the catalog that you would not ordinarily give your child, but try to be a bit more generous than before. If he's been getting a five-dollar-a-week allowance, I suggest that the amount in the catalog be raised to six or seven dollars. (The problem of the child who is already receiving an extensive amount of goodies without having to work for them will be discussed under the section on special problems.) Ordinarily I suggest that you do not switch your child too rapidly into this system; in some cases, instead of converting his entire allowance, you should let his allowance stay constant and simply add some additional money in the catalog which he can earn. The minor items in the catalog should be easily and readily accessible to the child; he should never have a contract that leads to his being deprived of these. I will talk about the conditions where he might wind up in deprivation later.

The major items in the catalog will allow for such things as a driver's license, a car, a trip, a new bike, a special toy, staying overnight at a friend's house, and so on. These are large important privileges or items that you would ordinarily allow your child to have, but which he is now required to save for—to delay, in other words. I suggest that he be encouraged to put approximately 20 percent of his weekly earnings into a fund to save for these major items.

There are many good reasons for having both major and minor items within a catalog. Sometimes the minor items become satiating; that is, the child grows tired of them. But there is always something large for which he can save, so the points will always have worth. You are teaching your child to look toward the future, to delay gratification, and to learn good habits of thrift early. These are very important skills that you can teach him by encouraging him to save for major items in the catalog.

In addition, your child can have the feeling of controlling his own destiny. Things that before were dependent upon your whim to give are now entirely up to him to earn or not to earn. There should no longer be a conflict between you and your child as to what he may have. Once it is established that something is in the catalog, it is available to him. He no longer can plead, beg, cajole, or manipulate you to get what he wants. He can obtain these things only by demonstrating that he has sufficient points.

The catalog allows no credit for there is no credit at all within the home contract system. I will return to that point later. The catalog is a cash system. That is essential. The child must have sufficient points to purchase something. But if he has them he can feel perfectly sure of being able to obtain the things that he wants during the contract period.

The menu is just a very simple catalog. It lists a few items with pictures of what the child may do, play with, or obtain, such as a picture of a ball (to play with for a few minutes), a picture of Mommy being pushed in a chair with wheels on it, a picture of a candy bar, or a picture of a favorite book. You should have a variety of these menus for young children so that you can keep them from becoming satiated with any particular activity. You also can teach the child to choose among a variety of activities and objects in order to build up his interest patterns and provide a larger consequence field with which to work. The menu lists a very few items at a time—as few as four to as many as ten—in order not to confuse a young child. The younger the child, the fewer the better. The items on the menu can be listed, described, or pictured, depending on the child's ability to read and comprehend the more complex kinds of consequences you may be offering. These positive consequences should be selected from among the things you are fairly certain the child will like or will grow to like. Their value is in backing up the point system.

Each week the catalogs and menus are renegotiated. Prices are subject to change with notice. The notice occurs at each weekly meeting. The only items which do not change in value from week to week are the major ones, for changing them would be unfair for a child although in real life changes in the prices of major items do occur. This system is more similar to a down-payment privilege to hold the price fixed than to an actual catalog in which prices can change on all items. I tend to withhold the privilege from the parent because I have found in my experience that many parents tend to abuse the privilege of adjusting the prices of major items. It is much safer to insist that the major item price stand as it is, and let the minor items vary from week to week. This is simply a little advantage that you give the child to give him a greater feeling of security.

You may find when the system has been in effect for a while that some things you thought would be highly desirable to the child are hardly purchased at all. You can take them out of the catalog and forget about them for a time. You may try reentering them sometime in the future, but usually the child will gravitate to things in the catalog that have real and important meaning for him. He may say he likes certain things, but if he won't spend his hard-earned points on them he really doesn't like them that much. Parents often are surprised to find that some of the things they were most afraid of, like overspending on ice cream, really do not occur. The child tends very quickly to spend his money much more wisely than parents would have expected. You can give bonuses for the wise use of money, thereby training your child to use his points more effectively. If he balances his spending and increases his savings, you might give him bonus points in the form of interest. When I discuss the actual use of the system with concrete examples I will go into various ways in which parents are able to adjust the spending behavior of their children.

Two of the components of the formal home contract system have now been covered. The requirements for the child's actions have been discussed under the heading of contracts and the consequence system for the child has been discussed under the heading of menus and catalogs. These two tools in the formal home contract system fulfill the requirements of complexity, precision, and practicality. It is possible to use such tools in any home by reducing or increasing the complexity according to the needs of the family and the needs of the child. But the basic form will remain constant.

RECORD SYSTEMS ✎

SCORECARDS ✎ The method by which these two areas—the contracts and the catalogs—are related is the record system. This requires special kinds of tools, and I have taken from the real world the kinds of tools used in the general economy. These are scorecards, bank books, and savings books. Let us look at the scorecard first since it is the simplest record system and the one most frequently used with young children.

A scorecard keeps a record of how many points have been earned so far. It is that simple. How you keep that record is up to your own ingenuity. Some mothers simply take a sheet of paper and list the days of the week on it. Every time a point is earned they make a check mark under the correct day. At the end of the day they count the check marks and total the amount. This tells the child what his daily balance of accumulated points is. It takes merely a moment. Some children have been trained to keep the records themselves, leaving even less record-keeping for the mother.

In our family we have five scores being kept on one sheet and we use the lumberman's check system. We make four checks and draw a line through them to make five. This simple scoring system tells us when our children have reached twenty-five points and are due for a positive consequence to exchange for the points.

Scorecards can be more elaborate. Some mothers like to make gold stars and paste them up to show a child visually how much he is achieving. In one school each child was given colored papers which he could then paste onto a larger sheet, so that the little slips of paper would visibly grow to cover the whole page. Some mothers use a piece of graph paper in which to make check marks. When every square of the paper is filled with checks the child is entitled to his exchange consequence.

Scorecards vary enormously. Their basic function is to keep a record. Very often I use a wrist counter for counting golf strokes, which can be purchased in any sporting goods store, but instead of counting golf strokes I count the appropriate behaviors of a child with whom I am working. At the end of any designated time period (hour, minute, or day), I simply note the number of points on the counter and write it down so that I have a list of daily total amounts without the in-between marks.

All of these are simply scorecards. They keep a count of the number of points. You can tell how fast a child is earning points and how effective your system is by the amount of time it takes to accumulate those points. This will be a function in part of how many opportunities the child has to complete the task. If we are counting the number of occasions he is on time to school, he obviously is going to have only five opportunities to earn his points in a week. It might be better to pay him on the basis of closeness to being on time. If he is exactly on time he would get five points, if he is five minutes late he would get four points, if he is ten minutes late he would get three points, and so on. Or you can make it even more precise and pay him five points for being on time, four points for being a minute late, three points for being two minutes late, and so on.

There are a variety of ways to arrange the payment of points and a variety of ways to keep the scorecards. All that I ask is that the scorecards be kept so that the child can understand them. Ideally, the parent should always do the entering. It is always a temptation, as the child gets older, to distort the scores in some way—to add a few points or even in some cases to forget a few points. It's a difficult task for most people to keep their own timecards, and most employers would not think of letting their help do it. You should have the same consideration for young children and keep the scorecards for them.

BANK BOOKS ⌒ As a child gets older and the system becomes more complex, you can begin to graduate to the record system I call bank books. These are patterned on the actual pass book used in banks for savings accounts. The bank book may be in the form of a composition book, a small binder, or any simulation of an actual pass book. The column headings should be as follows:

The *date column* is the first heading on the left. It's purpose is to present a visual time record of Johnny's efforts over the days of the week. Every transaction, whether a payment of points to him or a deduction of points for some purchase he has made from the catalog, is listed according to its date. This allows you to see if he is spacing out his work or frantically trying to accumulate points on one or two days and then coasting the rest of the week. It also tells you the preferred days of spending. Is he blowing all his points in one day and then going hungry the rest of the week? This is important information that allows you to adjust the contract in terms of the maximum number of points that can be earned in a day, canteen time when purchases can be made from menu or catalogs, and even prices paid and charged.

The *item column* is the second heading and calls for a brief description of the transaction, such as: "half-hour study, " "cut grass," "half-hour tv," "candy bar," or "polite to sister." All transactions should be noted, whether he was spending or earning points. This gives you a running record, by date, of his activity during each week. You will now have an accurate, objective history of Johnny's behavior to which you can both refer back during the weekly negotiations for new contracts. It allows you to see how he is earning and spending so that you can adjust the contract to strengthen weaker actions by paying more and to maintain newly established habits by bonus points rather than task points.

The *deposit column* is third and keeps the record of points received for a task performed. A quick glance at this column shows you the rate of work output on Johnny's part by telling you whether points were earned in clusters of activity, in large chunks, or in many smaller amounts.

The *withdrawal column* is the fourth column. Each time Johnny spends points for something from the catalog or puts points into the savings book an entry is made in this column. A glance at this column tells you immediately whether he is hoarding his points or spending like a drunken sailor. It helps you locate quickly any transaction dealing with purchasing items from the catalog and is a great aid in adjusting catalog items and prices to keep Johnny's motivation high. Under no circumstances should you take points away from Johnny unless he spends them.

The *balance column* is fifth. This is the column in which Johnny is most interested. It tells him his purchasing power at any given time. The number of points entered in the deposit column at each transaction is immediately added to the previous balance total, so that a running total is kept at all times. The number of points spent at a transaction is listed first in the withdrawal column and then subtracted from the running total in the balance column. If Johnny has a large balance he will be less motivated to work than if he has a very slim balance. Don't we all work the same way?

The *bonus column* is the sixth and last column. It is not simply merged with the deposit column because keeping it separate serves as a check on the parent. Are you being too stingy in giving bonuses? If you are avoiding giving bonuses under the mistaken impression that you want to be tough and make him really earn everything he gets, you are defeating the whole purpose. Do you tend to pile them up all at once instead of spreading them out over the week? For what are you giving bonuses? Are you maintaining a 20 percent ratio with task points? These questions are all answered by the numbers in this column and allow you to adjust your own behavior toward Johnny. The most desirable way of awarding of bonus points is in amounts of three, four, or even one at a time. If the bonus points are given because of a task especially well done, they should be related in some way to the amount being given for the task, just as a tip is related to the bill in a restaurant. The bonus is given also as a positive concrete sign of your approval and noticing of any of Johnny's effective behavior. The goal of the bonus is to give you an extra tool to build the relationship between you and Johnny in a very specific and concrete manner.

This is the area in which most parents initially fall down. Most of their efforts are spent on trying to get the child to fulfill his part of the contract, do his tasks, and earn his points. Somehow they seem to overlook their obligation to give as much as 20 percent in bonus points. When they fail to do so, they are failing to be effective managers. Just think what it's like to work in a business where all you receive is your regular paycheck without a word of praise or anyone noticing when you do anything right. Compare that with the office where even though your pay may be small, the bonuses for work done occur very often with a smile and a word of encouragement. People tend to work much harder in the second office than they do in the first. In fact, unless you need money desperately, it isn't likely that you would stay in the first office very long. Children also quit. Although they can't leave the office, they can effectively withdraw from a family. Be generous, but be contingent. Give as much as you can, but only when the child has earned it. Be generous to a fault, but don't let the fault be non-contingent management.

THE SAVINGS BOOK ᔆ Occasionally, when the balances are getting too large or when the child wishes to separate his savings for the large major items in the catalog from his daily spendings, you can institute an additional record-keeping book. This book is designated as the *savings book* and is somewhat simpler in design than the bank book. It has only the date, deposit, withdrawal, and balance columns. An interest column can be added for special purposes. If you wish to encourage your child to save, you can provide an interest rate of 5, 10, or even 15 percent.

Transactions are recorded in the bank book as a withdrawal and are entered into the savings book as a deposit. This is reversed, of course, when your child wishes to use some of the money he has accumulated in the savings book. The transaction is listed in the bank book under the item column as "deposit from savings" or "deposit to savings," depending on which it is.

This additional record book serves the purpose for both the child and the parent of keeping a check on how well he is learning to delay consequences and how effectively he is handling his own points. On rare occasions, when children have been too miserly, parents have paid negative interest. That is, at the end of each week or month they return three points for every four in the savings book. This system is used very sparingly and its purpose is to end inflation.

SAVINGS CERTIFICATES ᔆ A much better way of handling the problem of the miser is to use *savings certificates*. A savings certificate ties up his excess funds for a long period of time—a month, two months, or six months. You choose the period depending on your knowledge of the child and your desire to thin out his balance. The difference between a savings certificate and a savings book is that deposits in the former are for a specified period of time. This ties up the excess funds and therefore pays a higher rate of interest than does the normal savings book. The wise parent will pay any interest rate necessary to tie up the excess funds of a child who is miserly and beginning to lose interest because he has too many points. How many of us would not retire if we had enough money in the bank to last for a year or two?

One set of parents made the foolish mistake of giving five thousand points as a birthday present to their child who was working on a five-hundred-point-a-week system. That gift alone enabled the child to retire for a ten-week period. To remedy the error caused by their unfortunate generosity I suggested immediately that they should tie up the five thousand points in a savings certificate and pay whatever price they had to. Their child was a very hard bargainer. They came back and reported they had tied up the points for a six-month period and felt that they had made the best of a bad bargain. The next step was to find a major item for which he was willing to pay a large number of points, thereby using up the savings certificate at the end of six months. He chose to go to camp the following summer. The savings certificate serves as a back-up device for certain kinds of problems which we will discuss in greater detail shortly.

Remember that this is a fairly complex system, one you are not used to, and will take a considerable period of time to establish. Over a period of weeks you will work out many of the bugs in the system and get familiar with its procedures and problems. The next chapter will be devoted to the problems to be planned for and avoided, if possible, and to be dealt with when they do occur. I do not mean to scare you or to imply that this system in unworkable or too difficult for the average person. I'm simply saying that anything worth doing is worth doing well. Setting up a precise and effective management system requires going through many steps at first until you are used to it.

14 🎋
Starting Up From
Scratch

I hope that by now you have a good working knowledge of the principles of behavior, the problems involved in designing a management system for your family, some basic methods for changing behavior, and a set of tools to set up a home contract system. But before you plunge right in and start setting it up, I would like to discuss both the mechanics of doing so and some of the problems and common mistakes to try to avoid.

Both of you—husband and wife—should read this book, discuss its points, argue out thoroughly most of your differences, and prepare yourselves to confront your children in as unified a manner as possible. Resolve your doubts or else put them on the shelf for later revaluation. You can reappraise the system at any point and decide to scrap it. But a least give it a good try first.

Prepare your children also. Particularly if they are older, they need to be made aware of what is going to happen. Don't suddenly call them in, hand the system to them as an accomplished fact, and expect their full cooperation. They need to be convinced both of your positive motives in helping them achieve self-management ultimately and of the benefits they will derive from the home contract system.

Point out to them that all tasks will be clearly spelled out and that they can participate in setting up the requirements. Try to listen to them and, whenever possible, let them set the initial starting point for all requirements, no matter how low they appear to be setting them. Tell them that you will gradually increase requirements, change pay scales and add or delete tasks from the list. Reassure them that this will be done fairly and with their participation in the decisions. You, of course, retain ultimate authority, but they will assume greater and greater responsibility for their own behavior as they demonstrate competency.

Discuss the types of positive consequences that they desire and you are willing to put in the catalog. Try to show them you intend to be generous and fair. Give a little more than you intended. Set prices lower than you intended but be sure to tell them that only the major item prices are fixed.

Explain the system to them, show them the various tools you have designed, and enlist their cooperation in improving or changing them to fit your family better. If they want to read this book, let them. There is no need for secrecy about what you will be doing. The principles will work even better if they understand what is being done and why. If the children are very young, of course, it is not as necessary to explain in detail. Use your own judgment and your extensive knowledge of your children as to how extensive this preparation phase needs to be.

Next ask them to make up a list of things they want to go in the catalog. You and your husband need to discuss and prepare the initial list of tasks and the points you are prepared to offer for their performance. Make up your own list of consequences and assign prices to each item. Try to make the prices paid for tasks and the charges made for minor items balance. The 20 percent bonus requirement should provide enough left over to save for major items. Plan the major item prices so that it is possible, with reasonable saving, for your child to be able to obtain it in a reasonable amount of time. For example, you might set the price of a new bike at three thousand points, so that if he devoted *all* of his weekly savings of two hundred points to the purchase of the bike he could have it in about four months. He has the option, of course, of saving faster or slower by allocating different percentages of his income toward spending or saving. Now you and your child are ready to negotiate at the first session.

THE NEGOTIATING SESSION ∽

Remember that this is your very first session. Allow it plenty of time. Pick a time when no one is overtired and when you can be free to concentrate completely. Stay objective. Do not make value judgments about anything. Do not try to say what is good or what is bad, what is right or what is wrong. Speak only in terms of what you *prefer*, what is important to you, the way you would like to see things resolved. Stay away from such terms as "always" and "never." When you sit down to negotiate and to set up this very first procedure, be prepared to be shocked. He is going to take a very different view of matters than either of you will take. In all likelihood, you will assume that a task is worth very little in the way of points and he will assume that it is worth much more. He may not even like the nature of the task itself. He may bring up such issues as the other children in the family and what they are going to be paid.

You are carefully to steer away from discussing with Johnny anything but the immediate contract at hand. You will discuss at this time no other child, no other kind of contract than the one you are now negotiating. In this way you may avoid being manipulated for at least a short time. He will find a way to get to you, be certain of that, but be just as certain that eventually you can correct the matter if given enough time to plan ahead.

The first contract will be terrible. Nobody will like it. You will have one week to work out the bugs and start the revisions for the next time. In other sections of this chapter and the next I will discuss the various kinds of problems you will encounter, in the hope that knowing what to expect will help you avoid making errors. But you will make errors, and you must allow yourself the freedom to make them without becoming angry either at yourself or at your child.

Once the contract has been set, in terms of the types of tasks objectively described and the point values assigned, it is necessary to establish the initial catalog as well. You will find yourself going back and forth from catalog to contract because your child will frequently ask, "What is a point really worth?" There is no way to establish its worth until he finds out what it will buy and so he will ask many questions such as: "What is it going to cost me for TV time?" In his own mind he will be equating that with what you are paying him for his efforts at study or for the time spent in doing chores, such as cleaning up his room.

It is desirable, of course, that the same relative value system be kept in paying for work and charging for catalog items. Some people use the basic minimum wage and actual cost factor for their older children. That is, they pay $1.65 per hour for work performed and then charge him the real value of all goods and services available to the child. When you rent him the family car it is at the price of an average car rental cost, per hour or per day. They pay the child as though he had a full-time job. This may lead to as much as 6,600 points a week ($66). They arbitrarily assign value to special privileges, like staying up later, on the basis of what they think the privilege is worth in a real market. These prices are more difficult to determine than the price of the car rental or the cost of the hi-fi set the child is saving for. This system may then lead to charges of 6,600 points a week. Just keep wages and prices equal.

With younger children you can enact an arbitrary wage in terms of what they can make by baby-sitting; fifty or seventy-five cents an hour, depending on the neighborhood in which they live, their age and maturity. The prices of the items they wish also should be marked according to the real world. You are now teaching your child what basic economics are like and what he will experience all through life.

Some families arbitrarily have set lower prices than the actual real value. In some homes this makes a great deal of sense, particularly with younger children for whom you are merely trying to establish a consistent and logical internal system. You may choose a unit of a tenth of a cent, much as trading stamp companies do, and have in the catalog items at their real value or the wholesale value. The argument of many trading stamps companies is that the items in their catalog actually are cheaper than if you bought them with real money, so that you are effecting a savings. This makes the saving of the stamps even more desirable. Using this principle you can set any price you desire in a catalog and arbitrarily assign a relative value to the points, from a tenth of a cent to any amount at all. You can adjust the system in many ways, according to your own needs. I simply suggest that you find some consistent principle that meets your family's requirements and that you use it as the basis for beginning. You can always change it later.

You can create inflations or depressions and all kinds of other economic situations according to the way you shift wages and prices. Remember to assure your child that the consequences will be renegotiated at the end of the contract period. Minor items may appear or disappear on a weekly basis. Tasks and wages may change according to the weekly situation. Only the system is permanent.

In my work with families over the years I've discovered a number of situations that arise fairly frequently in most homes. Let's examine some of them.

STRIKES ∽

A *strike* is the most common type of problem that occurs in the home contract system. Your child simply refuses to work. He is testing the system. It may be a strike for higher pay because he needs more points since prices in the catalog are too high. This usually happens if he needs more spending money because prices have risen before a pay raise occurs. You can tie an increase in pay to an increase in activities on the child's part even if the pay raise is only to balance the increase in the cost of what he wants to do each week.

When your child shows that he is developing better social skills, better study habits, and better self-management procedures, he is more useful to your family. He requires less supervision and less time on your part. He is, therefore, entitled to more points, more pay for his work.

Very often children will attempt to obtain more money by threatening not to work. Strikes can occur very often at the beginning of the establishment of the home contract system when children are attempting to establish the best terms for themselves. They also may arise later on when you attempt to require more work for less pay, which will happen when you have been generous in the beginning and then desire to maintain his good behavior with less and less pay, trying to wean him to self-pride and other kinds of intrinsic consequence patterns. At this point, he may balk, showing you that you are going too quickly.

The way to handle the strike is to attempt to bargain, negotiate, and maybe make compromises or concessions. But if you discover that he is being stubborn, let him go on strike. You can outlast him. At the reformatory I mentioned earlier, where the boys were taught under this type of a system, a number of boys did go on strike. During the strike period they were entitled only to sit on a bench and wait. They could not enter the lounge area at all. They discovered that being on strike was no fun and that there was no way to win the strike. The only way to solve it was to return to work. One boy lasted as long as three weeks before he finally returned to work.

It is unlikely that your child will go on strike for more than a few days if he experiences a total absence of any of the consequences in the catalog while he is striking. You have selected the most desirable things in his life and put them under contract and in the catalog. When he refuses to work or to accept a reasonable compromise, you have merely to wait. You cannot, of course, give him or allow him to get any of the items in that catalog except by using points to purchase them, no matter how much he pleads or how much he needs them.

I have seen some families where the teen-ager would go on strike and the parents would refuse him the use of the family car. Then the mother would need some shopping done or an errand completed and, without thinking, she would give the child the car to use in order to bring back things for her convenience. The child very rightfully began to use this as a wedge to break down the negotiations. I was able to point out, for example, that if he was given permission to drive, he was satisfying his desire to drive. He managed to take a little bit longer each time and drove around to see his friends or show off the car to his girl friend. He really didn't want the contract system. He felt that in the long run he could manipulate the guilt his mother felt for using him to drive the car as a trade-off against his getting the car to take his girl out. You can see that the parents' poor handling of the situation made the strike last longer and let it become more bitter in the long run than it need ever have been.

With young children it is easy to get them out of a strike by simply throwing the contract away and starting on an easier contract. Since you are working with simpler systems, you could say, "All right, if you don't want to be paid for making up your room with fifty points, I'll pay you two points to make your bed and that's all you have to do this week." The child usually says "Fine, I want three points." You negotiate and finally even give in. You give him three points for making his bed. If he stopped to think, of course, he would realize that three points for making his bed and three points for hanging up his clothes only comes to six points, whereas if he had taken the original contract, he would have gotten fifty points for much the same work. When he does realize it he will find it much easier to accept a total contract without the threat of strike.

Remember not to be afraid of strikes and not to become angry at the child. In this system he is *entitled* not to work. Many fathers become angry at children's strikes and wish to rush in and punish the child. They want to return to the old maxim of "Spare the rod and spoil the child." They completely misunderstand the underlying principle that is being implemented. That is why it is so important for *both* parents to become familiar with the basic principles and techniques. The strike is only a temporary lack of effort on the child's part. He should be treated as a human being with the right to refuse work. You should no longer try to intimidate him and threaten him with punishment. He should no longer be thought of as an indentured servant. He's entitled to the rights and privileges of free employment.

The system is extremely effective. Given enough time and patience, your child will give up striking. He can no longer be angry at being punished unfairly and being forced to do things. He has been given the choice. It's not a difficult choice to make, however. If you choose to work, you get all the things you want. If you choose not to work, nobody's mad at you, nobody punishes you, but you don't get anything at all or only the barest minimum that your biological needs require. There is no need to rush in with punishment. In that reformatory I mentioned earlier no form of punishment was used for not working. The only thing that happened was that the boys did not earn any points, and without points they could not engage in the activities they wanted.

THE LOCK-OUT ◇

One of the weapons a parent has as a negotiator, similar to that of the employer, is the *lock-out*. An employer can close his plant down if he wishes, temporarily or permanently. This is the largest gun in your battery of procedures. You can say to a child, "You have refused to cooperate. You have been difficult. You have been engaging in behaviors for which we not only do not pay you but which we don't wish to see appear at all. It is time that we have a temporary lock-out period."

The lock-out is really a time out. Its purpose is simply to decelerate a very strong action in the child that you find undesirable. It is your major weapon for discouraging behavior. During a lock-out period the only thing that happens is that no points can be earned. It may be for one day or two days. It should never go beyond three. If you lock a child out for a week you are, in effect, punishing him completely. If you lock him out for a short period of time—a morning, an afternoon, or a day—all you are doing is cutting down the number of points he can earn. But you are still leaving the possibility of his returning to work, putting in extra work, and regaining the position he had lost. This is very similar, then, to the time out I mentioned in an earlier chapter. It is a strong negative consequence that a parent may have to use occasionally.

INFLATION AND RECESSION ◇

There are other tools that a parent has available for solving additional problems. These relate to attempts to produce more or less work on a child's part. In a real economy prices sometimes spiral upward so rapidly that the cost of living far exceeds any ability of the person on salary to meet it. You should have a slight cost of living clause so that there is a tendency to increase wages each week in order to account for the needs of the child with respect to rising costs in the outside world. But you can generate your own internal *inflation* if you find you want to.

For example, if you notice that your child is overusing a

particular consequence you can raise the price of that consequence over a period of a few weeks to astronomical proportions. In one school the girls were spending most of the points they had accumulated on soda. The teachers discovered a rapid inflationary spiral with respect to the girl's weight. Rather than taking sodas completely out of the canteen, they decided to leave them in but to raise the price. As the price went up, fewer and fewer girls purchased the sodas, until finally they were buying very few of them. Their weight dropped, everyone was happy, and the staff was proud of the girls. I should point out that the shrewd buying pattern of these girls is strikingly interesting because the girls were severely retarded. They were able to show good judgment and not waste their money on the excessive cost of the soda.

It is possible, then, for you to discourage the overuse of certain kinds of consequences by increasing their cost. This is an artificial inflationary spiral and should be handled very, very carefully because if everything in the catalog becomes overpriced your child may well react like many people do and simply stop buying. When they stop buying altogether the points begin to lose their value. If your child can't or won't spend his points because things are too expensive, what good are the points? If he has to earn enormous numbers of points before he can live well, what good is working at all?

Very often parents reluctantly will agree to allow a child to wear his hair long or to go away for the weekend unsupervised. However, the price they place on these consequences is exorbitant. Nevertheless, most children will accept that. They recognize that the high price is more a measure of the parents' reluctance to place that kind of consequence in the catalog than of anything else. But at least it is now possible for them to obtain that consequence, whereas before it was almost impossible to obtain. They were forced to cut their hair. They were never allowed to go on trips. Even though it's extremely expensive, it can be seen as possible and may have a very important effect in getting the child to work harder.

Recessions, on the other hand, are situations where the pay drops. The wise parent may use a recession as a way of reestablishing a more realistic balance in the pay scale and in the whole structure of the home contract system. Your child may have manipulated successfully by the threat of a strike or through effective horse-trading procedures to a point where the whole balance is disrupted. You can adjust by closing down a task in one area so that no points can be obtained by that task any longer. You can suddenly and strikingly lower overall wages, only to raise them more slowly within the next few weeks to a level more meaningful, more balanced, and more acceptable to you.

There is a variety of ways to bring about readjustments. The recession cycle and the inflation cycle are examples of the kinds of radical change that a parent may make to meet certain kinds of conditions. The conditions you may have to attempt to correct are overpayment of wages to your child, which has occurred through your having been manipulated over a period of weeks, or the overuse of consequences that you consider undesirable or possibly even dangerous.

Remember that, as a parent, you never have to put anything in the catalog that you don't feel you wish to. However, it is also true that you may reluctantly have to come to terms with some consequences and put them in, you may not like them. The catalog system allows you to regulate their use by making them expensive and using them as added incentives to sweeten the pot and produce more effort on the part of the child.

COMPETITION ◇

Without realizing it many parents establish a system of *competition* between their children. This is very bad. The children then can use it for manipulation and will learn many bad habits. One child may begin to complain that his sister or brother is getting more than he is for the same task. The parent unknowingly begins to raise the ante in order to give each child an equal amount of points. This is very similar to giving all the children a present on one child's birthday or making sure that everything always comes out equal between them.

Children are not equal. People are not equal. The idea of equality in our society refers to equality of opportunity and equality of justice. It does not mean that people are truly the same. This idea has been misinterpreted many times in our culture, but most often in the home. Parents are subtly manipulated by children into trying to make everything come out even. A three-year-old child is not as capable of staying up late as is a ten-year-old child. All children should respect the right of one individual to succeed.

One of the ways in which you can end competition among the children in your family and teach cooperation and encouragement as well is to award bonus points to the complaining child for encouraging another child to win more task-points for himself. Thus the children are taught to encourage each other and to enjoy each other's success. You must plan for this as you would plan for any other behavior and you must teach it systematically. You can use bonus points along with your praise as the initial consequence pattern. Later you can wean the complaining child to pride and self-respect in sharing in another person's success.

The main point of the home contract system is that it is not a competition. If one child gets some points, it does not eliminate the possibility of another child's getting some points. They are not competing for the same pool of points and they are not competing with each other.

The problem of competition occurs in two ways. One is when your children are attempting to get paid the same amount for the same work or effort, and the other is when Johnny becomes fearful that another child's getting points somehow uses up the points available to him and may even reflect parental bias. You constantly must reassure all your children that there are plenty of points for everyone, that points are paid for the successful completion of tasks only, and that each child is paid on his own pay scale. You can point out that the president of a company is paid a different hourly rate than is the janitor, the technician, or the engineer. Everyone gets paid according to his ability and his level of competence, according to factors that have nothing to do with "equality." There is an equality of opportunity in the sense the janitor should be able to become the president of the company with sufficient added skills and diligence. This is what is really meant by equality, not that everyone has the same skills or the same level of wages.

The problem of competition needs to be worked out within the family. It means trying to determine who can do what, who should do what, and what the pay scale is to be. If Johnny takes out the garbage he may receive ten points. When Billy takes out the garbage, he may get twenty-five points. When Tommy takes it out he may only get five. Why the different pay scales? Because of other factors, such as the amount of difficulty for each child in accomplishing that task and the desirability of the task itself for each child. You may prefer that Billy take out the garbage rather than Tommy or Johnny. So you offer the greatest incentive to Billy and the lowest incentive to Tommy. This means that Tom will most likely seek to earn his points by doing other kinds of chores, whereas Billy will gravitate toward taking out the garbage, the job you really prefer him to do.

It is possible by this differential pay system to so regulate the chores that each child is doing the chore most suited to him. Competition, of course, has many different characteristics and you can be sure that it will show up. But it can be handled. All that is required is that you think through what it is you want them to do instead of quarreling or competing.

80-20 VARIATIONS ⌒

When I established the relationship of 80 percent of all points being paid for tasks and 20 percent being paid as bonuses, I was arbitrarily suggesting a relationship that I have found to work fairly successfully for most situations. When I chose the 80-20 relationship for catalog prices—that is, 80 percent of wages were needed for minor items, leaving 20 percent of wages for major items—I was again picking an arbitrary division that seems to work best for most families.

The child, of course, has more of an option within the catalog end of the system because he can choose to put all of his money into future major items or spend all of his money on the daily items. Some parents may feel that 20 percent savings per week is too high and they may change the relationship. Others may feel it is too low and may encourage their child to save more by paying higher interest rates. They feel he should be taught to save for the future. As I will discuss later, the interest rates can be raised or dropped.

There are several reasons for raising the task and bonus percentages. Some parents may feel that they wish to provide more bonuses than task-oriented points because they want a more flexible system. They arrange it so about 50 percent of their child's income can be earned by tasks and the other 50 percent can be given as bonuses when they notice appropriate behaviors. In some ways the decision to be flexible and spontaneous is desirable, but what happens from the child's point of view is that the world becomes less certain and less predictable. Mother may find herself falling behind in giving points as bonuses and then rush to catch up. She may end up overpaying for a particular activity and then the whole system becomes unworkable. In most cases it is better to stick to the major share of points being earned by specific predetermined tasks set up at the weekly negotiation sessions and keep the giving of bonuses as a minor part of the over-all system.

With younger children it is more advisable to use a bonus system only. In our home we go from bonus to task-oriented point systems and back again. Sometimes we have them going simultaneously, but our children are young. With older children I much prefer to keep the 80-20 ratio since it seems to work more effectively. The older a child, the more capable he becomes of accomodating to the actual economy of our society, and for this purpose the 80-20 relationship offers better training. In his actual work career in the future the relationship between bonuses and task-oriented earnings is slightly different, probably closer to 95 percent to 5 percent. Employers are loathe to give 20 percent of a person's salary in bonus form, although some companies, calling it commission, in fact do.

MISERS AND SPENDTHRIFTS ∾

There are too few adults who can handle their money adequately. It is not surprising that two of the very frequent problems you encounter in the home contract system used with children are *overspending* and *underspending*. Either extreme can cause you troubles.

If Johnny overspends he is constantly short of points later in the week. He may become disgruntled or plead for a loan. He may take on "short-term" projects that you allow him as a way of earning more points. At first this can be a good solution. But he may make a way of life out of it so that he has very subtly increased his wages and learned to depend on windfalls to balance his insatiable budget.

The best solution for the spendthrift is to shape saving behavior. You can do this in two ways. One is to give him bonus points every time he puts points into a savings book or savings certificate. He can spend the bonus points immediately. The other is to pay a much higher interest rate than normally and increase the desirable major items in the catalog.

On the other hand, some children save their points and spend very little each week. Sometimes they aren't even saving for a major item; they're just saving. For the points to continue to have value it is essential that they be exchanged periodically for more tangible positive consequences. In addition, a compulsive saver may accumulate so many points that he retires and you suddenly find yourself unable to motivate him. Either way you are in trouble. You must force him to reduce his total balance in order to keep him lean and hungry.

There are two ways to do this. One is to increase the number of desirable items in the catalog. Perhaps you did not choose wisely initially. Find out what he is spending his time at and charge him for it. At the reformitory I mentioned earlier they charged the boys for homework, more difficult work, and study time. Use your imagination and your powers of observation. The other approach is to encourage him to put his money in a savings certificate which ties up his points for six months but pays a very high interest rate.

You can also cut savings by using an inflationary technique I call negative interest. For every four points he has in his bank or savings book at the end of a month, give him three back. Explain that in inflation money loses its value unless it is in a certificate which earns money faster than inflation decreases it. Use this technique very sparingly and only when all else fails. Be prepared for a strike.

LOOPHOLE PLUGGING ～

Resign yourself. *Loopholes* will happen. There is no way on earth that I know of for the child not to win in his bargaining with the parent many more times than the parent wins. For example, when you have set up a group of tasks in which hard tasks pay a great deal and simple tasks pay very little, he will quickly do the very simple tasks over and over, thereby earning as many points as if he did one of the very hard, undesirable tasks. You will realize at the end of the week that the hard task you are trying to get him to do has simply not been done, but he has still earned plenty of points by doing simple things repeatedly.

If necessary, you can change his contract so that only by doing the unwanted task can he earn points. You can prompt him into beginning one of the hard tasks and reward him with bonuses for doing any part of it at all. You can change the values of the tasks until you reach the critical point where he will seek out the harder tasks because that is the only way he can earn the total number of points that he needs.

Whatever you choose to do to plug this kind of loophole, be sure that the total number of points he can earn by tasks each week remains constant. Don't force him into lowered wages by removing tasks without compensating by increasing the number of points paid for performing other tasks.

Sometimes loopholes will occur when you have not clearly specified the task. You may pay for a "neat" room. His idea of neat and yours will probably be worlds apart. If he finds a loophole here, he may end up doing a very perfunctory job and demand payment in full. Next week write a better contract. Be more concrete as to how you want the job done. But this week you will have to pay him in full.

I cannot anticipate all the loopholes your Johnny will find. Just keep revising and improving the original contract. You can try giving bonuses for his not using the loopholes he finds, but in the final analysis, he will still increase your supply of your gray hair. Be a good sport and remember that you can always use shaping to bring him to a better level of performance.

DOWNWARD SPIRALS ∽

A very common problem is that of the *downward spiral,* the gradual deterioration in a child's performance of tasks. For many reasons his work may start to slip and he will fail to earn his usual amount of points one day. If he is ill his performance may be even worse. The trend may continue, gradually gathering steam until the child is no longer doing any work at all or the work output is so poor in quality that he might as well not be doing it at all.

In spite of how bad it looks, this is not a serious problem. Trained parents are not upset by this happening. In fact, they expect it to happen periodically. When it does happen they are prepared to adjust the contract system to take it into account.

This is done in the following way. The ratio of 80-20 percent requires that you give at least 20 percent bonus points. When a downward trend occurs and a reverse spiral is recognized, quietly increase the rate and percentage of bonus giving. Instead of giving 20 percent bonuses over the course of a week on a kind of random, sporadic basis, make an intense effort each day to make up in bonus points what your child has lost in task points.

Johnny has contracted for one hour of study each night. You notice that he has put in only fifteen minutes of study time and hardly completed his homework. You cannot under any circumstances give him task-oriented points. You can, however, say, "I notice that you are tired and you really made some effort. I appreciate that so I'm going to give you five bonus points." They go in the bonus column, not in the deposit column, clearly indicating for the child and for you that the five points have been earned as a bonus because you noticed him doing something appropriate.

Then watch for any activities that he does that indicate a positive direction, his first approximation of a possible reversal upward. You notice, for example, that he did not yell at his sister, even though he's down in the mouth. Give him some bonus points for that. He did put his dishes in the sink, very badly of course, but they are there. Give him some bonuses for that. By the end of the day, if you are working diligently at your task, the total number of points earned by Johnny should be roughly equivalent to the points he would have earned by a day of hard work.

If on the next day he is not back to his usual rate of work, continue giving bonus points and shaping him back to a high rate of work. Within a day or two he'll be back to his old self again and you will have avoided magnifying the downward trend. This downward spiral occurs occasionally in every point system.

SATIATION EFFECTS ∽

Downward spirals can begin because a child grows tired of the consequences available in his catalog, a satiation effect. It is necessary to find new and effective consequences periodically. If this is done, the satiation can be overcome. Sometimes a child will not value an object in the catalog until a sister or brother decides that they would like to have it. Do not expect there to be any magic in the incentives you chose originally or that the child told you he wanted. He may tell you to put something in the catalog because he thinks he wants it. But if you notice that he never spends any points on it, he really doesn't want it. It is having no effect on his behavior. If necessary, change the catalog frequently. Don't be afraid to try out new items. If they don't tempt Johnny, you can always remove them. Be prepared to watch for satiation effects. It is important to recognize that you can have too many consequences or too few consequences in the catalog itself. Just keep your eye on the withdrawal column and judge accordingly.

CREDIT ∽

Nowhere in the home contract system do I provide for *credit*. Children will plead passionately for an "advance" on their future point balance. They will pay you back when they get the points. How many times have parents heard that plea? "I'll pay back the money from my allowance next Friday." Next Friday never comes. It doesn't come for most adults, either. I know few adults who can handle credit very well. Credit is still too new in our culture for people to have developed effective skills. We are still floundering. Although we are becoming a credit economy, we really don't know how to use it very well yet.

Don't impose this difficult system on children, for it requires great maturity and self-control and the ability to see far ahead in terms of planning your behavior. It is beyond most children's ability level. You are much wiser to refuse any plea for credit. Under no conditions can your child borrow points. No matter how high you set the interest rate to try to discourage borrowing, children who are desperate will pay any amount. The best rule is no credit at all.

However, there will be occasions on which you will want Johnny to have those extra points. A sudden opportunity to make a good buy, go on a trip, or see a television special will all occur at one time or another when Johnny has too few points. But don't loan him any! You can set a special project up by which he can *earn* the extra points *before* he gets them. In this way you can be flexible, even generous, without teaching him any bad habits.

CANTEEN TIME ∽

I borrowed the *canteen time* idea from a hospital I visited once. They had solved the problem of children constantly wanting to exchange their points by limiting exchanges only to the times when the "canteen" was open.

Johnny may want to pay points to use the family car just on the night you were planning to go out. He needs to buy some money (by point exchange) from the catalog, right now. One solution is to make the catalog available for purchase only at predetermined times. The car and similar family-use items are available for rental only during certain hours. Majority rules on the program to be watched on television; points only buy a child the privilege of watching. Try as much as you can to accommodate him, but not at the cost of killing yourself.

Sometimes, when a child wants to purchase a trip within the catalog, Mommy must go with him on the trip. But what of the other children? She can't leave them alone. She may have to pay for a baby-sitter. If Daddy is not home to watch the children, she can charge extra points for going on the trip, thereby teaching her child a more realistic view of her problems in providing consequences. When you offer an item in the catalog you must take into account as to how practical it is to deliver it. If it is not practical to control and deliver, then it should not be in the system. But I have found by working with families that with a little bit of effort most families can control most consequences in a young child's life.

PLANNED CONVERSION ∾

Planned conversion is a way of helping the wary child to accept the home contract system. Sometimes even preparing him in advance doesn't help. You almost can tell what the previous relationship between a parent and child was by seeing how much faith the child has in the parent when they begin this new system. If the child is extremely leery of it, you can bet the parents have been inconsistent, threatening, or overindulgent. If a child thoughtfully accepts the system and tries it, you can almost bet that there has been a very good relationship in the past, although there may have been a certain amount of mismanagement through sloppy contract systems.

All children can be helped to accept good management. You can, for example, leave everything as is at first. Let him have his allowance for doing nothing. The next step is to offer him additional incentives. Put another twenty-five cents that he can earn over and above his allowance into the catalog. Make it very easy for him to earn it. Convince him that he can win. Set the task contract very low. Use bonuses very profusely. The child who does not value anything, as a way of controlling his parents, can be swamped with points and things given to him in exchange for the points so that he gradually reacquires a taste and an interest in life. He can find security in the fact that his own efforts are producing this and that his parents are no longer going to control him by withholding, but by creating, incentives. He then can return to desiring things.

You can make the shift to the home contract system gradual by allowing a period of time to work out the contracts, the tasks, and the catalogs so that each child participates in the process. Don't rush into it. You've spent a lot of time developing bad habits in the children; spend a little time in making the transition.

Parents frequently ask me if I approve of allowances. My answer is that I approve of them only if there is an unstated contract system in the home that is working successfully. Then the allowance is part of that system. Most often, however, it is not. It is simply given by the parents with no firm tasks requirements for the child. The parents believe in the philosophy that a child is "entitled" and they give it on that basis alone. This type of allowance-giving I am very much against, because it is destructive of the child. It teaches dependency, manipulation, and other bad habits. Unfortunately, most allowances are given routinely because it is the child's due.

LONG-DISTANCE MANAGEMENT ✷

Very often a parent is required to control her child at long-distance. The schools expect, for example, that the parent will turn over a well-behaved child with all the necessary prerequisite skills to fit into the classroom system. Baby-sitters expect that Mommy's influence over Johnny will continue even after she has gone out. The playground holds the parents responsible for how Johnny behaves.

Whether you should be held accountable for someone else's mismanagement or not is beside the point. You have responsibility for Johnny's actions at all times. But exercising long-distance control is not as hard to do as it seems. The only difficult part of it is getting accurate feedback as to whether Johnny is meeting the requirements set forth in his special contract.

Have the baby-sitter check off on a form how Johnny behaved in her care. Persuade Johnny's teacher to check "yes" or "no" on a short series of questions (no more than four) about his *daily* performances. You can collect the forms daily or weekly by having the counselor or teacher mail them to you in self-addressed, stamped envelopes. These forms become the record system which allows you to give Johnny points.

There are many ways to solve the problem of accurate reporting of Johnny's behavior. Once you have that, all you have to do is set up a contract, arrange for adequate positive consequences, and pray.

THE FEDERAL MEDIATOR ✷

Occasionally there are apparently irreconcilable differences. Usually they are over the kinds of tasks the child is to perform, how fair they are, and the number of points being paid. Sometimes the differences center around the high cost of living with respect to the prices you are charging for things in the catalog. Sometimes they are over what you are willing to put in the catalog. There is a great deal of difference in the perspective of children and adults as to what is best for the child. Children increasingly are demanding more and more say in how they will wear their hair, what clothes they will wear, what friends they will choose, and so on. When it becomes impossible to resolve these differences within the family, it is usually wise to consider consulting a *federal mediator.*

A federal mediator is simply someone whom both you and your child trust to be fair. It can be a family friend, minister, relative, or a professional family counselor. Both of you must agree in advance to accept any solution he offers to the dispute. I have served in this role many times and I have found that on the whole the difficulties are caused equally by both parties. Parents can be as emotional and arbitrary in their demands as can children.

BRIBERY, BIRTHDAYS, AND MOONLIGHTING ∽

By the time you are deeply involved in this system you probably will not be engaging in acts of bribery; however, someone else may be. Grandparents often give children money to be "good." Their bribe, of course, is in the form of another point system, usually the dollar bill. They will offer the child money, thereby violating the home contract system without even realizing that they are subverting it. By their giving the child money they are increasing his buying potential outside of the home in such a way as to defeat the tight control that the system provides for the parents.

Watch out for signs that the child is obtaining items outside of your system. Whenever this happens there is the danger of the system's breaking down. The child who is earning money by cutting grass or running errands is violating your system. He is engaging in illegal behavior that is not encompassed within the system. The people who are paying him to do this are not aware that they are subverting him. They are probably doing it for the best of intentions. The child also may not be aware of the ultimate effect. The effect it will have is that he will cease to work as hard for the points at home as for the dollar bills outside, because he will discover that he can buy most of the items in your catalog with hard American cash. The only thing he needs the points for are the privileges that you provide. Ideally, the child should not earn more money or even receive gifts outside of this system. I am aware that at Christmas time and birthdays he undoubtedly will get gifts, and you probably wouldn't want to put a stop to this even if you could. Therefore, it is likely that for a brief period of time after the holiday or birthday the child's work will slack off.

One of the things you can do, of course, is to use a savings certificate with high interest rate plus a great deal of bonus points to tie up that money immediately. In some situations you can arrange for double earnings as a way of encompassing the outside earnings within the contract system. That is, every dollar the child earns goes into his contract system. It is put immediately into the catalog. You add an additional 10, 15 or 25 percent to that dollar so that every dollar earned outside immediately was worth up to $1.25 in the catalog. He then has to use his points to get that money out. The inducement for him to earn it twice is the increased amount of money that is available to him because of his father's immediate interest payment.

Not all children will accept this. Some will refuse it on the grounds that it is their money and they wish to spend it. In some cases you simply may have to wait them out, encouraging them to spend it or tie it up by the purchase of stocks. If there is a steady rate of gift-giving by a grandparent, or an outside source of income, then it must be encompassed within the system in some way in order to avoid letting it subvert the system. Try to build ways for putting outside pay or gifts within the system. For example, if your child has a part-time job and he gets all of his money through that job, that becomes his source of cash. However, all his privileges come through the catalog itself, so that now he needs the points for privileges and the cash for outside buying power. Some families have compromised in that way. Some have used the dual system of earnings that I mentioned earlier. There are a variety of ways in which you can solve this problem for yourself.

OVERTIME ∾

Sometimes it is desirable to teach a child to engage in longer tasks or to engage in work during what would ordinarily be playtime. In order to accomplish this you need to create an extra incentive. The method is analogous to the payment of *overtime* wages. The child is paid time-and-a-half for overtime work.

You can greatly influence when the child works and when he plays by using the catalog alone. You can, for example, charge more for watching television during the week than for watching it on weekends. You can thereby shift his pattern to television watching on the weekends rather than during the week because it is too expensive. You then encourage him to use that time for study by paying more points for weekday study than for weekend study.

You can regulate his bedtime and his worktime by charging him three, four, or five times as much to stay up a half-hour later during the week as on weekends. It is also possible to pay him time-and-a-half or double time for work during periods when he would ordinarily be playing. A variety of possibilities lend themselves to the family to meet the problem of helping the child to organize his worktime and his own schedule in the most productive way.

"DADDY" POINTS ∾

Occasionally you need a separate source of points to meet a special problem. For example, if you discover that the kids are suddenly starting to fight or showing an unusual increase in poor social skills, it may become desirable to focus on this problem apart from the rest of the contract system. In our home we keep a special bonus point system called *"Daddy" points* for just such emergencies. "Daddy" points are exchangeable for special treats and privileges that only Daddy can provide by himself, such as going fishing with Daddy, going with him when he makes a trip, a special visit to the candy store with just Daddy, and so on. There are consequences that are not in the catalog. The points that are given are kept on a separate record. They are one-time points and they are given for a special purpose. The idea is to focus on specific problems, using a very powerful consequence for most children.

In my home "Daddy" points are valuable because Daddy does interesting things and it's fun to be with him. If Daddy is kind of dull and very uninteresting and doesn't really want to do very much except go to some dull museum, the children may not find this a very special or important type of consequence. In that case it might be wiser to pick a special event coming up and use the points for that. These *"event" points* are not exchangeable for anything but that one specific treat. This is what makes them different and unique from the usual bonus points.

Special types of bonus points are a good way of dealing with a specific problem that has arisen and needs to be dealt with quickly before the next negotiation session. These are usually set up in midweek when the emergency arises and the problem must be handled quickly, but actually they can be established at any time. Just remember to use this technique sparingly since it is dependent on the strength of the consequence. Too much exposure can bring satiation, with the children getting tired of Daddy or "special" events.

"SEWER CLEANING" ∾

"Sewer cleaning" is a special technique that allows the system to bend slightly. The home contract system makes no provisions for certain kinds of emergencies. These emergencies can arise either at the very beginning of the establishment of the system or periodically throughout its use. There are times when your child suddenly needs a large number of points for a special occasion, such as a trip, staying overnight with a friend, going to the school dance, or the sudden use of the car when it was not anticipated. If your child hasn't been able to earn the necessary points in advance, these situations tend to bring up suggestions about credit. Earlier I said credit was never to be allowed. So how is the child to go? The answer is that he can be given a "sewer cleaning" project. This is a single task at which he can earn a large number of points in order to have enough for the emergency that has arisen. But it is a most undesirable task. It is the toughest one you can think of that your child can do. If he had the time, he would much prefer to perform his regular contract tasks to get the points than to do this. However, this one-shot task makes it possible to earn points rapidly. Suppose you've started the system today and then find out the school dance is this weekend. What do you do now? He can't possibly earn enough points by the weekend to go to the school dance. Give him a "sewer cleaning" project that he can do in addition to his regular tasks to earn himself enough points by the end of the week. It will be very generous pay since it is a very undesirable task, such as cleaning out the garage, the basement, or the attic. In any event, it is a one-time thing and it is at your discretion that it is offered. Ideally, you should start the system after the dance, but sometimes you have already begun it. In my experience, most children do not object to putting forth effort to go to the dance since, in the past, going or not going to the dance was subject to the whim of their parents rather than their own efforts.

You may find that these emergencies begin to happen every few weeks. Johnny is not saving points sufficiently in advance and is always looking for a "sewer cleaning" project to pull him out of the point shortage. When you notice this happening, you simply refuse to give any more "sewer cleaning" projects in order to help him out. Inform him that he's been abusing the privilege and that it has always been your option to provide these special projects and you do not intend to do it on this occasion. This time he will fail to go to the dance or to have the use of the car. It only takes one or two of these refusals to assure your child that you mean business and that while you are willing to help him, you are not willing to be manipulated. You can thereby teach your child not to abuse such a privilege and not to rely on it to get him out of a jam. It is simply there as a way of helping him whenever you feel it is appropriate to do so.

THE MIDNIGHT RAIDER ⌒

Many families have children who are ingenious in obtaining goodies without working for them. They're the ones who sneak down at midnight, get into the cookie jar, and eat their fill. Cookies offered in a catalog or on a menu have very little appeal for such bandits since they can get them on their own. Older children may have their own sets of keys to the family car without your knowledge. They use them whenever they desire and pay little attention to the catalog system.

When this happens I can only say that if you cannot control the consequences there is no way to control your child. If your child is able to get what he wants by stealing or by manipulating, he may take that route. It seems much easier to steal than to gain things by honest effort, particularly if you have not taught him the value of self-consequences for honest behavior.

In many cases a child of eighteen or even sixteen discovers that he has the option of your home contract system or the real world contract system. He may decide to go out and earn his own money and thumb his nose at your system. He can buy whatever he wants and can even establish his own residence. Once this happens, of course, there is no way that you can control him.

The only way I know of to have any influence over people at all is to control the things that they either want or don't want. If you do not serve as the prime controller or the prime source of these consequences, you will have very little influence over your child. You might as well stop wasting your breath and you can even give up being frustrated, for there is absolutely no hope of success.

Younger children, of course, do not have the option of going out into the real world contract system and have to remain entirely under the home contract system. However, if they discover that they can obtain consequences without you, they will probably do so. My advice is to lock up the cookie jar and find some way of keeping them in their room at night. I know one mother who put a special lock on the outside of her child's door where he could not reach it, so there was no way for him to get out of his room to raid the cookie jar.

I would also suggest that if you have a "midnight raider," give him bonuses and a great deal of training and encouragement in not raiding the cookie jar as a way of solving the problem. Show him that by honest effort he can get more than by stealing (without the anxieties involved in stealing). If he enjoys the act of stealing because it is getting you angry, then you had better ask yourself why you are making your child want to make you angry. Perhaps you have been punishing him too much without realizing it or being more unfair than you realized. This is his way of getting even with you. The best way to stop his stealing, then, is to stop his anger by becoming more fair and more positive. If it is simply more convenient for him to steal, you can make it less convenient. If it is a case of his not having learned to value honesty, then you must teach him the value of honesty.

You must have complete control of the consequences and keep them under your control so that they can be obtained only by the points. Remember that no matter how angry you are at him, no matter what he just did, if he has the points and it is canteen time, you must let him use them to purchase what he wishes from the catalog. You cannot arbitrarily close the canteen in a fit of anger and expect the system to work. You may call a lock-out—that is your prerogative. You may make the canteen time very incon-venient—that is also your prerogative. But if you want the system to work, you must make the consequences available; you cannot withhold them to satisfy your own anger.

One mother reported to me that she had put cookies and milk into the catalog but her child was not spending any points for them. I told here to investigate and she came back red-faced the next week to report that her daughter had developed a very effective style of ringing doorbells, pleading poverty, and having all the neighbors feed her cookies, ice cream, and treats. It took a few phone calls on the part of the mother to solve the problem. Thereafter when the little girl rang doorbells she was met with a deaf ear. The only way she could get a treat was to return home and earn it. At first earning it was made so easy that she preferred to earn it rather than to go out and ring doorbells which produced no reaction. Later on, the mother increased the task level that was required of the child and brought her back into the system without any trauma.

WITHERING AWAY ∽

A formal home contract system is a teaching device for both the parents and the children. Each step in it and each of the tools used is designed to help the parents and the children to graduate eventually to an unstated contract system, with only the occasional use of bonus points. Ultimately, what should develop is that your family operates as though there were a formal contract system. I hope that your formal system will wither away. For some families it may never wither away. Some people wear corrective glasses only for a time and eventually they are able to throw them away; others go on wearing glasses for the rest of their lives. If you need a formal system, continue to use it. Don't give it up suddenly because you've grown tired of it. You may have to use it for a lifetime. The essential thing to remember is that it is a tool to aid you in the management of your children. It is a prosthetic device.

Remember also that there is no magic in the management of children, that simply because you have trained good behavior in your children today, it doesn't mean your job is done. If you want a well-run home with well-managed children, who are friendly, warm, assertive, and spontaneous and have all the traits and qualities that you strive for, you must continue to provide good management. This does not happen by magically changing your child in some way so that thereafter he is a good child. In order to have this kind of child you must work at it continuously. The process is endless, and yet it is extremely rewarding. There is a great deal of pleasure and warmth and love in a home that is well managed.

A formal contract system is one way of getting there. It is a way of learning automatically to give clear signals, always to be looking for ways to prompt behavior rather than to fill vacuums. It is a constant awareness of what children want, what is meaningful to them, and how you can arrange for them to have it. It is a way of looking at a problem and analyzing it so that you can solve it by a systematic step-by-step method. It's a way of setting goals that are realistic. It's a way of life.

The formal home contract system is simply a method of bringing you to the point where you automatically see the world in such terms as will make you recognize that nothing is gotten for nothing, that people should only get what they earn by their own efforts. Don't treat your child as a second-class citizen, as someone you can order around or use for your own convenience. Why not see your child as simply a temporarily less competent human being, a temporarily less effective student in the process of maturing and growing and passing through life?

15 🕸
Mistakes I
H ave Made

When I first suggested to a colleague of mine that parents needed training in methods of child management and in obtaining more effective obedience from their children, she was horrified. She said, "How can you put such a potent technique in the hands of the average parent? Parents can't be trusted. I have seen too many parents out to control their children and make them puppets. If you give them more effective techniques for doing so, you will be greatly damaging children. It is unethical to teach parents how to handle their children more effectively without first spending a great deal of time with the parents evaluating whether they can be trusted or not and whether their goals are appropriate or not." This attitude is still present among many professionals. Their fear seems to be that some parents are angry with their children and are frequently critical, nagging, and hostile. These professionals believe if you give these parents effective techniques of child management, they will use them to abuse the children still further.

This has not been my experience. Over the years I have found just the opposite to be true. Parents are angry, hostile, critical, and nagging because their children are disobedient and they are unable to manage them effectively. Once they are able to bring them under reasonable control, they begin to lower their expectations and the relationship among the members of the family becomes one of love, warmth, and mutual respect.

Why is this so? How does the miracle occur? The very nature of the management system we have been discussing in this book brings it about. To get the kind of control the parent wants of the child, the child must be involved in the process. The child must be treated as a human being. The management control system is effective. It brings the child to a point where he wants to obey and does. Once Johnny is obeying, Mommy and Daddy can relax. They are no longer as frustrated. They cease feeling and expressing a great deal of their original anger. They have time now to be nicer to Johnny and to notice him as an individual. They have to be nicer and more attentive to what *he* wants in order to bring about his obedience. Parents who use this system tend to lower their excessively high standards for children. Once they have objectified the standards they simply reevaluate them.

The children will now conform much more. Is this necessarily bad for a child? The conformity was not forced and the child always has the option of changing and of developing an additional set of values and skills as he gets older and able to handle it. As a matter of fact, what I find is that more and more parents using the home contract system are beginning to redefine conformity. The children can relax because now they know what to expect and how to earn what they want. Parents can relax because they don't have to hound their children constantly or feel the guilt that comes from yelling at them and punishing them. What many of my colleagues fail to realize is that parents are already controlling their children and are required by society to do so. All that I am trying to do is to give them a method for doing so which has no punishment in it. There is no way that you can hurt a child using this home contract system. The only way that you could hurt him would be to misuse or abuse it, and then you would be slipping into other kinds of systems which are the real source of abuse of children.

My answer to my colleague at that time was blunt. "It would be unethical *not* to teach this management system to parents, to withhold it from them, when this is the very thing for which they consult us. What right have we as professionals to say to a parent, 'You cannot set those goals for your child because I don't approve of them'? We may suggest and we may advise, but in the final analysis it is the parents whom society trusts with that decision. Children are too important to our society for it to allow parents to abdicate that responsibility. I think it is the role of the professional to provide the parent with management skills, to guide the parents, to coach them, to train them, but not to "treat" them.

Fortunately, most modern professionals would agree with me. There are some children who need such precise control systems that a controlled environment such as a school, hospital, or some other kind of institution may be called for. Here professional management of the child is quite necessary and appropriate. The majority of children, however, can function under effective home management and care.

I have found, of course, that parents do make many common mistakes. I would like to discuss these with you now in order to help you to avoid them or correct them. I do not hold you to an absolute standard of perfection; I would not even expect that you will be as competent in this type of management as a highly trained professional. Set yourself an error standard. You are entitled to "goof" at least 20 percent of the time.

If you reach this goal you will be behaving correctly toward your child the overwhelming majority of the time. You can repair mistakes. If you yell at your child, apologize. Instruct him in the future never to obey you when you yell because you don't wish to become a yeller. But also instruct him to obey as soon as you stop yelling. We do this with our children and it works. I know that yelling at my children will have very little effect, but as soon as I stop yelling they will obey. This helps to correct in advance the mistakes that most of us make because we are fallible human beings. Our own emotions sometime get away from us and we should allow for it occasionally.

Now let's discuss the most common kinds of mistakes that are made in using the home contract system.

GIVING UP TOO SOON ⌒

It is foolish to persist in a technique or procedure that is not working. It is just as foolish to give up too soon. A reasonable period of time is necessary to check out the procedure. I've seen parents who set a contract and then gave up the system entirely as soon as the child failed the first contract. They did not even bother to check to see why the contract had failed and they made no attempt to adjust it.

I have met other parents who, like grasshoppers, have gone from one technique to another, never stopping at one long enough to give it a chance to work. They are absolutely convinced that nothing will work with their child. They are amazed when I use one of their old techniques for just a little bit longer than they did and it works.

Patience is a virtue. It comes from knowing that the results you expect will occur. Often I am asked by teachers where I get my patience in working with school children. My answer is, "I don't have all that much patience. I just have confidence that this technique will work if I persist at it. I know the technique, I know the situation, and I know that it takes time. If I'm simply persistent, eventually I must change the child's behavior."

On the other hand, I am aware that sometimes I don't have absolute knowledge as to whether my technique will work or not and I'm merely giving it a trial. Under these conditions, I give a reasonable amount of time to the procedures that I'm using. I select an amount of time that I think should be fair. It is certainly not a half-hour or a single day. It may be three, four, or five days; sometimes a whole week, sometimes three or four weeks, depending on how often the behavior in question occurs. If it is a very frequent behavior, then I expect to see change very quickly.

For example, if a child is saying "you know" very often, my reply of "no I don't" should begin to change the behavior within the first hour. If I see it is not having an effect, then I know that I'm using the wrong technique for this child. On the other hand, if the child is late to school once a month, I must be prepared to give a full year to my procedure before I'm sure if it is correct or not as there will be only 12 trials in an entire year.

The amount of time you give for a behavior to change will depend on how frequently it occurs and how certain you are of your procedure. Don't make the common mistake of giving up too soon. Give the procedure a fair trail.

ASKING TOO MUCH ∽

Sometimes parents seem to have enormous certainty in areas in which I have the least amount of certainty. I am never sure what a given child can do. Yet I hear many parents, with absolute certainty, telling me "He can do that" or "He should be able to do that" or "He ought to be able to do that." They set the standard at a level which they think the child can achieve. Then they persist in holding the standard at that level in the face of the obvious fact that he is not achieving it and that he cannot. They insist over and over again "He could do it if he would only try harder." Frankly, I don't have that much confidence in my ability to judge what a child can or should do. I set a goal and a level of success for the first contract. Then I try it out. I use a trial-and-error procedure. If he does not do it, then either I set the standard too high or I used too weak a positive consequence. I always hold myself accountable for the child's failure to achieve the standard I have set. I always let the child determine what he can do. I avoid playing God and insisting that he should be able to do it.

This tendency to ask too much of a child is a very frequent problem with parents. They may be comparing the child to a neighbor's child, to an older child of their own, or to some idealized standard of the normal child. One of the biggest mistakes we have ever made in my field was to publish tables of norms of what the average child can do. I never met that mythical average child. Did you? Children differ in capabilities and developmental rates over a wide range.

I think it is best to let the children determine what they can do at any given point. Don't be afraid to discard an old contract and set a new one with a lower standard. But with each new contract, you should be working to increase the level of competence of your child. You should be helping him to improve his performance gradually. You should be realistic and let your child determine what he can do and how fast he can improve. Stop asking too much.

REVERTING TO OLD METHODS ◇

Let me warn you that there is a great temptation to revert to your old methods of handling Johnny. You have built up many habits over the years and they are strong. You are teaching yourself a new system. You may not even approve of all of the reasons for the new system. Many people still hang onto old moralistic concepts and theories about children and the ways of managing them. They do not like the idea of changing these theories and doing so is difficult for them. They are forced to use the home contract method because the method works, but as soon as the method appears unnecessary they will try to swing back to the old theories and the old methods. The effects can be devastating. Johnny may revert back to his old behaviors also, since he may not as yet have developed his own consequences for the new action pattern.

You should have positive reasons for using the methods I have been describing and you should spend time in thinking through why you are converting to the new system. It should not be simply to stop Johnny's bad behavior or to promote good behavior. It should be because you recognize that it is the natural system of life. Not only does it work, but it is the easiest method to use in the long run, once you have become practiced at it. Most importantly, it is the most humane system of all.

If you use the contract method for these reasons you will probably stay with it and not revert. Occasionally you still will slip into old habits, and when you do you will find that Johnny, too, will tend to slip backward, for his behavior is a function of how you are managing him.

When that happens I don't want you to feel guilty. I am against guilt as a method of controlling people. Guilt, like punishment, contains two parts. One part is the negative feedback that tells you that you are behaving inappropriately or incorrectly, and the other part is the fear of punishment. I am suggesting to you that you should have no fear of punishment, but you should welcome the negative feedback, since it is useful to you and can help you to change back to the new methods.

Be aware that if Johnny misbehaves, you have mismanaged him. Regardless of what triggered the behavior, it is your job to get him back to appropriate behavior as quickly as possible. It is also your job to try to arrange the system of management so that he seldom slips into bad behavior.

Of course you are not perfect, just as Johnny is not perfect. You will "goof." As I said, you are entitled to "goof" 20 percent of the time. Don't punish yourself when you do goof; accept the negative feedback but reject the fear of punishment. Reexamine what you have done. Set a new contract. Try another method. Teach your husband or your wife not to criticize, attack, or in any way attempt to punish you. Encourage your spouse, however, to give you the feedback in the most meaningful way possible without attacking you. In this way you will do much to avoid the natural tendency to revert and Johnny will continue to want to obey.

CHOOSING THE WRONG INCENTIVES ∾

Often parents believe that what they wanted as children, their children want today, or what they think is a pretty toy is what the child wants. How often have you had the experience of lovingly wrapping a beautiful toy in an old box, then giving a young child the gift-wrapped toy, only to find that he discards the toy and the wrapping and spends the rest of the day playing with the box? You chose the wrong incentive. The child will always tell you what he really wants out of life. He will tell you by what he spends the most time with, by what he chooses out of the catalog, by what he asks you to do.

You cannot choose an appropriate incentive for a child unless you know him well and unless he has demonstrated a history of continuous interest in something as a positive consequence. He still may lose interest in that positive consequence if he becomes satiated or develop other interests. Either way, a common mistake made by many parents is to insist on offering the old positive consequence as an incentive. They are reluctant to change the catalog. They are reluctant to offer the child what he wants.

Your child may want to play the guitar, but you want him to play the piano. Guess what kind of lessons your child may wind up being forced to take? Then you wonder why you can't use piano playing as an incentive to get him to work harder. Try him on guitar playing and see how fast you're able to change his behavior using that as a positive consequence.

Many a parent thinks that a child ought to go to college and develop the kind of professional career that the parent either had or wanted to have. But the child wants a completely different goal in life. Offering him an opportunity to go to school, then, will probably not be a very effective incentive. Over and over again parents impose their desires upon the child. The ultimate effect of this is to weaken the influence of the parent in managing him. It can even disrupt the family and alienate parent and child.

Remember that your child is a person and will eventually have the right to choose for himself. All you can do is influence, persuade, and create patterns and interests that you hope will sustain him through life. You cannot really force, and if you try to, the child may suffer because you may have chosen unwisely and he is not really suited for the incentive pattern that you have created.

If your child isn't working hard enough, take a look at what kind of incentives you are using and try to offer him things he really wants.

GOING TOO FAST ∽

Parents are very eager to reach the terminal goals they have set for the child. They want to get there in big steps. They are not content to be patient and move according to the child's ability to acquire behavior. As they raise the contract's requirements for success, they increase them too rapidly. How do you know when you have done this? Very simply—whenever the child fails to perform or gives evidence of being resentful because he is failing. He is rightfully attaching accountability to you. He just can't move that fast. He just can't do the new things that rapidly.

You may think that pulling up the bedcovers one day should lead to keeping the room completely neat the next day, but when the child fails, he is telling you that pulling up the covers is all he can handle at this time. Increase the standards for neatness gradually. For example, you can require him to remember hanging up his shirt, then hanging up his shirt and pants, then hanging up his shirt and pants and putting his underwear in the hamper, and so on—one small step at a time. It may be possible for some children to go in one big jump from making the bed to keeping the room neat; for others there may have to be many intermediary steps and many pauses along the way.

When you realize that you are going too fast, go back, require less, or even start over. Then go more slowly when increasing the requirements in each new contract.

Whenever your child fails a contract, apologize to him. You set it too high. But never give him any task-oriented points. You may give him a bonus point or two for being a good sport and for accepting the failure to earn the task-oriented points graciously, but he cannot get paid for failure. After you have apologized profusely, set a new contract, one at which you are certain he can succeed. You will always find some rate of increase that your child can tolerate. He may need several days at one level before shifting to another, or even several weeks. He will always tell you how fast he can go. Go at his pace, not yours.

GIVING UNCLEAR INSTRUCTIONS ∿

I have mentioned many times in the course of this book that signal-giving is a difficult skill to acquire. We tend to give vague signals, signals that do not convey enough information, or signals that are beyond the individual's ability to understand. It is important to learn to give signals clearly, to make our instructions such that the child can understand and follow them.

More parents fail in this area when the children are young. Parents have a tendency to expect the child to understand their adult terminology, which frequently contains words, concepts, and language beyond the child's comprehension. Sometimes the parents themselves are not clear in exactly what they want the child to do because they have failed to plan in advance. They give a vague admonition to be good or to try harder. These kinds of instructions do not convey very much information to a child and they make it very hard for him to succeed.

Take the time to ask the child if he understands by having him put the instructions into his own words. You must check to be absolutely certain. Unfortunately, many parents are too busy to take the time to have the child repeat the instructions. They simply hope that by some magic formula the child understood and will obey. He may be willing to obey under a contract system, but he has to know what to do before he can. Always take the time to ask the child to explain back to you what you have required of him. It's good practice for him and good practice for you.

ORDERS YOU CAN'T BACK UP ⌒

There is a saying in the Army, "never give an order you can't back up." This is a good principle to learn. Any request you make of the child must have a consequence attached to it that you control or provide. In addition, there must be some way of observing the act in order to be able to give the consequence.

How often have you told a child "now don't drive fast" as you gave him the keys to the car? There is no way you can back that order up. There is no way you can observe whether he is driving fast or not since he's out alone with the car. Better not to give that order than give it, because you are simply teaching him that he can violate orders with impunity. You are weakening your own authority.

Unless you can get some kind of direct observation of the child's actions by yourself or by someone else you trust (with accurate recording of the act, if necessary), don't bother to give an order. Similarly, if your child is able to get ice cream without your being able to stop him, don't even bother making a contract such as "I will not let you have ice cream unless you have earned it." And finally, don't offer something that you can't deliver. If you promise a child a trip without consulting your spouse first, you may find that it is impossible to let the child go. If that happens and you must tell the child his work was for nothing, you have seriously weakened your credibility and your authority.

Try never to threaten, never to promise, and never to set a contract that you can't back up, whether because you cannot tell whether the behavior occurred or because you can't control the consequences.

INCONSISTENCY, THAT OLD ENEMY ⌒

The home contract system is based on consistency. Positive consequences occur only when the behavior that precedes it is appropriate. Negative consequences or no consequences occur only after an inappropriate behavior occurs or the appropriate behavior fails to occur. You will find that occasionally you will slip into inconsistencies, overpaying in one case, underpaying in another, providing bonuses when nothing was really performed, and so on. Your goal should be to try to reduce the level of inconsistency and ultimately to be able to avoid it.

I would like to call attention to one subtle kind of inconsistency in which most parents engage. I am no exception. Just because I feel like loving my child and taking her for a ride is no excuse for doing so, because this directly effects another human being. To be consistent in what I am teaching it is essential that my child's welfare be considered. I cannot take my pleasure at her expense. If I wish to take my child for a ride or even if I wish to hug and kiss her, I must first be certain that she has earned it. It is my obligation to spend the few moments necessary to prompt appropriate behavior so that I may maintain the consistency and give my love and affection in a manner that does not cause damage or harm to her. It is quite possible to do so, but it requires the kind of consistency that too many parents are unwilling or unable to achieve.

I slip occasionally, all people do. You will, too. The goal is to strive as much as possible for consistency so that the overall pattern is maintained. Sometimes I may come home too tired to provide positive consequences, too worn-out to provide love and affection and the kind of care my children require and need. Those are my "goof-off days," some of the 20 percent of failure to which I'm entitled. The children have to know that Daddy is unable to give constantly. On these occasions, children should be encouraged not to seek positive consequences from the parent and should be given bonuses if they can wait patiently until he feels better.

On rare occasions, when Mommy or Daddy is unable to function in a consistent and positive manner, it is better to give up trying to manage the child then to try to go on functioning when doing so is just unrealistic. It is not always possible to pass control to someone else, but if it is, it should be done. There are occasions when I will say to my wife "Please take over, I've had it." I'm unable to continue functioning at the level I would like. I'm unable to show warmth and affection. I am unable to maintain a positive approach. When I see this beginning to happen in myself I remove myself from the care of the children and attempt to get myself back to where I would like to be. Sometimes I succeed immediately, and sometimes it takes longer. This prevents the child from being under an inconsistent system and takes into account the human frailties of Mommies and Daddies.

There are times, of course, when your spouse is not home to back you up. When this happens the children must be taught to understand that there are times when Mommy or Daddy is just completely unable to help them or to act in a positive and consistent way. The secondary behavior of avoiding Mommy and Daddy under these conditions should be taught to the child. It is a protective device for the children and actually for the parent as well, so that inconsistency does not become the rule but the exception. Children can learn to tolerate the temporary withdrawal of the positive social consequences of Mommy and Daddy's love and affection.

THE NEGATIVE FORM OF A POSITIVE CONTRACT ◆

Very often I will instruct a parent to say to her child, "If you work very hard today you can go to the movies in the afternoon." Later, the parent will call me and inform me that it didn't work. When I ask for an exact reporting of what the parent said to the child, the mother usually says, "I told my son that since he wasn't doing his work, he couldn't go to the movies." She has changed a positive contract into a negative contract without realizing it. Her method of stating the contract has reversed it. She is taking away from her child going to the movies which she has implied was already in his possession. Since he was bad, he can't go to the movies. That is punishment, not positive teaching.

Under a positive contract, movie-going remains in the parents' control and the parent gives it to the child only after the work is performed. The way this parent stated it made it a negative contract: Since her child did not perform at a level of which she approved, she is taking movie-going away from him. She is taking something that belongs to him away to try to teach him never to fail again.

There is a world of difference between stating something positively and stating it negatively. The emotional response of children will tell you almost immediately which one you are using. If the child resents the contract and is angry or sullen or hurt, you can be sure that he is aware that you have taken something from him that both of you agreed was already his.

When you use a positive contract, on the other hand, the child accepts failure to earn something with a great deal more resignation and with eagerness to try harder the next time. He can easily understand that by his efforts he can achieve the movie and that he must exchange his work for the movie. But he chose not to. He can accept the loss of the movie much better under these conditions. "You didn't succeed, therefore you can't," is a very prevalent speech pattern in our culture. However, there is still something you can do besides punish him for the failure or enforce the loss of the movie. You can say to him, "I'm sorry you failed to earn the right to go to the movies. However, here is a special thing you can do this time to earn the right to go if you do it really quickly. I'm going to bend a little bit to encourage you to work harder. I chose to do this for today only."

Then you can set up a special, rather difficult (but possible) project. Next time you should begin to prompt earlier in the day in order to get the child to begin the work and to keep him doing it. Set smaller tasks, if necessary, as a way of providing him with a good deal of self-confidence.

If you use a positive contract the child will begin to feel that you are his ally in helping him earn the privilege of going to the movies, and not his warden. If you use additional incentives besides the movie, such as bonuses for trying and praise for cooperating, the child can be helped and encouraged to work faster and more effectively. The end result is that he gets the movie with your help and cooperation. Can you see the difference between the two ways of stating a positive contract, the negative and positive forms? Always try to offer something and try never to threaten or take away something the child already has in his possession or has been promised.

PREPARING FOR FAILURE OR ARBITRARY REFUSAL ᠌

Because the positive contract approach is based on the attempt to avoid failure on the part of the child as he engages in the learning of new behavior, many parents may fail to teach the child what to do when he encounters failure in other situations.

One of the things that we did in the special school that I ran was to arrange problems for children at which we were certain that they would fail. This was done deliberately. When a child failed he was given bonus points. He was then told what he was to do during the failure experience. We would teach him other ways of thinking about his failure, what kinds of effective actions to take to try to overcome the failure, and how he was to evidence patience. If he was successful in these secondary behaviors, a constant flow of bonus points was administered. Each child in the learning environment learned that failure did not stop the flow of goodies coming and that there were things a person could do under failure. There were ways of redefining the failure experience. There were ways of involving themselves in alternate activities, or of seeking outside help, which can lead to a continuous flow of positive consequences. We were teaching them these skills because we realistically expected that no matter how hard we tried, failure experiences would occur both in our school and elsewhere.

When children asked for certain things, occasionally we would arbitrarily say no. When the children protested, we would teach them behaviors to use when people became arbitrary. We would show them, through the administration of bonus points, that it was all right to protest in certain ways—not by having tantrums or by insulting the staff, but by reasoning, debating, or offering alternatives. Finally we taught them to switch to another goal which was available. If they could do this they would receive the bonus points.

It was thus possible to strengthen the kinds of behaviors we wanted to teach—behaviors that enabled them to successfully encounter failure or refusal without reverting to the more primitive behaviors of giving up, sulking, or having tantrums.

One mother asked me how to solve a problem she had with a child who wanted to use sharp scissors. He was too young to handle sharp scissors, although he could handle blunt scissors. He saw other children in the family using sharp scissors and wished to do the same, even when Mommy was not there to supervise. Her question to me was, "What do I do after I say no?"

This becomes an occasion for teaching. I told her to set up a teaching situation at a time when she had plenty of free time. She was to make the sharp scissors available so that he could see them and ask for them. When he asked for them she was told to say, "No, you can't use the sharp scissors, you can use these others. If you use the blunt scissors without getting angry and you behave well, I'm going to give you a special treat." She was to give him one instantly, without allowing him a chance to complain.

I further told her, "Remember you are out to prompt and teach the new behavior, not to set a contest to see if he passes or fails. You are not to take any chances. You should give him the positive consequence immediately because for that brief instant he is not complaining. Of course, you won't give him a chance to complain, but that's the purpose of your prompting. As soon as he starts to complain, as he probably will, you are to point out 'I can't give you any more points because you're complaining. Now stop for a moment. Good. Now you're not talking. Here's another treat because you're accepting it well. If you take these scissors,' giving him the blunt ones, 'I'll give you another treat.' You are to pour on the positive consequences, using a very rich payment schedule. You should do this to teach him, as quickly as possible, the new skill of accepting the arbitrary refusal and to teach him to redirect his efforts into available consequences that are permissible. As soon as he demonstrates that he can do this, you quietly remove the sharp scissors and wait for another occasion to practice again."

The example I have just given can serve as a model for other kinds of situations you may encounter. The principles remain constant, only the situation and the technique may vary. It is very important to include preparation for failure in your management of Johnny.

CHRISTMAS AND FAMILY VACATIONS ❖

There are a number of occasions that occur in the course of family life on which it appears appropriate to give gifts that have not been earned. Holidays, birthdays, and vacations are examples.

By custom and tradition we try to make vacations available to our family because we feel that they are important. They break the routine of work and allow us to refresh and strengthen ourselves so that we can deal once again with the problems of everyday life. We feel that our children, too, should have this opportunity. It is very possible, of course, to arrange that your children have earned the vacation just as you have. You have earned the vacation by your hard work. You are taking a vacation not only as a health measure to strengthen yourself, but as positive consequence for work that you have done. By the same token, your children also are entitled to a vacation *if they have earned it.*

Of course, the whole family should not lose the chance to go to the shore or the mountains because one child has failed to earn the right to be there. That should not be made a part of the contract, because it is not practical to control the consequence of being at the vacation site unless you are prepared to leave one child home in an empty house or to pay someone a lot of money to care for him while you're away. However, when the undeserving child is at the vacation site there is still a great deal of difference between simply being there and enjoying all the advantages that the family traveled to obtain. So, for example, your child should not have permission to be in the water unless he has earned it for that day. In this way, it is possible to maintain a management pattern consistent with what is used at home. You can make the tasks much simpler and probably not related to school or study. Simply doing their chores and maintaining a happy and pleasant behavior pattern toward other members of the family would be enough. Sulking, sullenness, and angry outbursts should not lead to swimming. Swimming should be obtained by people who are pleasant to be with and behaving well.

With occasions like birthdays, Christmas, and other holiday occasions, the problem becomes a little more complex and more subtle. While you can control the consequences on family vacations, it is much more difficult to control the consequences on birthdays and Christmas. About the only thing you can do is to be less generous than you had planned to be. Remember that your child is earning prizes and gifts all year long. No matter what the hucksters tell you on the radio and television, you do not have to celebrate Christmas by giving a thousand gifts to your child. You should be trying to teach him about the spirit of the holidays and to understand the love and appreciation that you feel toward each other. Don't flood the child with a large number of gifts that will simply satiate him and weaken the entire home contract system. We have been used for too long to equating love with giving gifts to a child. It is better to act in loving ways and make him aware of your love by quality than by quantity. So it is possible on birthdays and holidays to give the child a gift in order to teach the meaning of giving and the depth of your love without weakening the overall system.

OUTSIDE WORK ∽

Many parents grew up during the depression years. They had to take jobs very early in life. They quickly learned that they had earn their way in life. They are proud of this fact and they want their children to have the same experience. At first glance the home contract system does not seem to allow for this, but it really does. It would be an error, of course, to let the two systems compete. If the child can obtain cash for his outside work, he can unhook himself from the consequence system that the parent is providing. There are several ways to avoid this error. One way is to concentrate on some method of incorporating the outside work into the system itself. For example, although he has already earned the cash outside the home, he cannot spend it unless he has earned the necessary points within the home.

Another way of handling this matter is based on the fact that, since he earns only cash through outside work, he can spend it only for material things. This means that you still can use privileges as the incentive system within the home—privileges he cannot buy with cash. Thus you are able to incorporate and accommodate into the home contract system a very desirable activity on the child's part, that of early training outside of the home in the economic system of our society.

There is another way in which this problem can be solved, and perhaps this one is the most desirable. As the child gets older and the contract system begins to wither away, it is possible to allow the child to move gradually outside the home for his external consequences and to maintain his behavior in the home by the social consequences of approval, love, and affection which you provide. Another source of motivation for him is found in the self-consequences that he administers to himself, such as pride in being an effective, loving family member or a sense of achievement for the way he contributes to the family. Hopefully, the intrinsic positive consequences of how good it feels to be close, warm, cooperative, and loving within the family structure will also guarantee good behavior. If this is achieved, he can take on all of the outside work he wants without affecting your home management system.

This should be the goal for all families, I think, and one for which it is worth striving.

WHEN YOUR CHILD LEAVES THE HOTHOUSE ∽

Let us be completely realistic. If you are able to achieve the goals this book sets forth for you and to use its techniques effectively and consistently, your child will be living in an artificial "hothouse." While in many ways the system approximates the real world, in many ways it differs from it. Some parents fail to realize this in their enthusiasm for the new approach.

You will be treating your child as a person. Everywhere else in the world he is a second-class citizen and will be treated as such. You are using consistent and effective techniques for teaching him. Very often the outside world expects him to learn by modeling or by learning magically on his own with no help whatsoever. You are using a consistent motivational system. The world can be capricious in the granting of positive consequences. Very often you can earn your way in life by cheating and manipulating rather than by honest effort.

The real world is quite imperfect. You are striving to build a home environment that is immediately and precisely responsive to your child. In addition, I hope you are teaching love, affection, and a sense of closeness that, unfortunately, too many people in the outside world reject and of which they even become frightened. Taking all this into account, it is nonetheless worth doing. There is no reason, as I see it, to make your home conform to the worst of what is outside of it. You are striving for your own goals within your own home. However, your child will leave his home, frequently too early in life to have major skills for dealing with an imperfect world.

We discovered this problem when our children went to school for the first time. They suddenly became aggressive, began to use negative contracts with each other, and all sorts of other bad habits appeared. We realized that this was happening because they were mimicking their teachers and the other children whom they met in school. We could not protect them forever.

In addition, we discovered that some people saw our children as "fresh." We found out why. They were going up to adults and correcting them. They were allowed to do so in our home, since we accept negative feedback from any member of the family regardless of age. We evaluate the feedback, not the source. So our children were correcting teachers and their friends' parents, all of whom objected to a child's right to criticize their behavior.

In addition, we found that they were meeting an arbitrary world which often was capricious and cruel. They needed explanations for this. They needed a way of coping with it. We found ourselves having to teach our children bad habits in order to help them to survive.

We taught them tact, which is a polite way of describing lying. Our children were tactless. They were willing to give accurate feedback whenever they observed something wrong in a person. In our home that behavior was acceptable, but we had to teach them that in other people's homes it was not.

They seldom met irrational or unfeeling behavior on our part. If they did occasionally experience it in our home, there was a rapid apology for it from us. Now they were finding their teachers scolding the entire class for one child's misdeeds and withholding privileges from all as a punishment (frequently on irrational grounds). Punishments were harsh and sudden.

When we realized what was happening and the error we were making, we asked ourselves what our children needed. Could we teach them a set of protective skills that would allow them to leave the "hothouse" and live in the real world? Could we teach our children to accept the irrationality of other adults?

We decided that we could, by teaching them compassion, by teaching them to look upon other people as imperfect, and by teaching them to look at the total repertoire of other people's behavior and to refrain from making judgments on the basis of one behavior. We taught them to keep their voices still and to sit quietly in the face of behaviors of others that aroused righteous indignation in them. We cautioned them in terms of their own competence level and their own ability to deal with the situation. We told them that as they grew older, they would be more effective in dealing with these kinds of situations. We taught them to sit back and watch another child being scolded by a teacher without attempting to interfere.

Our children frequently report to us their insight into what the outside world is like. It is almost frightening to see how perceptive they are of the failures of adults.

We hope that when it comes time for their children to be managed by them, they will select the technique that we are teaching them rather than the ones the outside world has tried to impose upon them. One of the things that happens is that other children try to talk them out of the contract principle. They report their allowances and laugh at the way my children earn their way and they tell our children that they are foolish. Our children, on the other hand, reply that ours is not a hitting family, that they never get punished. Look at all the things that they have. Let's compare who gets most out of life. We have yet to find that our kids would trade their system for any other.

Part 4

THE
WHY NOT of
BEHAVIOR

16 🎗
The Final
Emancipation of
Children

C) A final word about the management of children. Some people have objected to the use of any procedure which seems to indicate *control* of children. The word "control" to them seems to indicate a non-humanistic, dictatorial approach. They also object to any systematic procedure. They accuse the behavioral approach of being mechanistic and unspontaneous. This, they seem to feel, interferes with the development of a truly loving relationship between parent and child. If I understand them correctly, they are arguing for a sort of unplanned "doing what comes naturally."

I hope that I have been able to show you that a systematic approach, based on the realities of the processes of behavior and learning, does not have to be mechanical. It can be used flexibly and with full recognition of individual differences. It can be used in a loving way. I hope that I have been able to show you that "control" is not an ugly word but a fact of life. The contract principle is implemented in every home, sometimes badly and sometimes well. The purpose of this book is to help you remove the destructive or ineffective methods and replace them with methods that will help Johnny become an effective member of your family. A well planned and well managed home contract system allows Johnny the freedom to develop fully as a human being.

By now you should have realized that I strongly believe that children are people and not indentured servants. They should be emancipated and allowed to take their rightful place as citizens of the world. I do not mean that they should run the home. The fear created by psychologists during the 1930s that children would be irrevocably hurt if they were frustrated is nonsense. I think it is time that myths were put to rest once and for all.

I am not arguing for a laissez-faire policy, for allowing children to do whatever they wish whenever they wish. I am very much for an effective home management system, but I am just as vehemently for the emancipation of children. They are people. They are human beings. We forget this so often in the pleasure of ordering them around, of requiring comformity from them. We often do it

247

in ways that would be abhorrent if an employer tried to use them on us.

Our children are ours to share in terms of friendship and human closeness and warmth. They are there for us to guide; we are there to help them acquire competency. We have made that committment to them by bringing them into the world, and once they are here we are bound with ties of relationship that are profound and lasting.

It is possible to conceive of a future world in which children will be raised not by their parents but by the state. The parents merely breed them. I shudder to think of what kind of a world that system might produce. A number of authors have tried to conceive of such future totalitarian worlds. I find them inconceivable as permanent human systems.

The bonds between a parent and child are deep, and rightfully so. Yet they need to be reexamined and redefined in the light of what we now know about effective management and discipline systems. The goal is to help Johnny *want* to obey, not to teach him to obey. We should be interested in his full cooperation and participation, not in his blind obedience and subservience. I think that most parents would prefer children who cooperated willingly rather than those who merely obeyed. Cooperation given willingly is a sign of mutual respect. Even where there are differences in goals, cooperation is still possible through compromise or mutual aid.

It seems to me that we have made a fetish out of conformity. Some people seem to feel that the only way that cohesion can be developed within a group, particularly a family group, is to conform. Their children must think, act, feel, and behave in the same way as they do. I think that today this procedure only produces alienation between children and parents. I doubt whether it can be successfully achieved any longer. There was a time when such conformity appeared necessary in the light of the conditions of the times. It led to economic preservation of family goods and property. It led to social stability and personal security in an age where the only place to find such security was within the family structure. Such a system worked once, and perhaps it was justified then. But today it appears to me to be totally unrealistic, unnecessary, and undesirable.

The true meaning of closeness is based on mutual respect, and respect is not defined as obedience or awe, but as a valuing of the other person's beliefs and ways of doing things. You can attribute worth even to ideas with which you disagree. Agreement is not necessary for respect. Your child may disagree with you and still respect your position and you his.

What I am talking about is a family design where the goal is to permit differences and even to encourage them, and where each person develops a repertoire of behaviors suitable to his own structure and the ends that he has chosen for himself. Let Johnny be a person in his own right. Can you have that and still have closeness, still have a sense of commonality and the feeling of emotional security and warmth provided by close family ties? If the the answer is not yes, there is no hope for the future because we face then either continuous warfare among generations or total alienation.

The possible goal of complete uniformity among all peoples is as abhorent to me and seems to bode as ill for mankind's survival as nuclear warfare. Who is to pick the goals to which we are to conform and who is to guarantee that they will be the best survival system for changing times in the future? It has been said that the only way for mankind to survive is to maximize differences among people so that there would always be a varied pool of human resources. Thus many different ways of solving problems would be available from which to select in the crises and emergencies of a changing world. To me this idea makes sense. It makes sense even at the level of the family. For a family to survive it should have a pool of resources, human resources, that make it able to adjust, accommodate, and adapt to changing times.

Times change; in our age they change quite rapidly. The father who insists that his son think and act the way that he does is bringing the family close to destruction. For the family to change and to grow with changing times, there must be at least one member prepared to explain the new situations and to help the family adjust to different kinds of problems. Why not encourage your children to become adapted to their own peer group, to their own life style? Is it possible to do that and still remain close? Again, I think the answer is yes.

Look at your friends. Have you selected them only because of their similarity to you or have you achieved that kind of maturity that allows you to feel close to all human beings regardless of their superficial differences? People still hurt, still fear, still get angry, still strive and fail, regardless of their different life styles. All of us endure the human condition and all of us can touch one another at this basic level. Your interests may be different. You may spend your vacation time in different places. Your ideas in politics and religion may be different from mine. Yet we can enjoy and appreciate each other's enthusiasm, learn from one another, and grow in the process of trying to understand and to accept as much of each other's positions as possible.

You may wish to reexamine the way in which your family is designed and the values you have accepted and lived by in the light of this discussion. Take a good look at your family and ask yourself: Why not redesign my family? Why not implement the home contract principle in whatever form seems most suitable for my family? The end result, I think, would be a positive consequence for everyone.

The home contract principle is a positive method, based on incentives. It defines discipline in a realistic fashion. Discipline is not punishment. It is the training methods and the guidelines by which people live. It is the incentive system that helps people achieve the standards being set. It is the setting of realistic standards.

Ultimately you should want to go beyond the technique itself, beyond the formal home contract system to the kind of informal systems to which I have alluded many times. In an informal system there is a deep understanding and acceptance of the relationship between individual effort and the return of positive consequences. There is consistency in the implementation of the contract principle—so much so, that it hardly seems worth mentioning, for when this is achieved the use of points becomes unnecessary. The keeping of records becomes superfluous because the record-keeping is built into the way of life.

This is the ideal toward which you should be striving. Good luck.

Index